I Was Lucky:
I Got to Be a Pilot

by

Paul "PK" Kimminau

PITTSBURGH, PENNSYLVANIA 15238

The contents of this work including, but not limited to, the accuracy of events, people, and places depicted; opinions expressed; permission to use previously published materials included; and any advice given or actions advocated are solely the responsibility of the author, who assumes all liability for said work and indemnifies the publisher against any claims stemming from publication of the work.

All Rights Reserved
Copyright © 2017 by Paul "PK" Kimminau

No part of this book may be reproduced or transmitted, downloaded, distributed, reverse engineered, or stored in or introduced into any information storage and retrieval system, in any form or by any means, including photocopying and recording, whether electronic or mechanical, now known or hereinafter invented without permission in writing from the publisher.

RoseDog Books
585 Alpha Drive
Suite 103
Pittsburgh, PA 15238
Visit our website at www.rosedogbookstore.com

ISBN: 978-1-4809-7550-7
eISBN: 978-1-4809-7573-6

"You love a lot of things if you live around them.
But there isn't any woman and there isn't any horse,
not any before nor after, that is as lovely as a great airplane.

And men who love them are faithful to them
even though they leave them for others.

Man has one virginity to lose in fighters,
and if it is to a lovely airplane he loses it,
there is where his heart will forever be."

Ernest Hemingway

Contents

Dedication vii

Preface ix

Getting my Private License 1

USAF Primary and Basic Flight training 7

F-100 Fighter Pilot training (Luke Air Force Base, Arizona) 19

F-100 Fighter Pilot training (Nellis Air Force Base, Nevada) 27

Flying with the 31st Tactical Fighter Wing 33

Flying with the 79th Tactical Fighter Squadron
(RAF Woodbridge, United Kingdom) 69

Flying the A-1 Skyraider 95

Frag Officer, Hdqts 7th Air Force, Tân Sơn Nhứt Air Base,
Saigon, South Vietnam 135

F-100 Fighter Weapons School Instructor (Nellis Air Force Base, Nevada) . .157

Air Liaison Officer/Forward Air Controller (Fort Carson, Colorado) 165

A-7D Instructor Pilot (Davis-Monthan Air Force Base, Arizona) 175

Instructor, A7-D Fighter Weapons School (Nellis Air Force Base, Nevada) . .179

A-7D Wing Weapons Officer, Korat RTAFB, Thailand 187

Chief of Standardization & Evaluation, A-7D & A-10
(Davis-Monthan, Arizona) 205

Attachment 1 — Cocked Nose Wheel (by John Larrison) 215

Attachment 2 — Survival School (Stead Air Force Base, Nevada) 217

Attachment 3 — Weekend Trip around Turkey (Çiğli AB, Izmir, Turkey) ...223

Attachment 4 — R & R for a week in Greece 233

Attachment 5 — Student at F-100 FWS, (Nellis Air Force Base, Nevada) ...251

Attachment 6 — North Station/Lima Site 85 (Northern Laos) 261

Attachment 7 — Awards & Decorations 275

This work is dedicated to my wife, Lois,
and my children
Jon Alan, Lori Diane, Brian Keith, and Alex Paul.

After you read this, you will understand just how much
they had to put up with as the United States Air Force
had me going all over the world.

THANKS, Family.

Preface

I have been thinking for quite a long time about writing a book. My idea is not to write about my life, but to write about my life with aviation. A bit of background about me would probably help in understanding how I learned to love flying.

As a kid in Kingman, Kansas, I remember several incidents which made me THINK about flying. There was one guy who either lived in Kingman or had relatives who did, and he would "buzz" Kingman in his P-38 Lightning. This was just after WW II. Just seeing that airplane flying over and hearing the roar of the engines was a real thrill!

Another incident was when a Bell P-39 Airacobra flying over had engine trouble. He was forced to land in a field to the west of town near the golf course. He did not quite manage to stop in the field and a large corner fence post stopped him from jumping off the field into the road. I didn't really get very close to the airplane sitting there crashed into the fence post, but I did get an idea of just how big those airplanes were.

P-38 Lightning

P-39 Airacobra

B-36 Peacemaker

I came from a big family, one of nine: four older brothers, two older sisters, and a brother and sister younger than I. My oldest brother, Jerome (everyone calls him "Jerry"), was drafted into the Army Air Force just at the end of WW II. He was a crew member on a B-25 Mitchell. This was a twin-engine bomber. After the war was over (he never went to combat in the B-25), he got out of the service for a couple years. He re-enlisted and got into Aviation Cadets. (This was a program where guys without a college degree could go through pilot training and get a commission as an officer.) He completed pilot training and I am unsure just what aircraft he first flew. I know he ended up flying the B-29 Super Fortress and flew a lot of combat missions over North Korea. Before he retired, Jerry also flew the B-36 and B-52 bombers, as well as several other aircraft. He retired from the Air Force as a Major and worked for United Airlines for several years after retirement. [Note: When we lived in Scott City, KS, Jerry was checking out in the B-36 at Rapid City, SD. On one of his missions he flew over Scott City. I would say "buzzed" but you weren't supposed to do that. It was a huge airplane and I thought that the wing span went from one city limit to the other.]

My second oldest brother, Harold, tried to enlist into about all the services just after he got out of high school, but they all turned him down because of a "football knee." It is kind of ironic that he was drafted during the Korean War and served in the Army as an enlisted man in Korea. He tells the story that there were 18 guys drafted who all passed the physical at the same time; they were all lined up and someone came in. He counted twelve and said, "You are in the Marines." He was #13 in the line, so he ended up in the Army. After his time in Korea, he returned, got out of the Army, and ran his own drywall contracting business in Denver for many years.

The next two older brothers, Alfred and Leo, both enlisted in the USAF. Alfred was out of high school for a year or so doing different jobs, not really anything very interesting. Leo graduated from high school and was going to enlist in the Air Force, so Alfred enlisted at the same time. Alfred (everyone called him "Fritz") went to Radio Technician School and Leo went to Aircraft Mechanics School.

C-124 Globemaster II

Alfred, while in the Air Force stationed in England, met and married an English woman. After serving about 10 years in the service, Alfred got out and remained living in England with his wife and family. He lived there until he passed away in 2011.

Leo, during the early part of his time in the Air Force, managed to get into the Aviation Cadet program. He graduated from pilot training and flew several different kinds of cargo aircraft. C-119, C-54, and the C-124 (It had a nickname of "Old Shakey") were just three that he flew. After several years of flying the C-124, he was assigned as the Civil Air Patrol Liaison Officer for the state of Nebraska. He was stationed in Omaha, Nebraska. While serving there, he took classes to get a college degree and had almost completed that endeavor when the Air Force decided they needed him to fly an O-1 Birddog over in Southeast Asia.

After completing his tour, he got out of the Air Force as a captain, ineligible for retirement. While working in Wichita, Kansas, he joined the Kansas Air National Guard. He flew the C-54 while with the ANG. He also worked at Cessna Aircraft and flew along as a crew member in the T-37 trainer which they were converting into the A-37 attack aircraft. After getting enough jet flying time, he got checked out in the F-100 while a member of the ANG. The Kansas ANG was called to active duty during the Pueblo Crisis, and Leo was recalled to active duty. He remained at McConnell AFB in Wichita, KS, and flew the T-39 Saberliner. He got enough active duty time, was promoted to major, and retired from the Air Force.

The family moved from Kingman to Scott City in Western Kansas when I was in the seventh grade. Alfred had finished high school in Kingman and Leo finished his last year in Scott City. I finished grade school and high school in Scott City.

In the spring of my junior year in high school, I did not know what I was really going to do once I got out of school. I kind of felt like I should go to college, but my family sure did not have the money to send me to school. [My parents grew up and raised most of their children during the Great Depression. My Dad was a very strong Democrat and loved Franklin D. Roosevelt. One of Roosevelt's sayings when he ran for President was, "A chicken for every pot." My Dad used to say, "Well, we don't even own a pot to piss in and don't have a window to throw it out."]

One afternoon I was sitting in a Rexall Drug Store at the soda fountain, reading a paper. The town of Scott City was too small to have a daily paper (they did have a weekly), so the paper was the Hutchinson News Herald, from Hutchinson, KS. There was an article about Beech Aircraft Company Scholarships to the University of Wichita. I thought, "What the heck is this?" As it happened, I was in an English class that year and the teacher was also the scholarship counselor. I asked him the next day about this Beech Aircraft Scholarship. He didn't know anything about it, but said he would find out. He did, and that summer I managed to get to Wichita and take the tests for the scholarship. I did not win the big scholarship but did get a remission of tuition scholarship. My folks moved to Wichita, where Dad was taking a new job, so I was able to live at home and attend the University of Wichita.

When I started going to college, I decided that taking Air Force ROTC was the thing to do. My older brothers being in the Air Force probably had an influence on my decision. I guess the rest is history.

Now I'll start my story of flying.

C-54 Skymaster

C-119 Flying Boxcar T-39 Superliner

The B-25 Mitchell bomber that Jerry flew as an enlisted crew member before he went to pilot training. Leo also flew this aircraft during his pilot training for multi-engine aircraft.

The Cessna O-1 Birddog aircraft that Leo flew during his tour in Vietnam.

Chapter 1

Getting My Private Pilot License

I remember so well the very first time I flew in an airplane. My high school buddy (Gary Cook) and I were just fooling around one day. I don't remember if it was in the summer of 1952 or a weekend during the school year. We were out at the Scott City airport, looking around. There was this guy who owned a Piper Cub aircraft and he was getting ready to go flying. He asked if Gary and I wanted to go fly. We said sure! He strapped us both in the back seat. (It was really designed for only one person.) Off we went. I am convinced we never got over 50 feet above the ground for the entire flight. We were flying for probably 45 minutes and this guy was looking for coyotes! He wasn't hunting them that day, just scouting. He did normally hunt from the airplane. I don't remember being scared. Looking back on it, I should have been.

The next time I flew in an aircraft was in late October or early November 1956. My brother, Leo, was flying the C-124 out of Greenville, SC, and had to go TDY to Lebanon. He wanted Elsie, his wife, to come back to Wichita and did not want her to drive all that way alone. He got me an airline ticket and I flew to South Carolina. I know that was the farthest I had ever been from Kansas.

Piper Cub

Cadet "PK @ Selma

The thing I remember the most about this trip was going through the Atlanta airport. I saw drinking fountains and bathrooms for Blacks and Whites for the first time in my life!! This was really eye-opening for a naive young kid from Kansas!!

I got to fly in Air Force aircraft a couple of times while in college. Once the ROTC class went in a C-54 to Lackland AFB, TX, for a weekend orientation. This was much like flying in a commercial airplane without flight attendants. During the summer of 1957, I went to ROTC Summer Camp in Selma, AL. While there, all the ROTC cadets were given an orientation flight in a T-33. I don't remember a lot about this flight, so I suspect it was pretty much go up and flyaround without much maneuvering.

November 26, 1958, I started flying in the AFROTC Flight Indoctrination Program (FIP). This program was introduced by the Air Force to determine if a young officer entering the Air Force for pilot training from ROTC was in fact going to be able to fly. The flight school was a civilian company at the Wichita International Airport. I remember my instructor very well, though I cannot remember his name. He had been a civilian instructor with a company that taught Primary Pilot Training for the Air Force. He was probably 5'10" or 11" and a bit on the heavy side. Smoked a cigar all the time and could really cuss you out when you screwed up. Really a good instructor though.

The aircraft I learned in was a Cessna 140, a "tail-dragger." This of course means it was a tail-wheel aircraft, not a tricycle-gear aircraft. The main gear were mounted on what looked like flat pieces of spring steel. I don't remember just how much horsepower the engine had, but it was plenty for this light airplane. Several flights stand out in my memory.

Cessna 140

The dual cross-country flight was one such flight. We flew southeast from Wichita to Independence, KS, then to Wellington, and then back to Wichita. I don't remember landing at either of those two places, but we must have, because I think it was required that you land at a "strange" airfield before you went on your solo cross-country. When we were returning to Wichita, we were southwest of the airport about 15 miles when the IP (Instructor Pilot) said he had the aircraft, meaning he was now in control. He turned the aircraft to a heading of south. He adjusted the power (we were at probably 3,000 ft AGL) and told me to look outside. I looked down and we were right above this road running east to west, but WE WEREN'T MOVING. It was as if we were in a hover! We were indicating about 50 mph, so we were in a wind of about 50 miles per hour out of the south. When we got back to the airport, the reported wind was about 35-40 knots, right down the runway, so the IP did the landing. He stopped straight ahead on the runway and had a couple guys from his company come out and tie ropes on the wings and walk us back to the ramp. He was afraid that if we turned and had the wind coming from the side it would tip the aircraft over.

Another memorable flight was something of my own doing, and not real smart either! One day coming back from a solo flight practicing my maneuvers, I decided that, since there were flaps on the airplane, I would try to make a landing using the flaps. (I should not have tried that without my IP showing me first.) They, of course, increase the lift a LOT. Coming down final to land, the attitude of the aircraft is a lot different from a landing without using flaps, and you need to fly much slower. I did land OK, but decided not to tell the IP about that and to NEVER do that again.

Another memorable flight: I was getting pretty close to being ready for my CAA check ride for my Private Pilot Rating, so we were practicing maneuvers that the IP thought the check pilot might ask me to do. One of these maneuvers was "Wheel Landings." This required you to actually fly the airplane so the wheels were touching the runway before you pulled the power off for landing. (Normal landing, of course, was to fly it, slowing down to the stall speed, just as the wheels were about to touch the runway.) Wheel Landings were used when there was a crosswind; if you were flying slow at landing you would be required to be in a "crab" to keep from being blown off the runway, and since you did NOT want to land with the aircraft in a crab, you flew it keeping a wing down into the wind and landed it so you could get the tail wheel on the ground before you were actually slow enough for the wind to blow you off the runway. Anyway, we were practicing this and it seemed I was very good at getting the airplane to within a few inches of the runway, but then I would kind of push it down. Of course the wheels would touch the runway and I would pull the power off, but with the spring gear we would pop back up into the air a few feet. I must have tried five or six times on this 7000 foot runway. Getting close to the end, the IP was laughing and saying "Kimminau, you better land this thing, you are about to run out of runway!!" Well, sure enough, I did not get it landed and we had to go around. The IP told everyone in the place about me not being able to land a Cessna 140 on 7000 feet of runway!! EMBARRASSED, I guess!!

I got through everything the IP thought I needed, so we scheduled the check ride with the CAA. The day of the check ride I got there and the IP said there would be a weather front coming through later that morning; he was hoping that we could get the check ride in before the weather changed.

I briefed with the CAA Check Pilot, went out and flew the check ride, everything going just fine. Just when we got back to the airport for the landings, the weather front did arrive. In fact, the wind changed just as I was making my first landing. The wind switched, a crosswind, just as I was about to touchdown and was blowing me off the runway. I added power and went around. Now, of course, if I were going to land on that runway, it would take a wheel landing! I used my judgement and asked for the runway that was lined up with the wind. The CAA guy really liked that. In fact, when we got into the building for the debrief, he got my IP in with us and went on and on about how I had made a great call to go around from the first approach, then was smart enough to ask for the other runway. After he left, I and my IP had a good laugh, knowing good and well if I had had to make a wheel landing, maybe things wouldn't have come out so great.

OK, now I had my PRIVATE PILOT'S license. I had about an hour flying time left on the contract, so the company said I could use it up just flying solo or I could take someone up with me. I asked my Dad, because I really wanted to take him up. I don't think he had ever flown in an airplane. He declined, saying I should probably take my wife Lois up instead.

He was so funny. He got Lois one of those paper cups with a lid (like a take home soup thing) telling her she should have it in case she got air sick. I kept telling her she wouldn't get sick. The flight went just great until we entered the landing pattern, and then she got sick! She was thankful Dad had given her the cup!

Looking in my log book, it appears that I had enough time to also take my brother Jim up for a short ride. I think this last Cessna 140 flight was on 11 April 1959.

I graduated college in May 1959, but the Air Force did not have a slot in a pilot training class until February 1960, so I worked at Boeing Aircraft Company in Wichita until December 1959 when I went to preflight training at Lackland AFB, TX. After Lackland, it was off to Moore AB in McAllen, TX.

DATE 19 59	FLIGHT FROM	FLIGHT TO	AIRCRAFT MAKE AND MODEL	CERTIFICATE NUMBER	ENGINE	H. P.	CLASSIFICATION			DURATION OF FLIGHT	
										19	40
3-11-59	ICT	LOCAL	Cessna 140		Cont	90				0	45
3-12-59	ICT	LOCAL	"		"	"					45
3-17-59	"	"	"		"	"					30
3-19-59	"	CK [illegible]	"		"					3	05
3-24-59	ICT [illegible] HAYS	ICT	"		"	"				5	00
3-30-59	ICT	Local	"		"	"					55
4-2-59	"	"	"		"	"				2	00
4-4-59	"	"	"		"	"				1	20
4-7-59	"	"	"		"	"				1	00
4-7-59	"	"	"		"	"					40
4-11-59	"	"	"		"	"				1	[illegible]
										36	40

THE RECORD ON THIS PAGE IS CERTIFIED TRUE AND CORRECT:

PILOT [illegible] ATTESTED BY

CARRY TOTALS FORWARD TO TOP OF NEXT PAGE

INSTRUMENT		INSTRUCTION		DAY		NIGHT		DUAL		SOLO		REMARKS
		11	10					11	10	8	30	INSTRUCTOR SHOULD ENTER IN THIS COLUMN THE NATURE OF EACH MANEUVER IN WHICH INSTRUCTION IS GIVEN, AND THE TIME SPENT THEREON, AND SHALL ATTEST EACH SUCH ENTRY WITH HIS INITIALS, PILOT CERTIFICATE NUMBER, AND PERTINENT RATING.
			45						45			[illegible] LANDINGS. [illegible]
			45						45			20 hr Check Ride
											30	
		3	05					3	05			Dual Cross Country [illegible] ICT
										5	00	Solo Cx-Country
	05		55						55			Spins [illegible]
		2	00					2	00			
		1	20					1	20			School Final Check [illegible]
		[illegible]						[illegible]		1	00	went over everything for CAA Ride.
			40						40			CAA Check Ride [illegible] ASEL [illegible]
										1	[illegible]	Lois and Jim got [illegible] ride
	05	20	00					20	40	16	00	ENTER IN THIS COLUMN DETAILS OF ANY SERIOUS DAMAGE TO AIRCRAFT. IF MORE SPACE THAN THAT PROVIDED ABOVE IS NEEDED FOR ANY DETAILS OF FLIGHT INSTRUCTION OR AIRCRAFT DAMAGE, USE PAGES PROVIDED IN BACK OF BOOK.

CARRY TOTALS FORWARD TO TOP OF NEXT PAGE

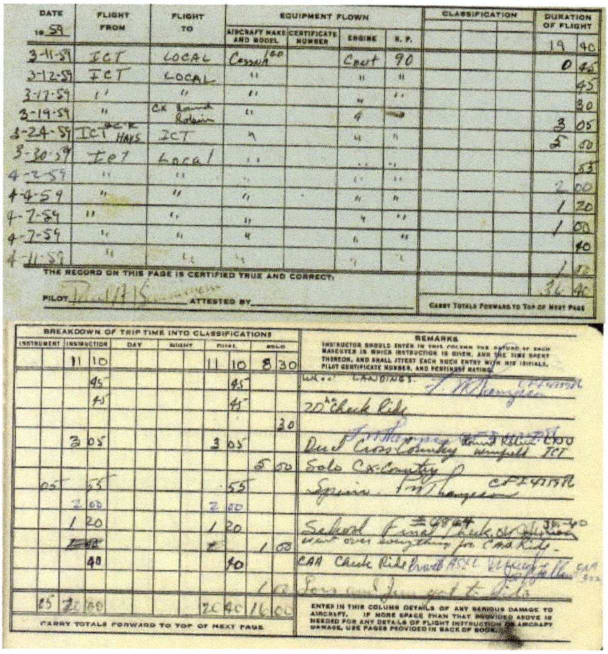

A page from my Log Book. Shown here as two pages since that is how I had to scan it. For example, the flight on 4-7-59 reflects a flight of 40 minutes, Dual, Instructions. In the Comments it's noted that it was my CAA Check Ride and I was awarded an Airplane Single Engine Land license.

Form ACA 301
(Rev. 8-48)

UNITED STATES OF AMERICA
DEPARTMENT OF COMMERCE
CIVIL AERONAUTICS ADMINISTRATION
WASHINGTON

School Graduation Certificate

This is to certify that **FRANCIS PAUL KIMMINAU**
(Name)

4302 EAST KELLOGG, WICHITA, KANSAS was graduated from the
(Address)

PRIVATE PILOT curriculum of the

UNITED AIRPLANE SALES, INC.
(School)

MUNICIPAL AIRPORT, WICHITA, KANSAS Airman Agency Certificate No. **6864**
(Address)

on **APRIL 7, 1959** ; that he has successfully completed the instruction required
(Date)

by the Civil Air Regulations and is eligible to apply for a **PRIVATE PILOT**

Certificate and **A S E L** Rating as issued by the Administrator of Civil Aeronautics.

The record of this graduate is as follows:

Flying time:		COURSES SATISFACTORILY COMPLETED	GRADE
Dual	20:00		
Solo	15:00		
Total	35:00		
Final flying grade	85		

I certify that the above statements are true.

UNITED AIRPLANE SALES, INC.
(School)

By _____
(Signature)

FLIGHT MANAGER
(Title)

Date issued **4-5-59**

Chapter 2

USAF Primary and Basic Flight Training

One thing about my assignment to Moore AB at McAllen that really had nothing to do with flying, but was somewhat important. Lois was pregnant with Jon and was required by the doctors to be near a hospital all the time. Since they had nothing but a clinic at the air base, we had to rent a house in McAllen. A lot of the student pilots lived at Moore, but the housing was so substandard that they didn't even take the housing allowance we were given as part of our paycheck. It was really a good deal if you wanted to put up with the housing, which was converted railroad cars.

Our House in McAllen

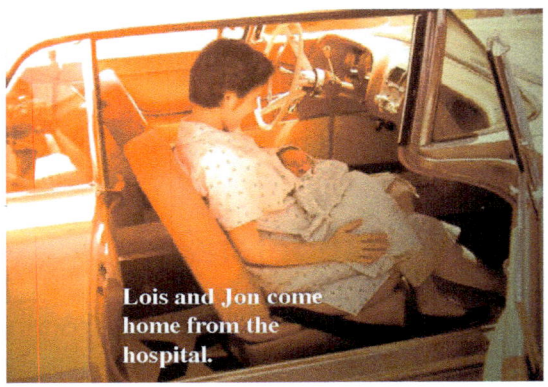

Lois and Jon come home from the hospital.

The instructors in the 3301st Pilot Training Group for our Primary Flight Training were all civilians. A lot had flown in the Army Air Corps, but some also had nothing but civilian flying time. My instructor, Leslie Ward, had over 20,000 hours flying time. That is a heck of a lot of flying!! He was rather a small man; he didn't smoke and I don't think he drank either. He was one heck of a GOOD instructor!

The first aircraft we flew was the T-34 Mentor. A single engine, tricycle landing gear, low wing, two-seat aircraft. The IP sat in the rear cockpit with the student in front. I don't remember how much academics there were, but I do know each and every airplane I flew, we had to learn all about every system on the airplane. After learning how to preflight, start, and taxi, we then went out and flew.

One of the first things we were taught was landings. Out in the flying area, we learned acrobatics, slow flight, stalls, and all the other things we needed to know. My IP, Mr. Ward, would, on just about every flight, when you least expected it, pull the throttle back and say "Forced Landing." He wanted you to be aware at all times that if you had an engine failure/problem that required you to land, you should have a suitable place picked out so you could make a forced landing. Often, there wasn't a really good field that you could use, but he wanted you to be able to pick the best one that was available. One other thing he made a point to remind you of ALL the time was: "If you don't have a specific task for the left hand, it better be on the throttle. The same goes for the right hand, no task, it better be on the stick."

Mr. Leslie Ward. A Christmas card with his family.

We also learned to recover from a spin. That could happen if you were ham-fisted and caused the aircraft to go out of control. It just so happened that the T-34 would not go into a spin unless you actually forced it to spin. The T-34 was so stable an aircraft that, if you just let go of the controls, it would actually come out of the spin all by itself. This is the only aircraft I ever flew that would do that.

There were some Air Force pilots also at McAllen. They would give all the check rides and would sometimes fly with students just to monitor progress.

I don't remember a lot about my solo rides in the T-34. Looking in my Log Book, which I just found, I see I flew in the T-34 the first time on January 27, 1960. My first solo ride was on February 10, 1960, after having eight dual rides, which was the minimum required.

Speaking of log books, I kept my own Log Book when I was going through the USAF FIP program in College, but at Primary Training I had a

Flight Dispatcher for our class, Melvin Kline, keep the log book. I don't remember how much he charged the students to do this, but I know it couldn't have been very much, because we couldn't afford much. He also drove the bus back and forth between Moore AB and the auxiliary field where we practiced take-offs and landings. On days we flew in the morning, he would pick us up and take us back to Moore for afternoon academics. If we had morning academics, we would ride the bus to the auxiliary field and fly with the final landing being at Moore.

The next aircraft was the T-37 trainer (nicknamed the Tweety Bird). It was a twin engine jet trainer. The two seats were side by side. It was a rather small airplane. The Log Book indicates that my first flight in the T-37 was 17 March 1960.

PK by the T-37

On probably my fourth or fifth flight in the T-37, we were flying down initial (flying straight and level, aligned with the runway) to practice landing. Mr. Ward said he had the aircraft (he was in control) and he asked me what was wrong. I said, "nothing." He said, "Why are you breathing so fast?" I hadn't noticed but I answered, "Well, I am just a bit worried that I won't be able to do this." He looked at me and said, "Hey, Mr. Kimminau, that is MY JOB. I'll be sure to tell you when I think you can't fly the way I want. Take the aircraft and just do it, and I'll tell you if you are doing anything wrong." I do remember very well that his saying that made a big difference in all my flying career.

I was the first one in our class to solo the T-37. I will always remember that day. We were practicing landings at the auxiliary field and Mr. Ward said to make this one a full stop. It was somewhat early in the flight so I didn't know why we would quit early. We taxied in and he asked me to stop. We shut down the right engine, opened the canopy, and he climbed out. Just before he disconnected his radio, he said to go make three touch and go's and then a full stop. Wow, I thought, he thinks I am ready. Sure enough, I started the right engine, asked the tower for permission to taxi out, and took off SOLO!! Looking back on that day I thought, "What a deal, here I am, a naive young kid from Kansas and I am soloing a jet aircraft!!" The Log Book shows that it was the 31st of March. It was also my sixth flight in the T-37.

PK taxis out for his first solo flight in the T-37. First in his class.

One other thing about the T-37. While the T-34 would only spin if you forced and held it in a spin, the T-37 would spin pretty easily. Once into a spin, the T-37 was a real handful to recover. We did practice some spins and had to demonstrate that we could recover from the spin to the Air Force check pilots; however, the civilian instructors taught us everything they could to NOT GET INTO a spin.

My log book reflects that I got 105.0 hours total time in the T-37 (179 landings, 8.2 hours night time, 41.3 solo hours, and 25.0 hours simulated instruments). I am pretty sure the rules were that we didn't fly in any bad weather, but I remember one day Mr. Ward let me fly in clouds and experience real instrument flying. I was in training in the T-37 from March until July 1960. My last training flight in the T-37 was July 13, 1960.

In August, I left McAllen for Laredo AFB, TX, where I would fly the T-33 trainer for Basic Pilot Training. I was assigned to the 3641st Pilot Training Squadron, Class 61-E.

I vividly remember the first time my three table-mates [Billy Kellum, Gilbert Holmes, and Dan Kimmel] and I met our instructor, Captain G. D. Monroe. He was a little over six feet tall and very good looking. He came to our table and all four of us jumped to attention. He said, "Sit down, and you don't have to do that anymore. OK, what do you guys want to fly when you get out of here?" We all had this kind of dumb look on our face and he said, "OK, you will all go to fighters!"

Kimminau, Kellum, Monroe, Holmes, Reinders

PK by the T-33

The story behind that is not about my flying but it is pretty interesting. Captain Monroe had gone through Basic Training in a class they called "Project Palm." The students in that class started and flew the T-37 jet trainer from the first day. Then to the T-33 for Basic Training and on to their next assignment. Captain Monroe graduated high enough in his class to choose to fly the F-86 fighter (highest class standing got first choice of assignments). After completing F-86 training at Williams AFB, AZ, his class was told they would not be going to an F-86 assignment because the F-86 was being phased out of the Air Force. They got a choice of going to B-47s or back to the T-33 as Basic Flight instructors. He chose being an instructor because he felt anyone flying bombers wasn't really a pilot, rather they were bus drivers. As it turned out, all four of us at that table would have gone to fighters if the Wing Commander had not changed some of the assignments.

The thing about Basic Training I remember most was the academics. They were tough and I really worked hard. I was number one in the class in academics and number two in the flying phase, so I ended up number one in the class getting to choose my next aircraft and assignment.

In Basic Training we were introduced to flying under "the hood" and formation flying. Under the Hood means we would be in the back seat (the T-33 had two seats one in front of the other) with a cover which pulled up and covered the canopy so you could not see out. The IP would take off and then you pulled the hood up and took the aircraft and flew by instruments. It was pretty hard work when you first did it, but as you did it more often, it really gave you confidence in your ability to fly in weather.

Formation flying was a lot of fun also. I remember the flight when we flew four-ship formation and were getting ready for our formation check ride. I had another Captain instructor (Ivy McCoy, a good friend and roommate of Captain Monroe's) as my IP. We would be in formation, would pitch out and all be in trail formation, then the leader would go into a turn and the other three would rejoin. I remember being number three and made such a smooth join up that Captain McCoy really was impressed and told Captain Monroe so during the debrief.

PK & GD on the way to the aircraft

The T-33 did not have nose wheel steering. The nose wheel was a "caster" meaning it would turn any which way and you steered the aircraft using brakes to steer. If you wanted to go left, you pushed on the left brake and that would cause the nose wheel to turn left, the right brake if you wanted to go right. Of course, if you wanted to go straight you did not use one brake more than the other and when you wanted to stop, you used both brakes to stop straight ahead.

Well, one day the Flight Commander decided I would go "fly" with him. Don't remember for sure but I believe there was weather that day and we would not be flying, but we went out to preflight, start, and taxi. I had NEVER had any problems steering the T-33 UNTIL that day. If you didn't let it roll a little straight ahead when you first started taxiing, the nose wheel would "cock." That is, it would turn sideways and you couldn't go anywhere until the crew chief would go push the wheel a bit so it would roll straight ahead. Sure enough, I had to cock the nose wheel with the Flight Commander, who then proceeded to teach me how to taxi for about 30 minutes.

Boy, was Captain Monroe pissed at me. I did not blame him either. He knew I had never had a problem and was a bit put out that cocking the nose wheel had to happen with the Flight Commander. [Note: See the story included as Attachment 1 written by an IP at another training base about cocked nose wheel.]

One other very memorable flight was the dual night cross-country flight. As we were coming back toward Laredo from our round robin flight, there was a cloud layer above us. We were at about 20,000 feet. The cloud layer wasn't level but angled up. When you looked out at it, you got the feeling that you weren't flying level but climbing. Looking at the instruments, you could tell you were flying level. This was my first case of vertigo. It was very strong and took a lot of willpower to look at the instruments and believe them rather than my feelings.

The morning of the big dual cross-country where all three of us at the table went as a formation [only three were now at the table; Dan Kimmel was moved to another IP because some guys had washed out and they wanted to keep the work load among the IP's equal], the weather was a bit low and they held us up. [Note: Later in training they did assign another student to Capt. Monroe's table. He is in the picture I have of our table.] It looked for a time like we might get canceled. However, we finally were cleared and off we went.

Lockheed T-33 Shooting Star

I again had Ivy McCoy as my IP. We got lined up on the runway and the heading indicator was not working. Ivy said, "Let's go anyway, we'll use the mag compass." Heck, who am I to argue with the IP? Off we go and into the clouds. We climbed out to the West and were in clouds up to about 15,000 feet. When we broke out on top of the clouds, we started looking for the other two aircraft. We had taken off single ship. Several miles out to our right we saw the other two. Our aircraft was in Mexico a few miles and we quickly joined up with the others. We landed at Davis-Monthan AFB in Tucson, AZ, to refuel. The IPs made the take off as a three-ship formation. I don't think that was authorized but they did it anyway. We went out to the West, found the Colorado River, and flew low level over the river up to Hoover Dam, popped up and landed at Nellis AFB, NV. That is of course in Las Vegas.

Lois pins on my wings.

This picture is "funny colored" because I developed the slide film myself and must not have done it correctly.

Both Monroe and McCoy had some students from previous classes flying F-100s at Nellis. We went to their BOQ rooms and started drinking beer. I mean, those other students and the IPs did most of the drinking while we other three were "Stepin Fetchit" boys! A night in town, and off the next day back to Laredo.

I can't remember the third IPs name, but he always liked to make VFR position reports to Center using a Shell road map. On our return flight to Laredo, we were at 20,000 feet going east toward Roswell, NM, and over Arizona. He reported our position as over Jackrabbit, AZ. There really is a very small place called Jackrabbit. The lady at the Center accepted the position report and without missing a beat, came back with the Jackrabbit altimeter setting of 29.92.

When the big day came for us to choose our next aircraft, they put the list of names up on the board in the order in which they would choose. My name was first. There were only six F-100 assignments for our class. There were B-47, Helicopters, T-33, etc. and several other aircraft to choose from. Our class was the first to have some F-101 assignments, and there were some F-102 assignments as well. The F-101 aircraft were Reconnaissance/Air Defense Command and the F-102 were Air Defense Command assignments. The F-100 assignments were to Tactical Air Command where you went to drop bombs and shoot the cannon. It was well known that all the fighter aircraft choices would go to the top guys on the list. Seems everyone wanted to fly a fighter. MY CHOICE was an F-100. I had never really been up close to an F-100 but had seen the USAF Thunderbirds Demonstration Team, which flew F-100s.

I don't know just how much later, probably within a week, they showed the class some film of different aircraft we would be flying. One such film was of an F-100 doing the "Sabre Dance" and crashing. This was a situation where the pilot got behind the power curve, i.e., got the nose of the aircraft so high that the drag of the aircraft was way more than the power of the aircraft could overcome, so the F-100 would weave back and forth. [If you didn't push the nose down (which would of course cause you to slam into the ground) to get some airspeed back, you would crash.] All the other guys in the class were then asking me how I felt about choosing the F-100.

One kind of funny thing about the choosing of aircraft: the guy that was second had worked pretty hard in academics also and just about beat me out for the top spot. Turned out that even if he had been number one, he was going to choose a helicopter, which he did even as number two.

Having chosen the F-100, I would be going to Luke AFB, AZ, for F-100 training. During leave between getting my wings at Laredo and going to Luke, we went to Wichita, KS, to visit my mother. While there, I went out to Boeing Aircraft Company to visit with a good friend who was in my class in college. (He actually took the job I had while working at Boeing for the six months before I went into the Air Force.) He took me out to a hangar there at Boeing, and I got to look at and climb up on an F-100. [Boeing had one there that was a chase aircraft for their big bomber aircraft test flights.] The thing that impressed me most was how BIG it was. I don't remember the number exactly, but the ladder must have had six or seven steps. (I do remember thinking at the time, the Cessna 140 that I had started flying in was a pretty small airplane. The T-34 and T-37 were a bit bigger, but still rather small aircraft. The T-33 was almost twice as big as those two, and now the F-100 was at least twice as big as the T-33.)

Chapter 3

F-100 Fighter Pilot Training (Luke AFB, AZ)

The first thing I remember about my time at Luke AFB, AZ, was really not flying but it occurred when I signed in. In line in front of me was another guy for the same class of F-100 training. His name was Jon Alan Reynolds. It struck me as kind of funny. Lois and I had picked out the name for our first son and thought it was quite unique. Jon Alan. Well, here was another and when I heard him say his name I asked how he spelled it. Yes, it was spelled exactly as we had spelled our son's name.

Also as I was signing in, I was checking my AF Form 90 [I am pretty sure that is the correct form]. It had just about all the information about you, and one of the things included was your "wish list," that is, what assignments you were looking for in the future. Imagine my surprise when I saw as my first wish a C-124!! I remember filling that out at Lackland AFB when we were in preflight training. I was thinking about my brother Leo and his flying the C-124. Of course I got that off there as fast as I could!

When we finally got to the training squadron, the 4515th Combat Crew Training Squadron, and checked in with the Instructors, we discovered that, even though we had gotten out of Pilot Training and had our wings, we were still STUDENTS! Looking back on it, I guess it was a good thing they treated us like students since we were still very new at the flying game.

One of the first things we did was fly about thirty hours in the T-33. Yeah, back into the same airplane we had just come from. Since we were now in Tactical Air Command and not Air Training Command, we learned how to fly instruments the TAC way, not ATC way. The procedures were just as safe, but, in most ways, cut short so you could get more aircraft landing in a shorter period of time than using the basic procedures we were taught in ATC.

4515th's Operations Building @ Luke

I mention that because it brings back memories of the ONLY time I ever cheated on a flight. We were making an instrument approach (I was in the back under the hood), and we were using a radio beacon for the approach. You would go over the beacon and as you passed over it (you could tell that by when the needle pointing to the beacon would swing from pointing toward the nose to pointing toward the tail) you turned to the outbound heading/track and would start your descent. When you reached a specific altitude, you would start your turn back toward the beacon and level off at a specific altitude which was safely above any obstacles. When you were over the beacon again, you would take up the heading/track back toward the airfield. Normally the beacon was a minute or so from the end of the runway. You would configure the aircraft for landing, gear and flaps, and descend to the minimum altitude for that approach. It was important to check the time you passed over the beacon coming toward the airfield because you were under the hood and you were supposed to tell the IP when you reached a point that you would be seeing the runway if you were really coming out of the weather and were now able to see the runway to make a landing. Well, I don't remember just what it was that I did, but somewhere during the descent, the Instructor started chewing my ass about something, I got pretty flustered and forgot to check the time I passed over the beacon going back toward the airfield. I got the gear and flaps down and made the descent to the minimum altitude but did not know just when to tell him we were over the runway. SO, I pulled up the hood on the side just a little and looked out. Seeing the runway, I told the IP we were over the runway. Well, I did pass the ride and of course never told the IP I cheated.

Now, on to the F-100. As noted on the cover page, Hemingway's saying about an aircraft is true, and for me it is the F-100. A tough airplane to fly to its maximum but as honest as the day is long!!

I can't remember exactly the number of flights in the F-100F we each got before we went into the F-100C/D. The F-100F is a two-seat aircraft that they used mostly for training. [It did see a lot of combat in the Vietnam conflict.]

On my second or third flight in the F, just about the time we were to touch down, the nose came up pretty high. The IP pushed the throttle forward, and we went around and made another approach and the landing. We were met by a bunch of people and I could not figure out why. Well, the guy in mobile control thought we had hit the tail of the aircraft on the runway on that first approach. After looking at the tail end, it was agreed by most of the people around there that we had scraped the eyelids of the afterburner. That made it a very nose high position and one you should NEVER be in. Since we were very close to touch-down, it wouldn't have been dangerous but the IP felt it best to go around. I did learn a valuable lesson and that was NEVER let the nose of the F-100 get that high when landing.

When you get on the runway for your first take off in the F-100C (or D), it is quite an experience! Every time you have gone solo up to then, the aircraft you are in is the one you flew when your Instructor was with you. Yes, he's not there, but the seat he used is still there. Now you are in an airplane that has just ONE seat, and you are in it!! It is a real thrill to be able to fly it and come back to the ramp and park, knowing you did it!

The training included going to the "Range" and dropping bombs, shooting rockets, and shooting the 20mm cannons. You were required to qualify in dive bomb, skip bomb, rockets, strafe, and nuclear weapons delivery. We did 45 and 30 degree dive bomb, level (50 ft) skip bomb, and 20 degree rockets. The strafing with the cannon was at a 20x20 ft. canvas target. Most of the time the dummy bullets you had were colored on the tip. Each student had a different color and after you strafed, the range people would count the colors and let you know how many hits you had. The nuclear weapons delivery was Laydown, LADD [Low Angle Drogue Delivery], and Over the Shoulder.

Sunset from our backyard at the place we lived while we were at Luke for my F-100 check-out.

Laydown was done at 300 feet level, and you used a "by guess" aiming method. You put a mark on the canopy just aft of the canopy bow and would bank up and when the target passed that mark you would release the weapon. Your 300 ft. altitude was a guess also since trying to fly a consistent altitude was almost impossible using the altimeter. A drogue chute would come out of the weapon after release and it would descend and stick in the ground, at the target hopefully. There was a timer, and you would fly as fast as you could departing the target area.

LADD was done by coming in very low, and at an Initial Point (IP) you would push the release button (Pickle Button), which would start a timer, then you would start a pull up and during the climb, the timer would release the weapon. You would complete a half roll, put the nose down and go as fast as you could away from the target. Again, a drogue chute would deploy and slow the weapon's descent, allowing you time to get safely away.

The Over the Shoulder delivery was completed by flying at 500 knots over the target, pressing the pickle button, and pulling 4 g's to complete a half loop. There was a gyro that you set that would release the weapon at the correct angle so it would come off at about the time you were vertical over the target. An instrument with a needle telling you that you were pulling the correct "g's" and keeping the wings level was what you used to tell that you were doing it correctly. After you completed the half loop, you rolled wings level and, again diving, you departed the area as fast as you could.

Low level navigation was another skill we learned. On a couple of these missions, we were in the back seat of the F-100F, and after IP made the take off, the student in the back seat, under the hood, would fly instruments, simulating we were in the weather, and, using a radio beacon and time, would fly at a high altitude (20-25,000 feet) for a set amount of time and then start a controlled let-down. We would let down on a specific heading, and when reaching about 5,000 feet AGL (above ground level) the IP would tell us to come out from under the hood. If we did it correctly, and the winds were as forecast, we would be in a position to visually determine where we were. You then let down to 500 feet and flew a set low-level route to arrive at the range to deliver your bombs.

This was where you learned to really pay attention to your airspeed and heading and TIME!!! If you could not determine your position after you came out from under the hood, you flew the heading and made sure you watched your airspeed and then turned on time. If you did this, somewhere along the way you should (and almost all the time did) find something you would recognize that was on your plotted course. Then you could get back on your route and complete the mission. This was difficult, and one of the funny things that just about EVERY student did was get lost. Seems that no matter how hard you tried, you would push up the throttle and the next thing you knew, you were going way faster than your planned airspeed. You were just getting lost faster and faster!!!

We did fly some air-to-air missions against other IPs and students, but, as I recall, not very many. I don't remember getting any cross-country flights while at Luke.

One thing that really sticks out in my mind about my time at Luke AFB was when Bob Hoover came to Luke to put on a demonstration flying an F-100D. I was told he just went out on the line and picked an F-100D that was used daily for training. He took off and did several low passes, sometimes doing a roll with gear and flaps down, and maybe even a loop. The one maneuver he did that I will never forget was, coming in for landing with gear and flaps down, he lit the afterburner!

[Anyone who has ever flown the F-100 in its early days knows that lighting the AB at low airspeed can be quite an adventure! Almost every time you would get a compressor stall. Fire would shoot out the front and back of the airplane, and in the cockpit it felt like the airplane had exploded!]

Mr. Hoover completed the landing at the end of the runway. He then pulled up and climbed to about 200-300 feet and did a roll! Completing the roll, he then proceeded to touch down again. He did not make a full stop, of course, but to be able to touch down, then do a roll and touch down again on a 10,000 foot runway, was to me the most amazing thing I had ever seen. With about 50 hours flying time in the F-100, I knew how hard it was to fly, and this seemed like an impossible maneuver.

One weekend while we were at Luke, we went to Oak Creek Canyon for a picnic. Here we have Jane Moyer and her little girl Debbie, Jon, Lois, and me. Bill Moyer was another guy checking out in the F-100 and a good buddy. He took the picture.

After he finished and landed, he came taxiing in and shut down before he had stopped the airplane. When it came to a stop, he stood up in the seat with his straw hat on. He was dressed in a white shirt, tie, and black slack pants with a sports coat on!! He looked as dapper as if he had just stopped by for a drink. What a pilot this guy was. (Note: I have met and talked to Bob Hoover a couple of times in my life and have heard some of his stories about flying. I have his book, signed by him, and will tell you he was one of a few true legends of FLYING!)

After finishing my F-100 training at Luke, I went to Survival School at Stead AFB, NV. My orders show I left Luke for Stead on August 15, 1961. That has nothing to do with flying and wasn't exactly a fun time. See Attachment 2 for more information about my time at Survival Training. [Lois stayed at Goodyear, AZ, with son Jon and baby Lori, who was 11 days old. Lois's mother came to help her while I was TDY.]

Chapter 4

F-100 Fighter Pilot Training (Nellis AFB, NV)

It was in late September 1961 that I checked into the 4520th Combat Crew Training Wing at Nellis AFB, NV, for more F-100 training. I don't remember if they called it "top off training" or not, but we did get training in requirements we needed to become Combat Ready before reporting to an operational unit.

The very first thing I noticed upon signing in at Nellis was that they treated you like a fighter pilot. No more student stuff!! They told us what we were going to do, and they showed us how to get ready for it, and then said, "When your briefing time comes, be there and be ready!!" Quite a growing up experience.

Wikipedia picture showing a KB-50 refueling an F-101 [Left wing], and F-100 [six o'clock], and F-105 [Right wing]

Another thing that sticks out about our arrival at Nellis was the in-briefing we got by the Wing Commander. Of course he told us we would be treated as Fighter Pilots, so act like one. He also told us this: "Tonight when you go downtown, go to Fremont Street and look at all the lights on the casinos. Ask yourself this, "Who is paying the light bill?" It didn't take long to realize he was telling us, you gamble, YOU pay the light bill.

We were trained in Air-to-Air refueling, Air-to-Air gunnery (Dart), tactical gunnery, and nuclear low level flying. Air-to-Air refueling was using a KB-50 tanker. They had a long hose with a basket on the end that you flew up to and put the probe into the basket. The KB-50 had three of these, one on each wing, and one coming out the tail. The hose had a take-up mechanism and brake system that allowed you to contact the basket and the hose would stay straight. If for some reason this did not work and you contacted the basket and pushed it forward, making a lot of slack in the hose, WATCH OUT! The hose would be like a big snake and there was no telling what would happen. Sometimes it would whip up and down, and if you did not disconnect quickly, it could tear the probe off your aircraft.

On one of the refueling flights, a good buddy of mine was hooked up and got a bunch of slack in the hose. It got tangled in between the wing and the slat. I thought he would be bringing a long piece of hose home with him, but as he backed away, it just cleared itself and everything was back to normal.

Refueling off the KB-50 and getting a full load was hard work; because we were flying so slow, it took a lot of power, and sometimes we just could not keep hooked up for a full load.

Since the time at Nellis was only three months, we stayed in a motel. This is Jon sitting in the door at the motel

The Air-to-Air gunnery, DART was fun. They had an F-100 that would tow a dart on a long cable, over 1,000 ft behind the tow aircraft. You would sit up on a perch and when the tow aircraft went into a turn, you would get on the inside of the turn, behind the dart, and shoot the 20 mm cannon trying to put a hole/holes in the dart. Sometimes guys would get lucky (or unlucky!), hit the cable, and the dart would go floating down to earth out in the desert. If it was the first guy (of the flight of four) the others did not get to shoot that mission, and that made the IPs unhappy. If it was the last guy, it sometimes made the IPs unhappy because they couldn't tell for sure if the others who had shot at it got a hit or not.

I think we had three dart missions, and you had to get at least a hit on one of the missions to be qualified. If you had a good radar (it was a range-only radar) and could get a lock on, it made it easier to get a hit. If you didn't, then you would crank it down manually and try to get to 1000 ft range (minimum) and shoot manually. This was a bit harder, because it forced you into a "tail chase" with the dart. The IPs watched that very carefully, because it would line you up with the tow aircraft and they did not want you shooting in that direction. Don't blame them!!

The Tactical Gunnery was dropping bombs and strafing on a range with tactical targets. The targets were old trucks or jeeps or tanks that would be placed in formations like one might find in a combat situation. On some of the missions they would simulate antiaircraft guns firing, and you would use different tactics. On one such mission, a mission where it was simulated that we were in an area where there were no antiaircraft guns present, we would get into a formation called a "daisy wheel." The lead would roll in and either drop his bomb or strafe, and about the time he was pulling off the target, number two would roll in, and then number three would roll in as number two pulled off, etc. This way there was someone always pointing at the target releasing ordnance. The IP briefed that you had to be very careful the first few times you did this, because everyone had the tendency to pull up and not extend out far enough to regain airspeed so the next time you rolled in, you would be slower than you should be to do it correctly.

I remember one mission when that was exactly what happened. All the students (even the IP) kept pulling in tighter and tighter, and on one of the passes (a strafing pass), just after I finished firing, I realized I was going pretty slow. I knew the pullout would be close and, as things would have it, there was a 400-500 ft hill right in front of me. I pulled up, but did not snatch and pull real hard knowing that wasn't going to help, and the hill in front went out of sight as the nose came up. I made it and really do not know how close I came to the ground, but I do know it was close enough that it scared the hell out of me and taught me a very important lesson.

This is a good picture of the Dart loaded on an F-5. During our training, the tow aircraft was an F-100.

The nuclear low level missions were quite interesting. You had to draw a map showing the route with markings for turning points, initial point, timing marks, and the target. The target and route would be displayed on a big map a few days before you were to fly the mission. You had to get the high detailed maps and put together the folder correctly, and show the IP during the briefing that you understood the route/target. I don't remember how many of these we did, but it was a real learning experience. It taught you a lot about low-level navigation and target study.

By December we had finished our training and knew which units would be our next assignment. Mine was the 31st Tactical Fighter Wing, 306th Tactical Fighter Squadron at George AFB, CA.

One other trip we took while at Nellis was to Disneyland. Here Lois gives Lori a bottle while Jon looks at Dad.

This is a picture of Lois with Jon and Lori at Boulder Dam. We took several week end trips while at Nellis. We were at Nellis over Thanksgiving and had several days off. We went to the Grand Canyon and stayed over night at the Lodge on the South Rim.

Chapter 5

Flying with the 31st Tactical Fighter Wing

It was January 1962 when I reported to the 31st Wing at George AFB, CA. I'll start this part by saying that the next year was probably the hardest/toughest for me and my family. When we arrived at Victorville, CA, rumors were flying around the Wing that the 31st was going to be moved from George AFB in the near future. When anyone asked the Wing Commander, his reply was something like "don't listen to the rumors." I don't remember for sure if it was Glenn Farnsworth or Jim Gorman (maybe both) who were thinking of buying a house and were really in a tight spot if the wing did move. I looked around for a place to rent, because I was way down on the list to get a base house. We finally rented a pretty large house in Apple Valley from a lady who was going to Los Angeles. It was a one-year lease that we could get out of if the wing moved or I was reassigned within the year.

Our house in Apple Valley

Lois with Lori in front of the Victorville house.

The house was heated with electric wall heaters, one in each room. With two little kids we tried to keep the house a bit warmer than if we had no children. WOW, the first electric bill came in about six weeks and it was so huge that we almost had a heart attack!! We got a cord of very cheap wood and started using the fireplace to get some heat into the house. That didn't work and we learned to live with a lot of clothes on when in the house.

OK, that really has nothing to do with flying but will give you a bit of background of what I was living with while trying to get established in my first squadron. The squadron had a bunch of really good guys with a lot of experience in the F-100. The 306th Squadron, to which I was assigned, was preparing to go TDY to Okinawa, so I was learning and doing missions to be fully combat ready—air refueling, going to the range, and night flying.

The Air-to-Air refueling mission took on a different look as we now started to refuel from the KC-135 tanker. It had a single drogue attached to about 10 feet of hose which was connected to the refueling boom that they used to refuel SAC bombers. When the hose/drogue was attached, they could only refuel fighters with a probe. The speed was quite a bit higher than with the KB-50 so when were up at 20,000 feet or more, it really took a lot of power to get a full load of fuel. We started refueling with the afterburner and partial speed brakes so we could have enough power to get the full load. This made the aircraft a bit sensitive and you really had to work at getting hooked up and staying hooked up.

One mission sticks out in my memory of flying around George. I was number two in a flight of four being led by Lt. Radamaker. (I think that spelling is correct; he was a Navy exchange pilot and a Navy Lt. is like an Air Force Captain.) It's a bit complex to explain just what happened, but to make a long explanation short, I was flying an echelon formation position which the Air Force flies, but the Navy does it different. WELL, Radamaker gave me a chewing out in the air to get in position, I thought I already was, but he had me move into the Navy position he wanted. This was a new position for me and very uncomfortable. I did it because he said to do it. He chewed me out some more during debrief. I was pissed off because I thought I was doing it correctly, but he assured me I wasn't. After debrief, I got a couple of the old head Air Force guys and asked them if I did it wrong or what? They listened to me and explained that Radamaker was wrong and they would explain it to him. He never said anything to me about this again, and I don't remember if I ever flew in a flight with him again.

I don't remember exactly the timing, but I think it was somewhere in mid March that the word came that the 31st TAC Fighter Wing would be moving to Homestead AFB, FL. The 306th was only about a month away from deploying TDY (Temporary Duty, normally 90 days) to Okinawa, Lois was pregnant, and the lady we leased the house from wanted it back!! What I was really hoping for was getting PCS orders for the move to Homestead so I could move Lois and the kids and still go TDY with the 306th. Well, the good old Air Force said that wasn't possible since I had already had a PCS move within that fiscal year. We looked around and found a house in Victorville that we could rent. I rented a U-Haul truck one weekend and a buddy helped me move everything from Apple Valley to the new house. After that weekend, I came to work on Monday and what did I find in my in-basket? Orders to Homestead!!! Crap!!! Now it was too late to move the family because I had already used up any money we had to rent the new house and to move. I was still going TDY with the 306th, but Lois and the family would be staying in Victorville.

Early April arrived, and I was scheduled to fly an F-100 to Okinawa. This was really a big deal! We would refuel 3-4 times and land in Hawaii. After a night's rest, take off and refuel several times and land at Guam. Then from there a couple refuelings and land at Kadena AB, Okinawa. For a pretty new guy in the F-100, this was really a good deal. Well, it didn't work out so well! Our first refueling just off the coast of California, my afterburner wouldn't light. I did get a full load of fuel with just mil power, but the flight lead said, go home! Crap, no, double CRAP!! Now one of the airborne spares took my place, I flew back to George.

View of Golden Gate Bridge taken from the C-54

I got all my stuff together and started a long trip with Military Airlift Command (MAC). Flew to Travis AFB, California, and then a C-54 to Hawaii. I can't remember just how long this flight was, I just remember it was a hell of a long trip!! (10-12 hours I think.) After a few hours on the ground and a crew change, we were off to Wake Island. Another long trip! Refuel and off to Okinawa. We did get to fly around Iwo Jima [*Iwo Jima, officially Iō-tō, is an island of the Japanese Volcano Islands chain south of the Ogasawara Islands and together with them form the Ogasawara Archipelago also known as the Bonin Islands. Wikipedia.*] and I took a couple of pictures. That was about the ONLY thing on the trip that was of interest.

Got checked into a BOQ room at Kadena, and then we had a welcoming party that the wing threw for us. The 306th was TDY to Kadena to fill in for one of the squadrons of F-100s stationed there that were going back to the states (Nellis AFB, NV) to check out in the F-105 aircraft. We, the 306th, would be sitting Nuclear Alert at Kadena in place of that squadron.

The flying around Okinawa was quite different from flying around George AFB. Right after takeoff, you were over water, and just about any place you looked, all you saw was more water. There was a gunnery range on Ie Shima island, which is just about 20 km west of the island of Okinawa. We did regular range missions and simulated nuclear weapons delivery missions on the island. (NOTE: In August 1945, the Japanese landed several Betty Bombers on this island with the surrender delegation going to Manila to meet with General MacArthur to get the ground rules for the signing of the surrender papers later on the Missouri.)

Each flight in the squadron would sit alert for about a week at a time. This involved eating, sleeping, whatever, in the quarters right next to where the aircraft were parked. We would get up and check out the aircraft every day, then back to the alert shack and play cards, study, whatever, all day. Then, sleep and start over the next day doing the same thing.

One mission that happened very early in the three-month tour sticks in my memory. I was scheduled to fly with Don Neary on a tour around the island. We were just going to fly around the island and see what everything looked like. The weather was pretty good and it was a very interesting tour. Coming back to land, a layer of clouds about 1,000 feet thick had formed up with the bottoms about 700 feet above the ground. Now I hadn't flown a lot in weather, especially flying in formation. This would be a new experience for me. We were going to do a GCA approach. (A ground radar station would guide you in, keeping you on a heading aligned with the runway, and when about one to one-and-a-half miles from the runway end, they would have you start a let-down of about 250-300 feet per minute. This would allow you to see the runway about a half mile out and you could make a visual landing.) On this day, since I was flying on Captain Neary's wing, I would make a formation landing. Everything went just as planned, except!!— the clouds were very thick and it was quite difficult to keep the wing tip of his airplane in sight. I had to keep moving in closer and closer. I did not know really how close and really did not care, I just wanted to keep him in sight and stay in formation. I can remember seeing the lettering inside the wing light on his aircraft. When we actually broke out of the clouds, we already had gear and flaps down, I was so darn close to his wing with my canopy, I was scared spitless! When we got back in and I told Captain Neary this, he said he thought I must be close because I was overlapped so much, that he was having to fight his controls to keep flying level.

The Island of Iwo Jima. Mount Suribachi at the tip of the island (far left in the picture). Mount Suribachi picture from Wikipedia

Maybe a little explanation about this sitting Nuclear Alert business is in order. Remember this is a single seat, single engine, fighter aircraft. One pilot. The nuclear weapon loaded on almost all the aircraft was an MK-43 (I am hoping my memory is correct here) and most were 1.1 megaton yield. We had maps with the route to the target showing time, headings, fuel, etc. Also included were large circles colored in yellow or red. There was a code word associated with each circle.

If you were flying the route and happened to be within the circle (yellow was a probably and red was a for sure) and you heard the code word, that meant that a nuclear weapon had been delivered and was about to be exploded. You couldn't really do a lot about it but you were warned that something was about to happen. It was a bit ironic in some cases because the bomb we were to deliver on the target would be maybe the fifth or sixth weapon to be dropped on that target. They wanted to be sure that target was destroyed!!

Kadena AB, Okinawa

I will tell you that not one other pilot that I ever sat alert with talked about maybe not going if we were launched. Each and every guy I flew with would take off and fly to his assigned target and deliver the weapon, PERIOD!

I can also tell you several of the targets were so far away that you only had enough fuel to deliver the weapon and make a safe escape from the blast before you flamed out.

Another interesting thing happened while on this TDY. A typhoon was headed for Okinawa and the squadron was to evacuate the aircraft to Japan. We were roused from bed about 4 a.m. and were at the squadron getting a brief on who was going to fly out and when. I happened to be sitting between guys smoking (yea, those were the days that smoking was allowed everywhere), on both sides, in front, and behind, and the smoke was terrible. Well, I don't smoke and the smoke was really bothering me, eyes watering, coughing, etc. The Squadron Commander saw me blinking and coughing and he thought I was either drunk or hung over. He called out, "Kimminau, you aren't flying today." OK, now I was going to be left behind with a bunch of others to sit out the typhoon.

I took this picture from the back seat of the F-100F. We have just completed an "over the shoulder" maneuver and are upside down. I am looking and taking the picture through the top of the canopy. The target isn't centered, it is at the lower right of the picture.

Left: The parking lot in front of our BOQ. The motor scooters we either borrowed or rented for our transportation around the base.
Right: The West gate into Kadena Air Base.

Left: Our BOQ at Kadena.
Right: My BOQ room. This was typical with two guys to a room.

A memorial plaque on Ie Shima island. Picture from Wikipedia

That is the air-to-air refueling probe on the F-100. The island is Ie Shima, an island just to the Northwest of Okinawa that had the bombing range we used for practice.

It turns out that the aircraft were launching at just about the time the winds were the strongest, about 60-70 miles per hour, and the weather really never got much worse. All of us who were left behind ended up in a house on base that a good friend of one of our guys lived in, but he was gone with his family back to the states. Jim Havey, a young guy in the squadron, was getting promoted to First Lieutenant (he had gone through Aviation Cadets, so he arrived at the squadron as a Second Lieutenant) and he had bought a bunch of beer and liquor to celebrate the occasion. Well, he was one of the guys flying an airplane to Japan, so those of us left behind drank all his booze to celebrate his promotion. He wasn't real happy when he got back.

Another happening while on this TDY was a bit funny. We could get Philippine beer (San Miguel) for about $2.50 a case of 24. It is a pretty good beer and I really enjoyed it. I also acquired a case of "Green Apple Quick Steps" soon after arriving at Okinawa. The first time I went on alert for a week, the diarrhea went away. Once off alert, and after a few beers, it was back. Yep, I had it figured out! If I drank San Miguel beer, I would get a case of the quick steps. Had to switch beers!!

This TDY was the first case of "wishing your life away." Yes, here you were away from your family and wishing the time would fly by so you could get back home. The experience was great and the flying a lot of fun, but not being with the family was NEVER any fun.

When we were replaced by another 31st Wing Squadron, we headed home. We were all loaded on a KC-135 and off to Hawaii. We were going to be at Hickham AFB for 12 hours, while the SAC crew had crew rest. Well, we were not going to be resting!! We hit the showers, changed clothes, and were in the Officers Club in about one hour. I and three of the other young guys had Mai Tais and when I went to the bar to get the third round, the bartender looked at me and asked if I knew what we were drinking.

After that round, we went downtown to see the famous Waikiki Beach. We had a couple more drinks and then stopped at a restaurant for breakfast. One of the guys, Wes Carey, had a cold and had been taking some cold medicine along with the drinking (not supposed to do that!), so fell asleep in the booth after eating. All the rest of us got up, paid the bill, and went outside. The booth we had been sitting in, and Wes was still sleeping in, was a corner booth with windows on both sides. We got up to the windows and pounded on them and Wes woke up, looked around to find himself alone and the rest of us outside laughing like crazy. Sounded funny at the time and probably was, but a bit mean to Wes.

Arrived back at George AFB in mid afternoon, if I remember correctly. Lois was there to meet me and she had Jon and Lori with her. Jon didn't even recognize me and held onto Lois. It really tore my heart out thinking my son didn't remember me. It didn't take long until he did come to me and then it was fun again.

Within a week or so, we packed up the house and shipped the stuff to Florida. Lois was pregnant with Brian, and couldn't make the trip by car, so I put her on an airplane with the kids and she flew to Homestead. I got into the car and started driving.

While it has nothing to do with flying, this happened during my drive to Homestead. I actually started driving about noon on the day I left. I don't remember if it was Interstate Highway 15 [I-15] back then that I was driving on but I was going northeast to Barstow, CA. There I got on I-40 and planned to be on that highway until I got to Arkansas. Just as I was making the turn from I-15 to I-40 I saw this guy in a sailor uniform hitch-hiking. I thought, what the heck, maybe he will help keep me awake through the night. This young guy had started hiking that morning at San Diego and was going to Albuquerque and was having really good luck catching rides. I told him I was going right through Albuquerque so he would have a ride all the way home. He said he was off an aircraft carrier that had just finished picking up one of the space capsules out in the Pacific and was taking some leave. It worked out really good for a while, but about the time it got dark, he decided to take a nap. The nap lasted a long time and I was starting to nod off to sleep, so I had to stop just short of Gallup, NM, to get a rest. After about an hour, I continued on, and it wasn't long before we were at Albuquerque and he was home. He was the first hitch-hiker I had ever picked up.

Our rental house in South Miami Heights

Jon and I on my Lambretta motorscooter in front of the house

The start of Highway US 1 in Key West, FL.

Watching the water skiers while visiting Cypress Gardens, FL.

In Key West looking South toward Cuba

Entrance to Everglades National Park

The trip took me a few days. (I stayed one night with my older brother Jerome who was in the Air Force and stationed at Clinton Sherman AFB, OK.) When I arrived at Homestead I discovered there was NO base housing available, so we had to hunt for and rent a house off base. Fun, FUN!! Did find a house in South Miami Heights and got settled in a few weeks before #3, Brian, was born.

Probably the biggest thing about flying while I was at Homestead would be the fact that in the two years plus I was there, I was TDY more than I was at home!! It started off with the 306th going TDY to James Connally AFB, TX, for some kind of close air support exercise. This was a Navigator Training Base near Waco, TX. (My orders show we went on this TDY starting October 9, 1962. Remember that date!)

A couple of interesting things about this TDY—a good buddy and I did not get to fly the F-100 from Homestead to James Connally; rather we had to go early in a C-54 carrying equipment and the crew chiefs. We were told by the Squadron Commander to meet the guys flying in with a cold beer when they arrived. Of course we did, and we asked what kind of beer? Well, when in Texas (at least at that time) Lone Star was the beer of choice. So that is what each guy got as he shut down and before he got out of his airplane.

This buddy (Jerry Smith) and I met a couple Army Warrant Officer pilots at the bar, either the first or second night we were there. They asked if we would like a ride in their O-1 aircraft the next day. Probably not the smartest thing we ever did, but we said yes. The next day they said they would fly us from James Connally over to the Municipal Airport, have a drink, and fly us back. Sounded like fun! WRONG!! I had never been as scared of flying as I was in that flight of about 20 minutes over and back!! Those guys wanted to impress a couple of jet fighter pilots and did they ever!! Never got more than 100 or so feet above the ground, and one time when we were flying over a pasture, they actually flew low enough that they were running the tires of the airplane across the ground. There was a tree line at the edge of the pasture, and they flew until they had to pull up very abruptly; of course they were having the time of their life scaring these two fighter pilots.

I cannot remember just how many days we were there, but one morning several days before we were scheduled to go home, we got the word to get back to Homestead as soon as we could. I did get to fly an F-100 back to Homestead and when we landed the DO (Director of Operations) met us and said get home and get some rest. We didn't know what that was all about but we got called out later that night and told to start planning and map making for a trip. Where to? Well, a U-2 airplane had pictures of Russian missiles in Cuba. It was the Cuban Missile Crisis. (President Kennedy gave his speech to the Nation and the World on 22 October. We were in place and ready to go!!) [NOTE: There were a lot of people now shaking their heads saying, "Now we know why the 31st TFW was moved from George to Homestead!"]

One of the fun times at Homestead. We had a picnic!

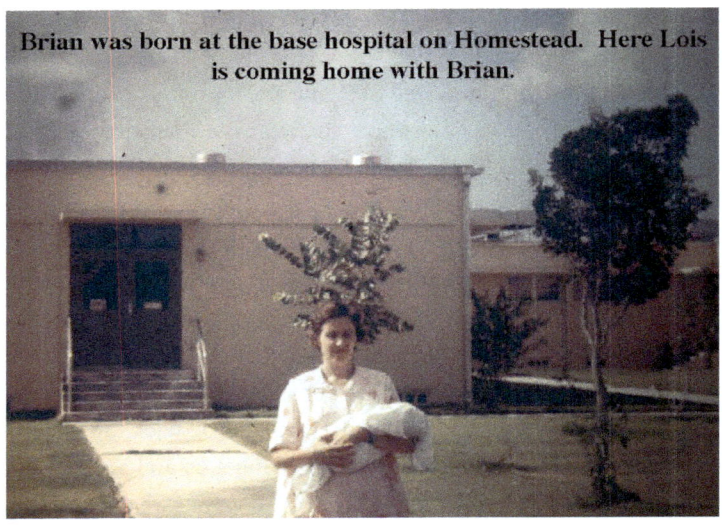

Brian was born at the base hospital on Homestead. Here Lois is coming home with Brian.

Remember I was living off base in South Miami Heights, about 5-6 miles north of the base. At the time I had a Lambretta motor scooter that I rode back and forth to work. Ten days in a row, I got up at about 4:30 in the morning, rode my scooter to work, preflighted my aircraft (in the dark), then went to the squadron and sat around waiting. At about sundown, we would go get our stuff out of the airplane, put it away, and I would ride back to my house, have dinner, and be in bed before nine o'clock.

Our aircraft were loaded with two large rocket pods holding 18 2.5 inch rockets, two canisters of CBUs (Cluster Bomb Units), and two external fuel tanks. (Can't remember right now if the tanks were 450 gallon or 335 gallon tanks.) My flight was in the first wave and we (if launched) were to hit our target at sunrise, return to Homestead, refuel and rearm, and go again. There were over 300 F-100s from all over the US now at Homestead and our landing from the first mission would be at about the same time the last flight in the third wave would be taking off. We were only one of several bases in Florida that had a lot of fighters that would be doing the same thing.

At the time we really did not think that they had any anti-aircraft guns that were of concern. Looking back on this time and realizing the experience guys in the F-100 had when they first flew missions in North Vietnam, I shudder thinking what might have happened.

There are a couple things that occurred during this period that are pretty vivid in my memory. One day, I think it was probably the 4th day we were sitting alert, about 2 o'clock in the afternoon we were sitting around playing bridge. (We played a lot of bridge!) They made an announcement that we should all come to the Ops desk. When we got there, they told us to get our "G" suits on. Next thing they said, "Go to the airplanes!" Well, off we went and got all strapped in and were waiting. [Everything was going to be radio silence, so no one was saying anything on the radios.] Next thing, I heard the first aircraft in my line starting up. "Ho Boy, this is it, we are going!!" Well, in about a minute, the line chief came by saying to start them up and run the checks to make sure everything was OK. (Actually this was pretty normal. The F-100 was notorious for hydraulic leaking seals if they weren't exercised every couple of days.) When we got back into the squadron, the Squadron Commander (Lt/Col John Madison) told us that was probably the closest feeling we would get about going to combat, unless we went. I know my heart rate was pretty high until the line chief told us we were just running up to check them out.

The other incident was pretty funny, and then again not so funny. All the pilots got briefed that we were going to practice starting up, taxiing out, lining up on the runway, running them up, and then taxiing back to the parking area. (If memory serves me correctly, this exercise was code named Elephant Walk.) One change we would be making was in the parking of the aircraft. Seems some news guy (either in a helo or a light airplane) had taken a picture of all the F-100s lined up on the ramp in very nice straight lines. The wing command structure decided that maybe we ought to not have them lined up so perfect in case the Cubans decided to come bomb or strafe us. [What a joke that was!!] Anyway they went through this elaborate briefing about how each flight would be parking in a different place, but close enough so we could still do everything in radio silence.

I can close my eyes right now and see what happened that day. We got started up and started taxiing. We got 36 F-100s on the runway (11,000 ft long and 300 ft wide runway) and all running up at full power at the same time. My flight was probably the 4th or 5th in the line up. That put 16-20 F-100s running at full power in front of me. I saw covers of the rocket pods, rings and seals from somewhere, and all kinds of stuff flying by my airplane. It is a wonder we didn't ruin a lot of engines that day.

That done, we taxied back to the ramp. Oh, someone FORGOT to brief the crew chiefs and ground personnel about the new parking arrangement. Here we were trying to go to the new briefed parking spot, and our crew chiefs were all at the spot where we were originally parked. Confusion?? I guess!! This first group of 36 aircraft got all bunched up at the end of the runway and no one was out there to tell the ground personnel of the new parking plan. I think we sat there for over 30 minutes waiting for something to happen. I remember seeing one guy, I think it was an Air National Guard guy, just shut down his airplane and climb out. The F-100 did not have parking brakes, so how this aircraft kept from rolling off somewhere, I'll never know. I do know it was one heck of a mess to get corrected.

Well, thank God we did not have to go. When things had settled down, President Kennedy came to Homestead to visit. We all (the pilots and crew chiefs) were standing out by our aircraft and he came driving by in his car. I did get to see him, but that was all. He was only at Homestead about an hour. I remember all of us standing out in the sun were sunburned pretty good!!

Birthday party at on base house, Homestead AFB.

After things were back to somewhat normal, our wing had a couple of F-100s that sat alert in case any aircraft were to launch out of Cuba. Several times going on orbit just north of Cuba, we were close enough that I could see the city of Havana. During one of these orbit missions, we got a call from radar that an aircraft had taken off in Cuba. They did not know just what type aircraft it was, but it did get our attention, and our search for any aircraft in that direction took on much more intensity.

One other interesting tidbit: After things had settled down somewhat, the US was still watching the removal of the missiles from Cuba. To do this they had U-2s and some Naval Reconnaissance aircraft flying over Cuba taking pictures. Since Cuba still had SAM (Surface to Air Missiles), our wing had a flight of four sitting alert to strike any SAM site that would fire at US aircraft.

Well, as things had gotten so political, after a week or so of sitting alert we had a team of "experts," civilian of course, come to Homestead and have the flight lead of this flight of four brief them on what and how they were planning to do the attack, if it ever came to that. Back then we did not have the fancy electronics to be able to put on a real "dog and pony show," so they had a big map of the area in Cuba where there was a SAM site. They put that thin, colored tape (different color for each aircraft) showing just where each aircraft was going to fly and what he would do.

The briefing was something like this: "We all go in in spread formation and on lead's call, we'll all dispense the CBU. After passing over the target, we'll take spacing, jettison the empty canisters and roll in, each from a different direction to launch the rockets. Again, after passing over the target after the rocket pass, we should have spacing to jettison the empty rocket pods and align for the strafe pass. We'll all be headed out on the opposite heading that we originally came from to do the strafing, and we'll join in spread formation for the trip home." One of the "Experts" asked how many of the people at the SAM site would be killed? The Squadron Commander answered, "Every damn one of them!!" Boy, that wasn't the politically correct answer!!

Someone up in Washington had figured out that if they did it correctly and hit only certain of the buildings at the SAM site, they would only kill four and one-third men. No one asked how you kill only a third of a man, they were too dumbfounded. The Squadron Commander was the leader giving the briefing. He was a crusty old Lt/ Col and actually served in WWII. Of course the "politically correct crowd" had him replaced.

Then it was more TDY.

Looking at a set of old orders, I find that I was scheduled to attend a Combat Operations Specialist Course (FAC, Forward Air Controller) training at Eglin AFB, FL. This course would have started April 14, 1963. For the life of me I cannot remember ever going to this course. I have another set of orders showing me going to Nellis AFB, NV, on April 1, 1963, for 30 days of GAM-83 training. I know I went to this training.

A few interesting memories about this TDY, starting with the trip out to Nellis: some Air Force Reserve C-119 unit was going to fly our equipment out to Nellis and I sweet-talked them into taking my Lambretta Scooter with us. I remember one night that Wes Carey and I rode the scooter to the Stardust

Casino and had the Valet park it for us. When we got ready to come back to Homestead, that crew did not want to let me put it on their C-119. I had to agree with them that if anything unusual were to happen, I would have to jettison the scooter.

Another unusual thing was very sad. One of the guys at Nellis checking out in the F-105 was a pilot who had been in the 306th when I arrived at the squadron at George. He had an assignment to Okinawa and was back checking out in the F-105 aircraft. His name was Kosterman. I remember him real well because one day after work at George he invited me over to his house for a drink. I was really impressed because here was an "old head" inviting a new guy for a visit with his family. It turns out the reason he wanted to talk to me was rather a funny reason. Seems when they got a copy of the orders sending me to the 306th he looked at the spelling of my last name and assumed I was Hawaiian. He was from Hawaii and was really happy to be having another Hawaiian in the squadron.

[I wondered just why he thought I might be Hawaiian. Much later in my career while at Davis-Monthan AFB in Tucson, AZ, I think I figured out why he may have thought that. I was looking at the box scores of a college World Series game between the U of A and the University of Hawaii. Just about all the Hawaiian names had a bunch of K's, I's, M's, and U's. My name with the I's, M's and U just had to look Hawaiian to him.]

Anyway the sad event was that he was in a flight of F-105s returning to Nellis to land, and as they turned initial his aircraft had a mid-air collision with a light aircraft that was in a place it should not have been. Of course both aircraft were destroyed and Kosterman and the man in the light airplane were killed. (I remember later when I was stationed in England I was telling this story and one of the guys in the squadron, Ron Sumner, said he remembered that accident also. Seems the guy in the light aircraft was his Uncle. Ron Sumner and I had gone through the F-100 training at Luke and Nellis together.)

Somewhere around June or July the 306th was again going TDY to sit alert for a squadron that was coming back to the states for F-105 check out. We would be replacing the 308th Squadron already in place at Itazuke AB, Japan. I remember a few interesting events about this TDY.

One day when there was a full schedule for flying in the local area, the weather was bad and forecast to stay that way, so the squadron cancelled flying. All the old head guys took off to shop or play golf or whatever, leaving the young guys behind at the squadron. As sometimes happens, the weather cleared up and the Squadron Ops Officer wanted to fly some sorties. Looking around, he saw four of us young guys sitting around and he told us to get ready to go fly. I am very sure I had never had a formal check out as a flight lead but he said, "Kimminau, you lead." Well, I briefed and we went flying around Japan. The weather was still scattered to broken clouds at a couple thousand feet so we were sometimes going through a few clouds. I think I screwed up only once. I flew through a gunnery range without ever contacting anyone. It was fortunate that the range was closed. I also remember flying up and looking down on Hiroshima, which was quite an experience. I could not tell from the air any difference between it and any other town we flew by.

Since Japan did not allow any nuclear weapons in their country, the alert we pulled was at Osan AB, Korea. If I remember correctly, we would sit alert for a week at a time. We would get flown over in a C-124 since the aircraft were already there and loaded with weapons.

The way it worked, you normally did not have much time at Osan except sitting alert. As soon as you got there, the crew, who had been on alert for a week, were anxious and ready to go back to Itazuke, so you went right on alert. After a week, you were the ones eager to get out of there. One time, however, the C-124 had a bit of maintenance problems so the four of us got to go to the Officers Club. After several drinks and some rough weather going back to Itazuke, we never did that again. Flying your own airplane in weather is one thing, but flying in the back of "Old Shaky" in the weather is something I never want to do again.

I remember another interesting occurrence that turned out to be nothing, but it could have been serious. One night they had to change out the weapon on one of the aircraft. This was a normal thing they did because of the requirement to check the weapon occasionally; they could not do that while it was loaded on the aircraft. They changed out the weapon and were towing the aircraft back to its hangar when a strange and unusual thing happened. They had cut the taxi way and had dug a ditch across, I guess to put in a new water line, and had covered it with new concrete. They had used the steel plates over the new concrete for several days and thought it cured enough. Well, it wasn't! Sure enough as the main gear got to the new strip of concrete, they just sank down, and the aircraft was sitting on top of the weapon. This could have been a serious thing, like a Broken Arrow, meaning a damaged or some kind of accident with a nuclear weapon. They were able to jack the aircraft up and get it out of the hole and discovered that the weapon was in no way damaged or hurt. Maybe a little paint, but nothing major. I do not know if this was ever reported up the chain or not.

We were not back very long from the Itazuke TDY until we were off on a 3 week TDY to McChord AFB, WA. (This was in November 1963.) This TDY was to support a Close Air Support exercise at Ft. Lewis. I don't remember too much about those missions. I do, however, remember a couple missions where the weather was so bad we did not even try to go to Ft. Lewis. One of the missions we launched as a four-ship, and I don't remember just what we did, but when we got ready for landing, the weather was such that the flight lead decided we would each make our own approach and landing. We were in formation to the south of McChord and the flight lead had each flight member break off under radar control. I was on the left side of the formation and was the last one to start my approach. I was flying formation off lead and he received a vector from the radar control to turn right. He did, I was then flying as a single ship. There was a cloud bank (we were at 20,000 ft) and when I was no longer flying formation, I got a case of vertigo that was the worst I had ever had! Everything seemed wrong. Looking at the instruments and then the clouds was so confusing that I almost got sick. I stuck my head in the cockpit and started flying instruments as best I could. It took every ounce of concentration I had to believe the instruments. I entered the clouds and made the let-down feeling that everything was wrong, but I believed the instruments. When I finally broke out of the clouds at about 1,000 ft AGL, I was so relieved to see I was flying wings level toward the runway. I was one happy camper!!!

On one other flight we knew before we took off that the weather was not good. We probably should not have even tried to fly that day. My flight of four briefed and the Squadron Commander decided we should give it a try. I was number four with Fred Erickson as number three. We briefed real well on making a formation approach and landing. He briefed me that he would fly instruments right down until he could see the runway and then he would look over at me. When he did that, he said, I could now start looking for the runway also.

OK, out we went, and just after take off, we were told that there would be no one else taking off from McChord that day. In fact, I think they wanted to close the field but decided to wait until we were ready for landing to see if the weather would improve.

We went out and flew around for about an hour or so and then started our approach. Sure enough, the weather was really bad right down to the surface. I flew close formation to Fred and he was very smooth. I could hear the GCA (Ground Control Approach) guy talking to us and he was telling us how far out we were and what our altitude should be. I knew we were getting close to the end of the runway, and, sure enough, Fred looked over at me. I then started trying to pick up sight of the runway in my cross check but saw nothing out the front except clouds!!! Next thing I knew I saw the big white stripes that meant the end of the runway, and then my airplane touched down on the runway. I looked out front and pulled the drag chute; Fred disappeared down the runway and I saw his drag chute deploy. I followed the center line and the white line back to the parking spot. Right after we touched down (the other two had already landed), the tower announced that McChord was closed because of weather.

When I got in the debrief, I asked Fred if he saw the runway when he had looked over at me because I sure couldn't. He said, NO, he hadn't seen the runway, but we were at minimums and he didn't know what else to do but look to see if I was still in formation. That was probably the worst weather I had ever had to land in.

We weren't back too long from this TDY (of course, we had Christmas in between), when the wing got word that the 308th (one of the other squadrons in the wing) would be replacing a squadron from England AFB, LA, that was then TDY to Çiğli AB, Turkey, sitting nuclear alert. (Çiğli AB was near the town of Izmir, which is on the west coast of Turkey.) One of the young guys from our squadron, I don't remember his name, was selected to go with them. One day soon after he was assigned to the 308th, he got killed in an accident shortly after take off. Yea, you know right off the bat, huh? I was picked to replace him.

I was originally selected to be a ground spare. You know why? Because they came up with the extremely lame excuse that I had not refueled over water before! Huh, what the hell, did they lose the record of me refueling west of California way back in 1962?? I probably shouldn't be so upset over the Air Force and their screwed up thinking.

This was pretty close to my birthday (9 February) and Ash Wednesday (it was the 12th of February) in 1964. [Kind of an interesting side note: Since this was the start of Lent, I had decided to give up drinking. I know, this was pretty DUMB! No drinking while TDY with a Fighter Squadron??? I actually DID IT!!]

I sat in the aircraft, engine running, fuel truck hooked up, for about 2 hours while the 24 aircraft launched. The Air Force in their great wisdom had us launching about 10:00 at NIGHT. Why? So we would land in daylight when we got to Turkey. Did I get to fly? NO! After all the waiting, I got to take off my Poopy Suit (this is a rubber suit much like a swimmers "wet suit", which we were wearing because we were flying up pretty far North in a Great Circle Route to get to Turkey), get all the stuff I had packed in the F-100, put it in a KC-135 and fly for about 12 hours to Çiğli AB.

A rather funny weather brief before we went to the airplanes that night: The weather guy briefed the weather for take off and what we could expect in Turkey and then briefed the en route weather. When he talked about the conditions up around Newfoundland, he said something like this: "The waves will be about 10-12 ft and the temperature of the water will be about 39 degrees. If you have to bail out, Good Luck, Charlie."

I got to Çiğli AB in time to get checked into the BOQ, get a bit of sleep and then go out and preflight, start up, and check out several F-100s that the England AFB guys were going to fly home. One of the shittiest deals I ever had in the 31st Wing!! [NOTE: When I first went over to the 308th while at Homestead to fly with them, my name and some information about me got posted on the scheduling board. I mention this because by that time I had a little over 500 hours flying time in the F-100. I thought this was pretty reasonable. Well, to my surprise, almost every guy in the 308th had 1,000 hours or more flying time in the F-100!! I was a new guy.)

There were some interesting things about flying in Turkey. One I remember was going to Konya Range to practice weapons delivery when we weren't sitting nuclear alert. We only had 4 aircraft on alert so we did have plenty of other aircraft to fly. Normally we would fly a low level route to the range, complete the range work, and fly back high altitude. The funny thing about flying low levels in Turkey was watching what the herd of sheep would do when an F-100 flew over. Almost anywhere in the world, if you fly low over a herd of animals, they scatter to the four winds. Well, in Turkey we would have one of the aircraft flying the low level route and another flying a couple thousand feet above checking for other aircraft or whatever. Many times I saw the low level plane pass over a guy herding some sheep and, instead of the sheep all running away in different directions, they would all run TOWARD the guy herding them! You would see all these little specks scattered all over, and as they heard the airplane approach, they would all compress in a circle around the sheepherder. I often wondered if the sheepherder got hurt when this happened. None of us ever wanted to have to bail out and count on one of these guys to help us.

Another interesting flight I had while there. One day, Carl Young and I were going out to do an air-to-air mission. We would practice maneuvering on each other trying to get into a position to shoot the other guy down. We had just started the maneuvering out in the area, probably 60-80 miles from the base, when Carl asked me to join up on his wing. He then asked me to adjust the power settings so he could check his engine against what mine was showing. Long story short, it appeared that something was amiss with his engine. He set it for 80% and started a gentle descent toward the base. We declared an emergency and he made a straight-in approach. After he touched down, he pulled the power back and the engine ground to a stop! Seems the ring around the aft turbine had come loose and was rubbing against the turbine, causing the engine to overheat. All the turbine blades were very brittle and would come to pieces if you touched them. We were very lucky he was such a good pilot.

While we were there in Turkey TDY, Greece and Turkey got close to going to war with each other. I saw a real big deployment of military stuff one day when we were on the Konya range. The Turkish Air Force flew some of their F-86s into Çiğli for alert which caused us to get a bit worried. They had their enlisted Army people on the ramp to guard their aircraft and we were very uneasy about going out on the ramp while they were there. [NOTE: Just as an aside, we found out that the USAF spent more money per day taking care of the dogs the Air Police had than the Turkish Army paid their enlisted people.] It also caused us to think very hard about ferrying the nuclear weapons out of Turkey. The only place we could really take them would have been Italy, and to get there we had to cross Greece.

I did get to take an R & R to Greece while we were there. I and another pilot got about 10-11 days in Greece. It was fun and I got to see a lot of places you read about in history. Several times we just went to downtown Izmir for sight-seeing around the town and eating at good restaurants. I also got to travel a little bit around Turkey on weekends. I saw some very interesting things such as Roman Ruins and one of the Seven Churches mentioned in the Bible. At Attachments 3 and 4 you will be able to read about some of the trips as best I can remember where we went. But again, most of the time was spent wishing my life away!!

The day at Itazuke that I got to lead a flight for the first time, I took some pictures. The upper one is looking down on Hiroshima. The lower picture is of Iwakuni Range. I was very lucky since the weather was such the range was closed because I did not check in and ask permission to over fly the range.

The top picture shows Wes Carey looking very studious. Actually I think he was reading Playboy. On the bottom is a picture of the Main Gate at the Annex (From *Wikipedia, the free encyclopedia*). This was several miles from the Operations/ Runways. It was where our BOQ's were and most of the "Shoe Clerks" worked here.

When we deployed back to Homestead, we did not take the F-100s; those remained behind for the next squadron that replaced us.

We went back on a SAC KC-135. I mention that because of something that happened on the way home. I had bought a camel saddle and it was quite unique in that it had a white leather covering. Well, it kind of stood out in all the baggage we had loaded on the KC-135 and I kept my eye on it. About halfway across the ocean coming back, I went by where the luggage was stored, and what did I see but a brown leather cover on my camel saddle! After raising holy hell I found that one of the SAC slime bag crew members had exchanged his seat for mine. I got mine back.

I don't remember exactly when we did get back to Homestead, but I think it was late April or early May. I took two weeks leave and took the family around Florida. I think this was the ONLY time I had any leave while I was stationed at Homestead.

Hodges, Neary, Cabaniss, Kimminau at Osan just off Alert.
Waiting for C-124 to take us back to Itazuke.

In early June I was back in the 306th and we went TDY to Elmendorf AFB, Alaska. This was for Exercise Diamond Lil XII. We would launch a flight of four F-100s out of Elmendorf, climb to around 30,000 feet, and head west. We would fly until we just about got to the Bering Sea, let down to low level, 200-300 AGL, and then fly back to Elmendorf low level. About an hour or so behind us would be a flight of four that would fly west at low level and, when about at the Bering Sea, climb up to high altitude and return to Elmendorf. This was, of course, to confuse the Russians who could see us on radar when we flew high altitude going out but would lose radar contact when we let down to low level. Then an hour or so later they would pick up on their radar those guys who had flown out low level and were now climbing up to altitude to return. I guess the game was to scare them into thinking we were coming close to their coast because of the hour or so they did not have us under radar contact. It kind of worked because they told us that after we would let down going west, the Russians would launch a bunch of aircraft thinking we were coming that way. It was fun anyway.

One day I was in the flight coming back at altitude, at about 27,000 feet, and I looked out at Mt. McKinley and then did a double-take looking at my altimeter. It sure did not look like we were at 27,000 feet! You could see the glaciers on the mountain very plainly and they looked very close. In actual fact, they were kind of close since the mountain is 20,320 feet!

One weekend while at Itazuke, Jerry Smith and I took a tour around the country side. We stopped at this park and had a couple beers.

One of the days we were the flight that went out high and were returning low level when another incident happened. The Air Defense aircraft stationed at Elmendorf and some of the auxiliary fields would be vectored in on us just for practice. We normally flew about 360 kts at low level, so, for them to intercept us, it did not take a lot of extra airspeed. I don't remember just why, but this day my flight commander was leading and he decided we would push it up and fly at 400 kts. This made their problem of flying an intercept a bit more difficult. Well, this F-102 was running an intercept on us and he had to push it a bit too much. One of his drop tanks ripped off the aircraft and hit his wing. It did a little damage but we escorted him back to Elmendorf with him having no problems. The pilot of this F-102 happened to be the RAF Exchange Officer assigned to that Squadron.

One very funny thing happened while we were there. Some of the "old heads," my flight commander (Cabaniss) included, went downtown one night. Remember this was late June and the sun sets very late and comes up pretty early. It got to be around midnight and my flight commander told the other guys he was going to the car and they would find him there when they decided to go back to the base. He fell asleep and woke up at about 3:00 am. Seeing it was pretty much daylight, he thought it was afternoon. They were on the schedule that afternoon so he ran back inside and yelled at the other guys that they have to get back right away or be late for the briefing. They laughed and told him it was still morning. He was a little embarrassed.

This was June 1964. A huge earthquake hit Alaska on Good Friday in 1964. There was still a lot of evidence of the damage caused by the earthquake. I got a lot of pictures of the area around Anchorage showing the damage. [See page 66-67.]

I got back from this TDY with the 306th, and, what do you know, I got assigned to the 308th again for a TDY! This one was actually in Florida, at Tyndall AFB. It was an Army exercise called Indian River II. I did not tell you about the Squadron Commander of the 308th before but this TDY was something!! This guy had the nickname "Flubber" (this was what the squadron pilots called him). He was just fine as long as things went just as the schedule called for. Let one little thing change and he bounced all over the room!!

As an example, one day while we were TDY, the weather was bad and not forecast to get any better, so the Ops Officer canceled flying. Yea, you guessed it, it cleared up later in the day and we could have flown at least one mission. Old "Flubber" hit the roof. Now, a few days later the weather is really bad again and not forecast to get any better, and again, you can guess what happened!! The Ops Officer was not about to cancel flying. So, we briefed and when it came time to go out to the airplanes, it was raining as hard as could be. Here we were, pre-flighting the aircraft in the rain, getting soaked to the skin, stuff in the cockpit getting wet, but we were going. We got started up and started to taxi out and guess what?? Yea, now "Flubber" got into the act and canceled flying. We taxied back, got our stuff out of the airplane, IN THE RAIN, and went back into the squadron. This guy should not have ever been put in charge of a bus much less a squadron.

Jerry took my picture standing next to this ugly thing.
I title this picture "Pick the real ugly one!"

I think the only other thing that happened on this TDY that really made a difference in my life was something I did that was stupid and nearly got me killed. Remember earlier I said something about having a bit over 500 hours flying time in the F-100? Well, I have talked to a lot of fighter pilots and did a lot of thinking about this, and have arrived at a conclusion: If you get around 500 hours in a fighter you get to feeling pretty cocky. You think you really know what you are doing and can really fly pretty well. Don't you believe it!!

One day, I was #4 in a flight and we went out and did the close air support part of the mission, then returned to Tyndall as two-ships for instrument approaches. Since I was #4, I flew chase while #3 made a GCA approach. He landed and I went around for a visual overhead pattern. OK, get this, here is a hot fighter pilot from TAC at an ADC base doing a visual pattern. 'Boy, I'll show these guys just how to fly a tight pattern.'

I came down initial at the proper altitude and airspeed and pitched out. I pulled really hard and made a really tight pattern. In fact, I even impressed myself in how close I was to the runway. I kept the power full up, put the gear and flaps down, started my base turn, and the airplane kind of bucked. This was very unusual. I looked at the airspeed and was dumbfounded to see it down around 160 kts. NOT good!!! I let off the stick and let it float around base but saw I was going to overshoot the runway, so

I applied a little back pressure. Nose wanted to buck again. Looking at the airspeed, I made an immediate decision that I couldn't make it.

I let the airplane float around the turn, hoping and praying that I could get some airspeed. I rolled out wings level about 100 feet to the right of the runway and still descending. When I got to what I thought was about 50 feet I put a little back pressure on the stick and was very happy (and LUCKY) to see the descent stop. I was now in level flight and gaining airspeed like a snail. I got all the way to the other end of the runway and finally had enough airspeed that I felt OK to get the gear and flaps up and start a shallow climb. I went out and came back and made an Air Lifters pattern! This was one of those times when you do something really stupid and are lucky to live through it.

Another flight that is kind of funny and shows just how silly "Square filling" can be. It was getting close to the end of the year and we needed to get some night air-to-air refueling missions. We took off just after official sunset, climbed up to somewhere around 25,000 feet, and joined up with our tanker out to the west of Homestead. We started refueling and when we were on the westerly heading you needed sun glasses! The sun was just going down over the horizon and it was still plenty bright. It counted as a night refueling.

If you have read this far, you'll realize that way more than half my time in the 31st TFW was spent away from home! I talked it over with Lois after I returned from this latest TDY and submitted my resignation. I also had contacted Pan American Airlines and got an appointment to interview for a job.

Right after I put in my resignation, the Wing Commander asked me into his office. Seems I was about the 10th guy in the wing to resign. In discussing with him just WHY I was doing this, I mentioned that with the latest TDY to Turkey, I had gotten a new overseas return date and now probably couldn't get an overseas assignment very soon. He asked if that was really what I wanted. I said I wasn't sure, but it seemed that guys in my position overseas were having more fun and less TDY than I was. I guess he remembered this.

About a week later, I was at home getting ready to go to Miami for the PAA interview when the phone rang. It was the Wing Commander's Executive Officer and he told me the Commander would like to see me. I told him right then wasn't a good time because I was going for this interview. He asked me to hold a second, and the Wing Commander came on the phone. Making a long story short, he had an overseas assignment to the 79th TFS of the 20th TFW at Wethersfield, England, and I could have this assignment if I wanted. I looked at Lois and asked what she thought. She looked back and said: "OH, NO, you make this decision." Well, it took a couple of seconds, but I told the Commander I would take it. He said, OK, he was sending my resignation back to me and Personnel would be in touch about the assignment. I think it was about a week later I had orders sending me to RAF Woodbridge in England.

The Squadron I was assigned to for my TDY to Çiğli in 1964.

From Wikipedia, the free encyclopedia
The 1964 Alaskan earthquake, also known as the Great Alaskan Earthquake, the Portage Earthquake and the Good Friday Earthquake, was a megathrust earthquake that began at 5:36 P.M. AST on Good Friday, March 27, 1964. Across south-central Alaska, ground fissures, collapsing structures, and tsunamis resulting from the earthquake caused about 143 deaths.

Lasting nearly three minutes, it was the most powerful recorded earthquake in U.S. and North American history, and the second most powerful ever measured by seismograph. It had a magnitude of 9.2, making it the second largest earthquake in recorded history—the largest being the 1960 Valdivia earthquake in Chile.

The powerful earthquake produced earthquake liquefaction in the region. Ground fissures and failures caused major structural damage in several communities, much damage to property and several landslides. Anchorage sustained great destruction or damage to many inadequately engineered houses, buildings, and infrastructure (paved streets, sidewalks, water and sewer mains, electrical systems, and other man-made equipment), particularly in the several landslide zones along

Knik Arm. Two hundred miles southwest, some areas near Kodiak were permanently raised by 30 feet (9.1 m). Southeast of Anchorage, areas around the head of Turnagain Arm near Girdwood and Portage dropped as much as 8 feet (2.4 m), requiring reconstruction and fill to raise the Seward Highway above the new high tide mark.

An F-100 with Mt. McKinley in the background

Above is a picture of the coast line showing how it slid into the ocean during the Good Friday earthquake of 1964.

Chapter 6

Flying with the 79th TFS at RAF Woodbridge, UK

I talked to another pilot in the wing who had been at the 79th previously, and he said it was probably THE best F-100 assignment in the world! It turned out that the 20th TFW at Wethersfield had 3 squadrons, but the Wethersfield complex was only big enough for two squadrons. Therefore, the 79th was actually stationed at Woodbridge. The 81st TFW stationed at Bentwaters RAF (they had F-101 aircraft) had the same problem and had their 78th squadron at Woodbridge. Bentwaters and Woodbridge were only about three miles apart as the crow flies, but probably five miles driving.

The trip to the 79th Squadron was an experience in itself. We were to depart the US from McGuire AFB in New Jersey. We (my wife Lois, and 3 children, Jon, Lori, and Brian) got there a day early and spent a night in the Visiting Officers Quarters. The next day when we reported to the departure building (the weather was really bad, really bad fog) we found that our aircraft was actually at the Philadelphia airport, where we would be taken by bus.

In the late afternoon, we finally got on the airplane. Shortly after that an announcement was made that they couldn't put enough fuel on board because of the shorter runway there in Philadelphia, so we would fly the short distance to McGuire to refuel! Realize that not only I with my family of three small kids are on this plane, but there are many families with small kids on board. It made a very long day for them!

The officer who was my Squadron Commander at the 306th when I reported in at George AFB and at Homestead [John Madison, a Major then but newly promoted to Lt Col] was also on the plane going to the 79th squadron. He was going to be the Operations Officer until the current Sq Co. was reassigned. His children were a little older (10 or 12) and were a big help playing with and watching Jon,

Lori, and Brian. Finally we took off from McGuire to Mildenhall RAF Station in England. When we were several hours out, we had an announcement that we would be landing in Shannon, Ireland, to spend a couple hours on the ground. There was a quiet hour rule in effect at Mildenhall and our delayed takeoff caused us to miss our window to land, so we then had to wait until morning in England.

While on the ground at Shannon, we were allowed to get off the airplane but were restricted to just one large room in the terminal with no access to buy anything. One time when taking my oldest son, Jon, off the plane I looked into the cockpit and the pilot was sitting there. I asked if we could come in and look around. He said, "sure." He even put Jon, 4 years old, in the pilot's seat and he made some light come on. Jon got the biggest eyes you ever saw and I was one happy Dad because this pilot was such a great guy.

We finally got to Mildenhall, were met by our sponsor, and told we would be staying in a hotel close by the base until we could find housing. It was the Woodhall Hotel and we actually enjoyed more than six weeks of a heck of a lot of fun at that place. [See the "contract" we received from the hotel on page 71. Where could you stay with a family with three children now for $16.80 a day, including meals??]

The back of Woodhall Hotel.
The small set of windows on the left was our room.

A.A. and R.A.C.
(LICENSED)

PHONE:
RECEPTION - SHOTTISHAM 283.
VISITORS - SHOTTISHAM 278.

WOOD HALL HOTEL
SHOTTISHAM. WOODBRIDGE.
SUFFOLK.

19.9.64.

Dear Captain Kimmenau,

    Our daily terms for you and your family are £6 (U.S.Dollars 16:80) per day. The terms include breakfast, luncheon and dinner and also a Service Charge so that tips to the staff are not necessary. We can probably give you two rooms in the very near future if you would prefer this. There would only be a slight increase in terms as there is a slight reduction in your normal terms very shortly when we go off "Seasonal" rates.

    We have reserved accommodation for you for two weeks. If you wish to stay longer will you please let me know as early as possible and I will try to arrange this. There are no extra charges of any kind except that tea or coffee, other than with breakfast, are charged at 1/-d. per head. Heating, lighting and room service is free. As we have a number of quiet elderly people staying we would appreciate it if, at least for dinner, the dining room was kept quiet. In this respect we shall be only too pleased to serve any meals for the baby or your children (or yourselves) in your room if required.

    The terms are special "family terms" as it is assumed that Fathers often miss luncheons and have only light breakfasts during the working days - but they are entitled to and are very welcome to full meals whenever they are at home. We hope you will enjoy your stay with us and we will do everything we can to make you comfortable.

                            Yours faithfully,
                              T.G. Hopkinson

Resident Proprietors: Mr. & Mrs. T. G. Hopkinson

The back of Woodhall Hotel.

Arriving in England in August 1964, the family and I expected to see some rainy weather. Everyone said that the weather in England seemed to always be cloudy, cool, and rainy. That year the weather up to early November was the best fall weather they had had in England in many years. People talked about how it was so great and much different than normal.

When we finally got housing, it was one we rented in the village of Woodbridge because there was no base housing available at that time. The address of the little house we rented was 9 Through Duncans, a quaint little house, but that is a long story by itself.

The kitchen. Note the really small stove.

Brian, Jon, Lori, and Steve in the backyard. Steve is my nephew. My older brother Alfred lived in England

When I arrived at the 79th, I was a little unique. I was already a bomb commander and had about 700 hours in the F-100. Up until my arrival in the squadron, the new guys they were getting were either old heads (mostly from Air Training Command) newly checked out in the F-100 or young guys just out of pilot training/F-100 training. The squadron was quite happy to get an experienced F-100 guy.

Flying in Europe was quite different than flying in the United States. I remember the first flight very clearly. We were scheduled to just take a tour around England, the IP in the back of an F-100F and me in the front seat. The weather was pretty bad, so they decided that maybe I would just go in the back seat and get some weather flying experience. We took off and really did not get out of weather until we were at 24,000 ft. We just flew around and the IP said "Let's call up one of the RAF bases and make an approach."

In the US and at US bases, if the weather is below minimums for landing, you can't attempt an approach even if you have no intention of landing. The UK has no such regulation. If you wanted to make an approach, you could. So I called up this base (I don't remember which one but it was up toward the middle of England), and the guy read me the weather at the base and asked if I wanted to make an approach. I answered, "sure".

He did a great job of talking me down and letting me down to the runway. I had the proper altimeter setting and knew what the field elevation was, so as we were getting down to about 200 feet AGL, I went around. I could just barely see the ground between broken clouds below us. Of course we weren't going to land anyway but this was way below minimums. As we were going around, I said something to the IP like, "wow, that weather was right down there." He took control of the airplane and asked me if I had copied the weather he had read off to us before we started the approach. I said yes, I had it. He said, "Read it off". I did and sure enough it said broken clouds down to 200 feet.

A "Hero" picture. Note the patch and helmet visor cover reflecting the Squadron "Tiger" identification.

It was the first time I had actually heard and copied weather given to me by an English Controller. They did it a little differently than the US does and, at the time I was writing it down, it did not dawn on me that the weather was that low. I said something about that to the IP, and he told me in England if you want to make an approach to a field that is zero, zero, they will vector you in for the approach. Learned something that day. Also got a lot of good weather flying.

On another early flight at Woodbridge (may in fact have been my second flight), I was in an F-100D (single seat) on the wing of one of the flight lead and we were just up flying around over France, Belgium, and Germany (just a mini get-orientated flight) and all at once I had a French fighter flying formation with me. Over there (at that time) if you saw some other fighters, it was not uncommon to just join up, or actually sometimes they would get into a turning fight for a couple minutes. Somewhat of a surprise to me. He flew along with us for a couple minutes, then broke off and went about his business.

Another flight I had concerned the weather also. In fact it was a "Weather Day," i.e., the weather was such that the only flying you would do was go fly in the weather and practice instrument approaches. I was lead for a flight of just two aircraft. We had been airborne for about an hour just flying around England in the weather. We made a Tacan let down and were picked up by GCA (Ground Controlled Radar). They would guide you to the runway giving you directions so you were lined up with the runway and at the correct altitude to make a landing. We had enough fuel to make several GCA approaches but for some reason I decided to have the wingman land on our first approach and I went around. I planned on landing on the next approach. On the downwind leg of the pattern, the weather was so thick that you could not see anything outside the cockpit. It was a very strange feeling. I could hear the engine running and see the dials on the instruments move but I could not sense any movement. It was like being in a simulator. When I was on final approach, I heard other aircraft from Wethersfield and Lakenheath calling for landing permission. The weather had gotten below minimums at all the other airfields in England and Woodbridge was the only field open. I was very lucky in making the decision to have the wingman land first and me land on the next approach.

Our house on base at RAF Woodbridge. That is Brian on the three wheeler.

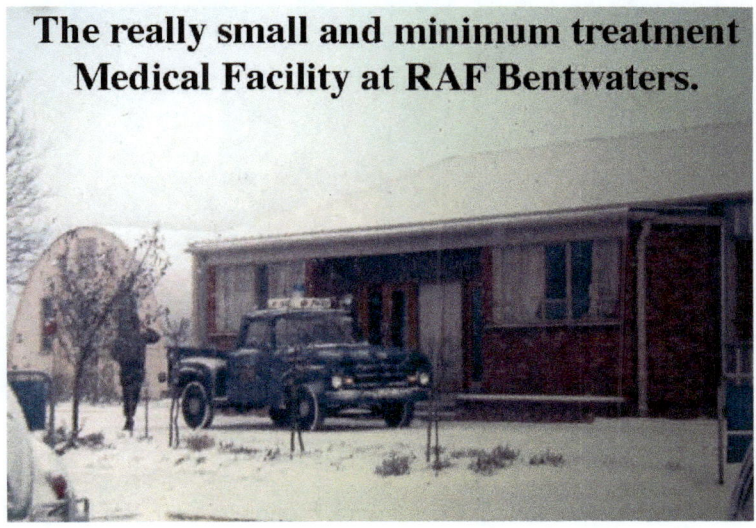

The really small and minimum treatment Medical Facility at RAF Bentwaters.

PK with Lori, Brian, & Jon.
One of the many castles we visited
while stationed in England.

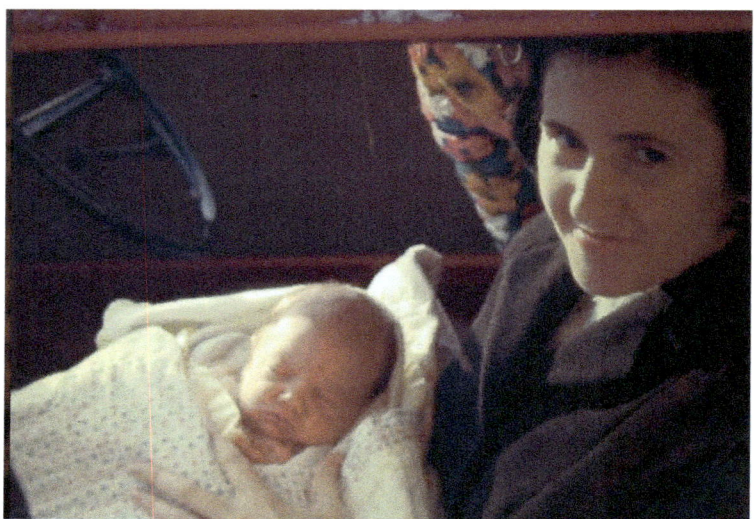

Alex comes home! Note the right hand drive Hillman Imp car. We bought it new because we did not want a big American left hand drive car while in England.

Propeller from Lady Be Good, at a memorial site on Wheelus AB, Libya

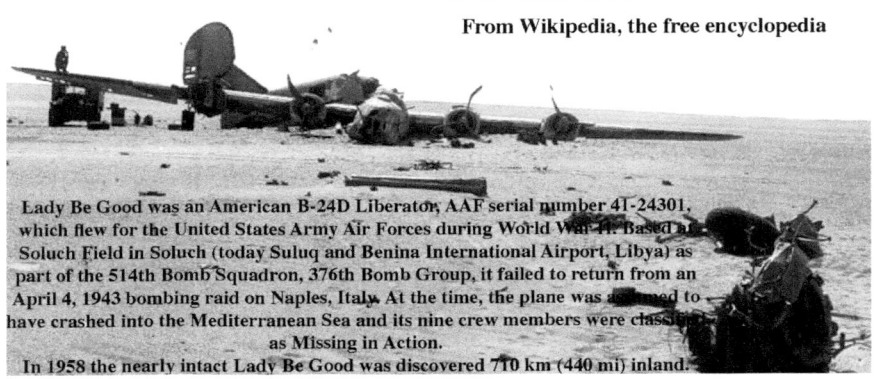

From Wikipedia, the free encyclopedia

Lady Be Good was an American B-24D Liberator, AAF serial number 41-24301, which flew for the United States Army Air Forces during World War II. Based at Soluch Field in Soluch (today Suluq and Benina International Airport, Libya) as part of the 514th Bomb Squadron, 376th Bomb Group, it failed to return from an April 4, 1943 bombing raid on Naples, Italy. At the time, the plane was assumed to have crashed into the Mediterranean Sea and its nine crew members were classified as Missing in Action. In 1958 the nearly intact Lady Be Good was discovered 710 km (440 mi) inland.

From Wikipedia, the free encyclopedia
Lady Be Good was an American B-24D Liberator, AAF serial number 41-24301, which flew for the United States Army Air Forces during World War II. Based at Soluch Field in Soluch (today Suluq and Benina International Airport, Libya) as part of the 514th Bomb Squadron, 376th Bomb Group, it failed to return from an April 4, 1943 bombing raid on Naples, Italy. At the time, the plane was assumed to have crashed into the Mediterranean Sea and its nine crew members were classified as Missing in Action. In 1958 the nearly intact Lady Be Good was discovered 710 km (440 mi) inland.

When we went to Wheelus Air Base (near Tripoli, Libya, where we would complete our gunnery training), we would generally fly non-stop from either Wethersfield or Woodbridge. We would leave in the morning and fly southeast across France, into the Mediterranean, down alongside Italy, then south into Libya. At the time (early 1960s) France's radar control/coverage was not very good. We would file to fly airways, but you could go just about anywhere you wanted and give a position report, and they would give you the OK.

Although I don't remember ever flying to Wheelus with Ron Sumner (good friend from F-100 training) he told me something that was very interesting and proved to be true. He said that if you took off from England in the morning and kept the nose of the airplane pointed at the sun as it came up and went across the sky, you would fly directly toward Libya. I kept a close eye on it one time flying to Wheelus, and sure enough it did appear that if you kept the sun on the nose you would go right into Tripoli.

Flying at Wheelus was great!! Weather was almost always good and there is nothing more fun than going to the range to drop bombs and shoot the gun. On a trip down one Friday with two F-100Ds, me leading in a 79th aircraft and Ray Ryder in a 55th squadron aircraft, we got off a bit late and, as luck would have it, the winds were against us, so we had to go into Aviano, Italy, to refuel. Actually we spent the night, which wasn't all that bad. I told Ray that I wanted to be up early enough to make sure we got to Wheelus before noon. Ray had never been to Wheelus before and he asked me why the hurry. I told him I didn't want to miss the blabbermouth punch party on the beach. He asked me what was this blabbermouth punch stuff?? I told him to just wait and find out for himself. We made it and went to the beach party; Ray learned just what blabbermouth punch was.

Our detachment at Wheelus was always made up of six or seven guys from the three different squadrons in the 20th TFW. If I remember correctly, you would spend three weeks at Wheelus. Every week there was always a new group of guys from one of the squadrons arriving and another group leaving, taking four aircraft back. The Commander, Operations Officer, and Weapons Officer were generally from different squadrons also, and they were there for about six weeks.

I only show this picture to illustrate the fact that for a while the 79th wore the orange flying suit. Actually, I believe almost all USAFE units wore the orange flying suit.

It was the responsibility of the squadron guys who had been there for a week to make the punch and get it to the beach. It was made in a 5-gallon plastic bottle and consisted of whatever they wanted to put in it. Most often it was frozen concentrated lemonade, rum, vodka, ice and soda water. Actually each Saturday the punch was different but on the beach, in the sun, it made no difference what was in it, it was always good. Very often the first five gallons were gone and they would have to go back to the base and make another batch. You really had to watch out because it went down very easy and you could get drunk pretty fast.

Sure enough, about 2 hours after we arrived at the beach I went over to talk to Ray and all he could do was blabber. I asked if he knew what blabbermouth punch was, and he allowed that he had learned what it was. As a side note, he got really sunburned and suffered for a couple days.

The week you were to return home, you would fly an early morning mission with two external fuel tanks (all the gunnery missions were with a clean aircraft with only a pod with the practice bombs on the center line station) and a practice nuclear weapon on the center line. You would fly a long low level, ending up running in on the range at your range time, making a simulated nuclear run. Most often it was an over the shoulder. This way you checked out the external tanks, making sure they would feed when you departed and headed back to England. The low level was to the east toward Benghazi, then south out into the desert (I mean there was NOTHING out there!) for some time, then turn back to the northwest and fly to the coast just to the north of the range.

A 20th TFW F-100 0n takeoff at Wheelus.
Picture by Dave Menard

One of the times I was in the group scheduled to take an aircraft back to Woodbridge, I flew one of these missions. It was very interesting, because when I called off on top it was somewhat unusual. Normally you would feel the weapon release from the aircraft and you would make the call: "Off on top, wet." This meant that you had completed the maneuver and the bomb was in flight and the range officer could watch for it. With the practice weapon, the time from when it came off the aircraft until it hit the ground was well over a minute. You were going almost straight up when the weapon released; you completed the maneuver until you were inverted and had the nose pointed down about 10 degrees, you would roll until you were right side up and then turn either left or right depending on which range you were on. Sometimes after you rolled out you could actually see the weapon still going up. It was great fun to watch it go up, kind of stop, turn over and start down.

Well, this day when I was doing my maneuver, I felt what I thought was the weapon releasing, and when I relaxed the "g's" a bit I felt something again like the weapon coming off. I guess what happened was one of the lugs released and one hung up and as the g's were released a bit, that lug also released. I called the range officer and told him I had had a late release and I was pretty sure the bomb wasn't going to land where it was supposed to land. Sure enough, it hit the ground about half way between the bomb circle and the range tower.

The thing about the low level, sometimes you would see a small cluster of tribal people with some goats, sheep, and camels and you just could not resist flying over them. It was really mean because the animals would all scatter all over the place. If you remember earlier I told about the sheep in Turkey and how they would cluster around the herder; well, these animals took off running in all directions. We always said we for sure did not want to have to bail out near these people. I don't know what they might have done to us!!

On one of my TDY's to Wheelus several of us got to go to El Uotia Gunnery Range. We flew out in a U-6 Beaver and landed on the gravel runway at the range. Got to observe several flights making weapons deliveries on the range. On the way back to Wheelus, we flew north to the coast and had a look at the Roman Ruins on the coast. [From Wikipedia: *Sabratha, Sabratah or Siburata, in the Zawiya District in the northwestern corner of modern Libya, was the westernmost of the "three cities" of Tripolis. From 2001 to 2007 it was the capital of the former Sabratha wa Sorman District. It lies on the Mediterranean coast about 66 km (41 mi) west of Tripoli. The extant archaeological site was inscribed as a UNESCO World Heritage Site in 1982. Besides its magnificent late 3rd century theatre that retains its three-storey architectural backdrop, Sabratha has temples dedicated to Liber Pater, Serapis and Isis. There is a Christian basilica of the time of Justinian and also remnants of some of the mosaic floors that enriched elite dwellings of Roman North Africa (for example, at the Villa Sileen, near Khoms). However, these are most clearly preserved in the coloured patterns of the seaward (or Forum) baths, directly overlooking the shore, and in the black and white floors of the Theatre baths. There is an adjacent museum containing some treasures from Sabratha, but others can be seen in the national museum in Tripoli. In 1943, during the Second World War, archaeologist Max Mallowan, husband of novelist Agatha Christie, was based at Sabratha as an assistant to the Senior Civil Affairs Officer of the Western Province of Tripolitania. His main task was to oversee the allocation of grain rations, but it was, in the words of Christie's biographer, a "glorious attachment", during which Mallowan lived in an Italian villa with a patio overlooking the sea and dined on fresh tunny fish and olives.]*

I should mention this about the range missions at Wheelus. Every six months, the 20th Wing would review the scores of all the events flown at Wheelus (and any range missions flown in the UK, if you had any) and rank the pilots of the wing on how well they had performed. I don't remember exactly the number but think it was the top ten pilots in the Wing, that would receive a plaque naming them "Select Crew" for that six month period. During the time I was at Woodbridge, I was a select crew three times.

An incident that I thought at the time was going to be very funny could have been pretty serious; I was mighty happy it turned out to be nothing. When we sat nuclear alert at Woodbridge, there were four pilots on alert. We had what they called four lines to cover. One such period when I was sitting alert, I was the Senior guy on alert. Each morning we would go to the alert hangar where our aircraft were sheltered and under armed guard 24/7. With our crew chief, we would preflight the aircraft and start it up and run the normal preflight ground checks. You were never allowed in the alert hangar with the loaded aircraft alone. It was a "two man" concept and everyone paid close attention to this rule.

Top Left: Tripoli, Libya circa 1965.
Top and Middle Right: This and the picture above of Sabratha I took from the U-6 on our return flight from the range to Wheelus.

The other three pictures of the Ruins at Sabratha were taken from a site on the internet.

Each hangar had an intercom box that was connected to the alert building where the VADO (Victor Alert Duty Officer) manned the communication center. This was where he would receive the launch word if we were to launch. Each morning we would make some kind of call into the VADO just to ensure that the intercom was working.

This particular morning, for some reason, I was a wise ass, and when I talked to Harold (the VADO that morning) I told him that someone must have gotten into the hangar over night because the weapon was missing from my aircraft. He answered back in a normal voice and I thought nothing of it. About an hour later while sitting outside the alert building, Harold came up to me and asked if maybe we should tell someone about the weapon being missing. MY GOD, he had believed me! I was so shocked I almost fainted. I told him about just kidding around and made a decision that very moment to never kid around about something like that again.

I am not sure just when, but I think it was in the first year I was at Woodbridge, the Squadron Commander, Lt Col John Bartolf, was replaced by Lt Col John Madison. (Remember, he was my first Sq Cmdr and came over to Woodbridge on the same airplane.) This was a really good break for me. In mid 1965, the 20th TFW had a slot to send someone to the F-100 Fighter Weapons Instructor School at Nellis AFB, NV. It was the 79th's turn to select someone to go. Madison asked me if I wanted to go. Of course!!! What an opportunity!! It was actually a reasonable selection since I had the most F-100 flying experience of any of the younger guys that could be selected. I went off TDY to Nellis in September 1965. Three months of the greatest flying anyone could ever wish for. [See Attachment 5 for my experience of flying at the FWS.]

I got home to Woodbridge in late December and took Lois to the hospital at Lakenheath. She spent a couple weeks in the hospital (did get to come home for Christmas day) and Alex was born on 6 Jan 1966. I cannot remember just how many times I drove up to visit Lois, but I do know I had the route memorized and the car could just about drive itself to Lakenheath. I don't remember how long Lois stayed at Lakenheath but she came back to the small dispensary at Bentwaters and then we brought Alex home to our on-base house at Woodbridge.

Lois tells the story of that trip home from Lakenheath and it wasn't very pretty. Seems the vehicle they used to bring her from Lakenheath to Bentwaters was a station wagon with the rear seats down. She was on a gurney and her nose was only a couple inches from the roof of the vehicle. Made for a very uncomfortable ride. [We had moved on to RAF Woodbridge as a base house became available for us some time in the late summer of 1965, before I went to the FWS.] Guess that has nothing to do with flying but thought I would include that information anyway.

I had a couple of very interesting flights (or attempts at flight) when I returned to Woodbridge. One of the first was a natural mistake but pretty dumb on my part. While flying at the Fighter Weapons School, there were a couple things that Tactical Air Command did differently than we did it in United States Air Forces in Europe (USAFE). One such detail was formation takeoffs. In USAFE when you were the wingman, after you were lined up on the runway, the leader would give the run up signal. When he was ready, he would look at you and if you were ready, you gave him a nod of the head. He would then nod his head for brake release, look over at you, and if you were in position, he would nod again signaling to go outboard with the throttle, thus lighting the afterburner. In TAC (at Nellis) the lead would give the run up signal and when he got the nod from you that you were ready, he would nod, release brakes and light the afterburner. Then he would check to see if you were in position. Well, having done it that way for three months, the first time I was on the wing at Woodbridge and I got the nod to release brakes, I did, but I also started to light the burner. Then I remembered and pulled the throttle out of burner. Then the lead looked at me and nodded again, and I again went outboard to light the afterburner. NOT GOOD! I got a heck of a compressor stall and fire came out both ends of the airplane!! The lead's eyes got as big as dinner plates and I called "I am aborting." Did not hurt the aircraft or engine any but sure made me feel stupid.

The second thing was a few months after I was back; it was time for my TAC Eval Check. This is a check ride where you plan a CPM mission, fly the planned route to a range, and practice nuclear delivery with a 25 lb practice bomb. The planning and briefing were standard. Take off, climb out, and cruise to the let down point were perfect. Then the differences with TAC procedures and USAFE kicked in. In TAC (and all the CPM missions I flew at the Weapons School) when you did your let down to the low level portion of the mission, you pulled the power back to 80%, put the speed brake out, and let down holding the correct airspeed. Well, in USAFE you did the let down the same EXCEPT you DID NOT use the speed brake. Doing this of course had me getting to low level several miles BEFORE I should have. When I started to look for check points to make sure I was on course, NOTHING looked like it should. I almost panicked!! Remembering that holding a heading and airspeed were very important, I at least did that. It took several minutes but I finally started seeing some familiar check points and realized I was about two minutes behind where I was supposed to be. I pushed up the power and tried to make up the time. I made it to the range at the proper range time and the rest of the mission went OK.

When I got back, I was debriefing and told the check pilot I just couldn't figure out how I got so far behind in time. He looked kind of puzzled and asked me if I had used speed brakes on the let down on purpose. Man, then it dawned on me what I had done. I did pass because I completed everything as I should have, but the IP was pretty perplexed when I explained that I had fallen into the habit of doing it the way I did it at Weapons School.

Another very good deal that I happened into while at the 79th was going to Tiger Days. During the late 1950's and early 1960s the RAF 74th Squadron and the USAF 79th Squadron had a couple of Dining In events that ended in some rowdy parties. Somewhere in this time frame, a couple of the Squadron Commanders had a discussion about making these parties a regular thing. Then it came down to some of the project officers taking it a step further with the idea of maybe getting together to fly together and discuss tactics. (The first USAF project officer that set up the meet in 1961 was Lt. Mike Dugan who became the Chief of Staff of the USAF later in his career.) The French Air Force was invited and the FIRST Tiger Meet (as it was first called) was held at RAF Woodbridge on 19 July 1961 with the RAF 74th, USAF 79th, and the French 1/12 Squadron. [NOTE: The reason it was called "Tiger Meet"/"Tiger Days" was the fact that each squadron that participated had the Tiger as their squadron emblem/mascot.] As they say the rest is history.

In 1966, when I went, the RAF squadron hosting the Tiger Meet was at RAF Leuchars in Scotland. We had the 79th Squadron with F-100s, the RAF 74th Squadron with Lightning F Mk 6, EC 1/12 French AF with Super Mystere B2, 31st Squadron Belgian AF with F-104G, 53rd Squadron USAF with F-4D, 439th Squadron Royal Canadian AF with CF-104G, 432nd Squadron German AF with F-86, and AG 52 Squadron German AF with T-33. [The two German Squadrons were in the midst of conversion so they could not bring their current aircraft which would have been the F-104 in AG 52 Sqdn and the G-91 in the 432nd Sqdn.]

The T-5 Lighting I got a ride in.

Our departure from Woodbridge to Leuchars was delayed by a practice load out (nuclear weapons exercise) so we did not arrive when we should have. However, we (there were three of us: Tom Orman, Omar Fahey, and me) had dressed in black slacks and white shirts with tie; then we put on our flight suit over that. We crammed a very bright yellow Tiger Blazer in the cockpit. I wanted to make a tactical pitch up upon arrival and when I called the tower and requested permission I got an answer I did not understand. (As I learned later, the tower cleared me for a "Running Break." This meant that I could come enter the pattern in formation as low as I wanted and pitch up to down wind. This was exactly what I wanted but did not understand the term.) Anyway, we entered initial for the pitch out with me flying the number three and number three leading the formation (it could probably be called a reverse echelon) so that he gave me the call to pitch out and I went first followed by the other two. Not quite as I wanted but enough different that those on the ground thought it quite funny. We all stopped at the end of the runway after landing and keeping our canopies closed got out of our g suit and flight suit, then put on the yellow blazer. (Since the F-100 did not have a parking brake, this was quite a feat!) Taxiing in for parking, we kept the canopies down until we were all parked and opened them at the same time standing up in the seat as the canopy came up. There we were, all dressed up, ready for a party. One of the reporters from an Edinburgh paper asked if this "flying kit" was normal: We all laughed and said, "no, it was just something we did special for the Tiger Meet."

The newspaper article and a picture with the
79th Sqdn Liaison Officer and Tiger Days Commander.

I also got a ride in the RAF Lightning aircraft and received a certificate showing I have gone 1,000 miles per hour. Very impressive aircraft with so much more power than our F-100 had. The 74th Squadron "Boss" held three straws for the three of us from the 79th, with the short straw getting the ride. Somehow, and I don't know how he did it, I got the short straw and the ride.

Two pictures of the Unit Commanders at the Tiger Meet.

The take-off was to be a full afterburner takeoff. However, they normally did not use afterburner for takeoff because of the amount of fuel it used. My pilot released the brakes and was rolling down the runway, and after about 1,000 feet he remembered he was supposed to use burner. He lit them both and I am telling you, the acceleration was fantastic! He got to rotation speed, pulled the nose up, got the gear up, and we were going straight up! We entered the clouds at about 1,500 feet and continued going straight up. At about 20,000 we came out of the clouds, still pointed straight up.

During the flight, he wanted me to be able to get the 1,000 mph certificate, so we were about 30,000 feet and he lit both burners and started to accelerate. Once he got to 500 knots calibrated he had to start a shallow climb to maintain the 500 calibrated because of the refueling probe on the aircraft. It got to Mach one and kind of hung there for a few seconds, then it started climbing again. I think we got to 1.45 or 1.5 Mach and I mentioned to him that I had heard the F-4 had a problem when it was in burner above the Mach, because moving the throttle very fast would cause compressor stalls. He said, "Watch this." He pulled both throttles to idle, shoved them back forward and lit the burners and did it again. Engines ran just as smooth as can be. He pulled them to idle and started a level turn. I don't know for sure how many "Gs" he pulled but know it was up around 4 gs. After rolling out after a 180 degree turn, we were still above the Mach. Really an impressive airplane!

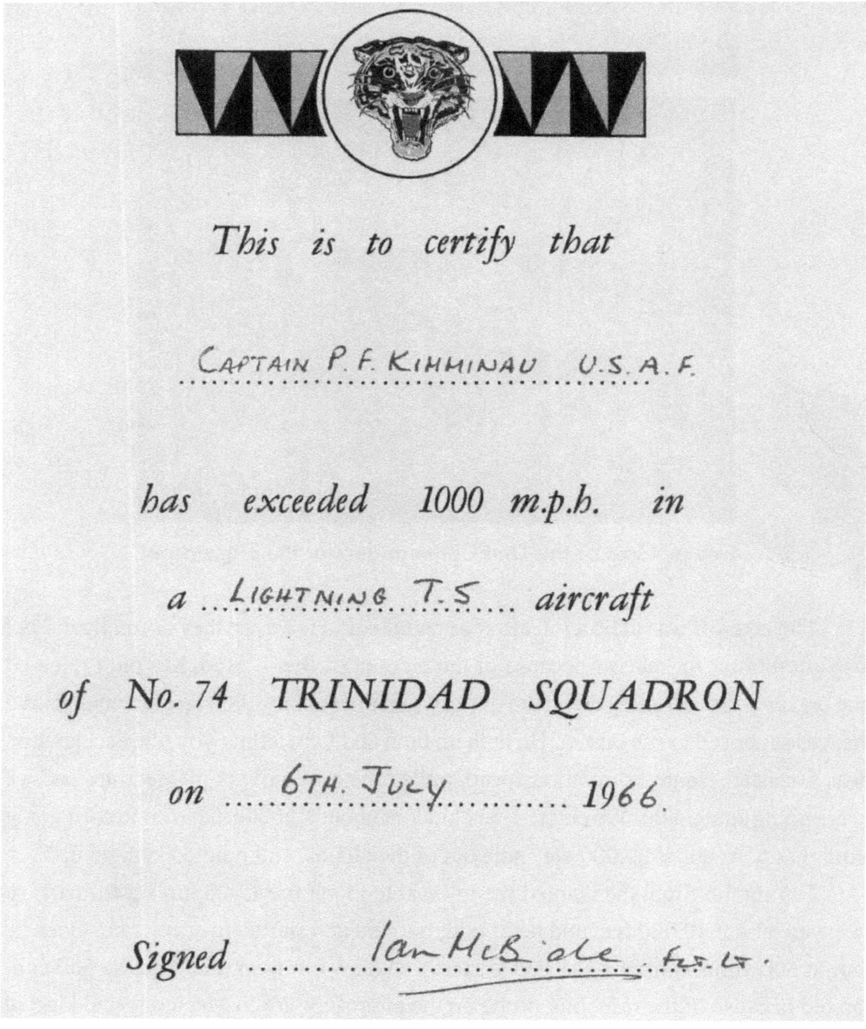

This is to certify that

CAPTAIN P. F. KIMMINAU U.S.A.F.

has exceeded 1000 m.p.h. in

a LIGHTNING T.S *aircraft*

of No. 74 TRINIDAD SQUADRON

on 6TH. JULY 1966.

Signed Ian McB'ole Flt. Lt.

The meet was great fun. We got to meet a lot of really good guys and had a great time. I even got to play a round of golf at the Old St. Andrews Course. We had a really sad occurrence on Friday morning during the practice for the air show on Saturday. The French Super Mystere demonstration pilot crashed and was killed. The French requested we go ahead with the Tiger Meet in memory of Capt. Joel Dancel so things were conducted as normal as possible. [On 12 July, Fahey and I took an F-100F to Laon, France, to attend the funeral for Capt. Dancel.]

A sad moment at the Tiger Meet. The cloud of black smoke is from the crash of a Super Mystere B2. I was watching the performance and had my camera and got this picture. I just happened to be in such a position that the smoke is above one of the other Super Mystere's.

In early September 1966, the 20th Wing was tasked to sit two lines of nuclear alert at Çiğli AB in Turkey. When the 79th's turn came, I was sent along with two of the young guys (Kerkman and Duncan). It was an uneventful TDY except for the trip home. We were to bring back one F-100D and one F-100F (The "F" was a two-seat aircraft.) I told the young guys that I would ride in the back seat of the F and they could fly home. Going over Italy we had to change our flight plan, because one of the airways over a range was closed. In changing the flight plan, I messed up one of the radio calls and these two young guys remembered this forever. Of course they never told anyone in the squadron. NOT!!

Also while we were there I tried for the first time to grow a mustache (it turned out to be the LAST time also!!). My mustache would never grow in even. It was very light and grew in patches. It looked like a dog with mange. One time the three of us went to the barber for a hair cut and I was going to get my mustache trimmed. These other two young guys got to the barber before we arrived for our hair cuts and asked the barber to do them a favor. When it came time and I asked him to trim my mustache, he looked real surprised and said, "You have a mustache??" Kerkman and Duncan were on the floor laughing.

Either in late September or early October, the Wing received a message asking for volunteers to Southeast Asia, i.e., Vietnam. The aircraft available was the C47 "Goony Bird" or the A-1 "Skyraider." I realized that it was not going to be very long until I got an assignment and, looking into what this A-1 was, decided that flying this big old single engine prop aircraft might be fun. Making sure that if I volunteered for one that they wouldn't then put me into the other, I volunteered for the A-1. Probably the quickest action I had ever seen in the Air Force. Within a week, I had an assignment in the A-1. I was to report to Hurlburt Field, FL, in February 1967, check out in the aircraft and report the end of May to the 602nd at Nha Thrang AB in South Vietnam. Before I had finished my A-1 checkout at Hurlburt, the orders were changed to report to the 602nd at Udorn RTAF Base, in Thailand.

Chapter 7

Flying the A-1 Skyraider

The family and I packed up and went back to the states in early January 1967. After a visit with our families in Kansas, we went to Ft. Walton Beach, Florida, where we lived in a motel for about three months while I got checked out in the A-1E. This was a two-seat aircraft with what they called "the blue room" behind the cockpit. This was an area big enough to hold at least six fully armed troops or whatever cargo you wanted to put in it. When we flew combat with this aircraft, we had nothing in the back.

Flying at Hurlburt was actually a lot of fun. The aircraft was big and had a very powerful engine with a 12-foot propeller. It developed a heck of a lot of torque and you really had to be on your toes when you flew it. Landing was very easy UNTIL you got on the ground with the tail wheel. Yea, it was what they call a tail dragger. You could lock the tail wheel for takeoff and landing but had to unlock it to taxi. With the relatively poor brakes on the aircraft, it was pretty tricky to taxi.

My first ride in the A-1 was somewhat interesting for what didn't happen. Since this was what they called "a dollar ride," it was more or less just an orientation in the airplane. However, one of the things the instructors liked to do was impress you with how much torque would affect you if you didn't pay attention. You would pull the power back to idle and pull the nose up. You held the nose up until the aircraft stalled, then you pushed the power full on and relaxed the back pressure. If you did this and didn't know about how to use the rudder to counter the torque, the airplane would just flip over. The IP was watching very close so he could catch it before it flipped over on its back. When my IP (I think his name was Curtis) had me do this, he was very surprised when as I pushed the throttle forward I pushed the rudder hard enough that the aircraft did not roll much at all. He asked me what aircraft I had flown because every pilot he had checked out before that had flown jets would never push the rudder in time. I told him about the F-100 and how if you didn't know how to use the rudder you were in big trouble.

Express 36 my A-1 class at Hurlburt
Back Row (L to R): Capt. "PK" Kimminau, Capt. Berkstrom, Maj. Jenks, unknown, Capt. Ward, Maj. Frank Armstrong III (KIA 67/10/06), Maj. Bonds
Front Row (L to R): Capt. Bozarth, Maj. Castle, LtCol. Pearce, Capt. Smedley, Maj. Westfall

One of the very interesting check-out rides while at Hurlburt was night range missions. We did rockets and dive bomb under flares. With the smoke generated by the flares, sometimes when you came around base leg and were rolling in on final for the delivery, if the flares were in the correct position, you would see your shadow on the smoke clouds and it would appear as if another aircraft was coming right at you. They briefed you about this but the first time it happened, it scared the daylights out of you. In fact, every time it happened, it scared me. It looked so real that you could not convince your mind it wasn't another airplane going to collide with you.

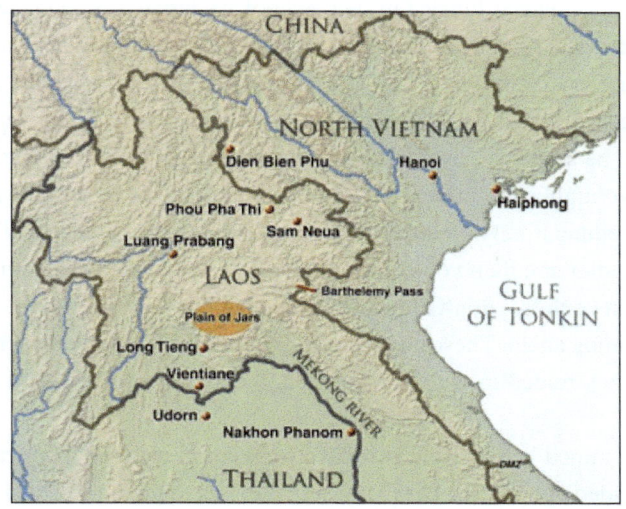

After I completed the A-1 check-out, I took the family to Wichita, KS, where they were to stay while I was in Vietnam for a year. It was supposed to be pretty simple to just rent a house and get the stuff moved into it, but that isn't how it happened. It is a long story and I won't attempt to put it in here.

As I mentioned earlier, while at Hurlburt I received a change of orders. I was still going to the 602nd but the Squadron was now at Udorn Royal Thai Air Force Base in northern Thailand. The primary mission of the Squadron was Search and Rescue.

A-1H with "Sandy" ordnance load.

En route, I attended Jungle Survival School at Clark Air Base in the Philippine Islands. Clark AB is on the same island as Manila, the capital. This was a very interesting but very crappy week. It was raining hard when we landed and got off the airplane at Clark. It was raining the next day when we started classes. It was supposed to be a couple days in the classroom then out into the jungle for three days and two nights, with the last two days and one night on your own, trying to evade local ethnic tribal hunters trying to track you down. If they caught you, you gave them a chit and then you continued. They could catch you again and again. If you ran out of chits, I don't remember for sure, but I think you had to go through the field training again. These guy were really GOOD. They could even smell you and, since they traded in the chits for food, they really worked hard at tracking you down.

Well, it rained hard for the two days we were in class and was raining hard when we loaded up in the trucks that were taking us to the field. The day we went to the field, a couple guys in the class before us, which was still out in the field, got killed by a hillside collapsing on them. We went into what they called "static camp" where the local tribesmen taught us things about the jungle, i.e., how to make a shelter, find something to eat, make a fire when it was raining (which it still was), and things like that. We suffered through two days of really WET weather and then they came and got us. It was deemed too dangerous for the evading phase of training. I think I got to play one day of golf, even though it was wet, and then off to the war.

The last two pages of this Chapter reflect the missions I flew with the 602nd. I kept a log of all my missions but did not do a very good job of the details of a lot of the missions. I refer to the log several times while writing about my time with the 602nd.

I arrived at the 602nd in early June 1967. I don't remember just what day I arrived but my flight log shows I had my first ride on the 10th, so it must have been a few days prior to that. (NOTE: In the column Area/Mission you will see I have Barrel Roll listed for almost every mission. The 602nd, with the help of the Road Watch Teams [and the "secret guys" briefing us], helped Vang Pao and his Army. We flew a lot of times in the Eastern part of Ban Ban Valley, from Ban Ban to the Fishes Mouth, around the edges of The Plains de Jars, up around Sam Neua, and even way up North just South of Dien Bien Phu, conducting our own strikes and being a FAC for aircraft sent to us by 7th AF. We flew into the Southern part of Laos (Steel Tiger) sometimes. I guess I should say, I only flew there a few times. In my original handwritten flight log, I have a lot of question marks for the area into which the mission was flown. I decided to put Barrel Roll in place of the question marks for this log. (Also in looking at the log today, I can see where I only mention successful SAR's a couple times. I remember very clearly that I participated in six [6] successful pick-ups.)

The 602nd SOS July 1967

This is a listing of the names of the guys in the picture. It is tough to get them in order so I'll just list them as I got them off a handwritten note. The writing wasn't very good so the spelling could be suspect. Starting in the lower left and going right: Gray, Col Skelton, Kiehle, Skeels, Shumard, Ensellin (Wing Safety). Now the guys standing: Mehr, Miles, Stark, Gould, Trimble, Sikorski, Raush, Leonard, Carr, Thomas, Doc Kottle, Zevin, Cochran, Dinwiddle, Fleis—, Burden, Kimminau. I think there were a few missing when the picture was taken. For example I don't see Westbrook, Carlson, or Jenks.

If my memory is correct, I think at the time there were not enough rooms so we could have just two guys per room. I am pretty sure I had the top bunk and there were three guys in the room. Made for pretty close quarters. This did not last long and I had just one roommate, Jack Cochran. I don't remember who my roommate was after Jack returned to the States. Another note about the flight log. Almost every one of the missions that shows "Strike" probably included the Firefly's FAC-ing (acting as a Forward Air Controller.) for either F-105's or F-4's. Sometimes these would be diverts from the big Strike Force scheduled to go into North Vietnam or spares for the Strike Force which were not used. We did have some resources which were scheduled to strike targets in Barrel Roll or Steel Tiger which we did FAC into scheduled targets.

This is probably a good time to discuss a little "History." What would that be?? Well, in my combat log you will see a few different call signs. When we were flying a Strike mission of our own, or flying a Strike mission which included FACing other fighters and we were in the Barrel Roll area, we used the call sign "Firefly." That one mission with the call sign Dragon Fly was in the Steel Tiger area, and I believe we used Dragon Fly when going to the Steel Tiger area.

Remember how these little gals would wash your clothes pounding them with a rock. After a couple weeks they were thin as cheese cloth!

So what's with this "Sandy" call sign?? The 602nd was at Bien Hoa (at one time they were actually flying sorties out of four different locations) and had sent some aircraft up to Udorn in late 1965 to fly/sit alert for SAR duty and they did not use the call sign Sandy. Here is an article from Skyraider Association Newsletter, dated November 1988: *Although several groups had flown SAR missions out of Udorn Thailand in late 1965, they did not utilize the call sign "Sandy". Capt. W. I. "Doc" George led four replacement A-1E's to Udorn and his Bien Hoa departure call sign was "SANDY." On his arrival at Udorn, Doc was asked what call sign he would like to use while there. His reply "SANDY" is history. The other initial SANDY pilots were: Harlan Davis (deceased), S.P. Knickerbocker, Ronald*

Linder, and *Kenneth Ruhr.* S.P. Knickerbocker was the author of that article. So that is how the SAR mission call sign "SANDY" came about.

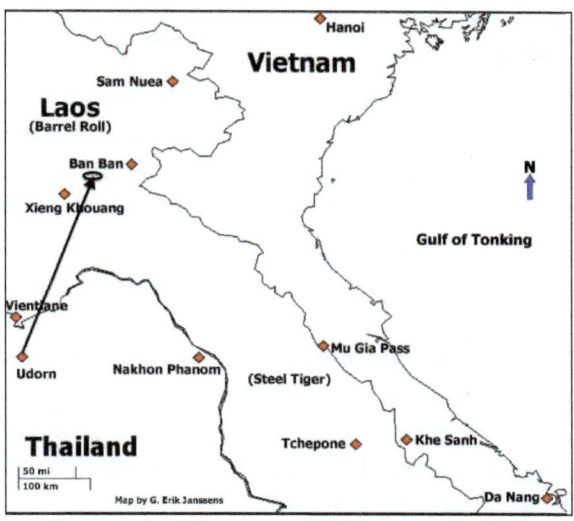

My first mission with Larry M.

Again, looking at the flight log you will see in the "remarks" column some reference to "Stories." Like the mission on 10 June with Larry Mehr, being my first (or my Dollar Ride). Here is the story:

This isn't really a funny story but as it turned out somewhat memorable, I'll tell it. This first ride I went with Larry Mehr to the briefing. It was to be a strike mission to the Barrel Roll area and also FAC (Forward Air Control) a flight of F-105s on a target. Since they had 750# bombs, it would be a "road cut" mission. The target was located at the NE corner of the Plain de Jars. When Larry had contact with the F-105s, he started his brief. Going through it, I listened and thought to myself that if he did it as he was telling the F-105s, he would be rolling in right over the only gun position we were briefed on. Being the new guy, I didn't think it was right for me to question him, especially right while he is talking to the F-105s. Sure enough, he rolled in and hardly got in position to shoot the marking rockets when we had this "stuff" going past the canopy. I said, "Hey, what is that?" Larry replied, "Hell, they are shooting at us!" He pulled out and after that we rolled in from a different direction. After landing, we found one hole in the right flap of the aircraft. It was the first time Larry had been hit during his tour. He was mad and, as I remember it, he always saved a bomb for that position if he possibly could.

On my second mission I was with Sandy Zevin and got to drop some bombs. Sandy had been there quite a while and knew how to bomb so he was quite vocal in telling me how to do it. Here is that story:

My first ride, in the left seat, was another strike mission to the Barrel Roll area. This was on a truck park by a river North and West of Sam Neua. Sandy Zevin was the IP in the right seat. We found the target and I rolled in on it. Going down the chute, Sandy was hollering that with the ball all the way to the right I sure wasn't going to hit the target. After I pulled out and we watched the bombs hit right on target, he commented: "I don't know how the hell you ever hit the target." I don't know why, I just never thought the pass was so bad and I guess the results proved I was right. Thanks anyway, Sandy.

While I am telling stories about Sandy Zevin, I might as well include this one. On another mission with Sandy, he was leading us to escort a couple Army Helo's to destroy a Huey Helo that had been crashed in the jungle in bad guy country. The mission was actually in South Vietnam. It very possibly could have been just into Laos. It was west and maybe a bit north of Da Nang, and it seemed to me we were doing a lot of messing around to get the job done. Later I realized why. Sandy had a couple of friends who flew F-4s that were stationed at Da Nang and he wanted to visit them. We played around long enough so we had to go into Da Nang to get fuel. It also happened to be lunch time so we had lunch with his friends.

While we were getting ready to leave, we had a guy come up to us, a young Air Force Captain, and ask for a ride to Udorn, if we were going there. Having A-1Es, we had a lot of room. In fact, we also took along a couple aircraft tires that were needed at Udorn. Anyway, this Air Force Captain, Greg Etzel, was a Jolly Green pilot coming to southeast Asia for his tour, and he had gotten to Da Nang and was waiting for a ride to Udorn, his duty station. He rode with me; it was just a normal flight back to Udorn, no ordnance delivery anywhere. Greg's first rescue turned out to be the first SAR that I was on. I tell the story of Pintail 2 later.

Somewhere along here I have got to tell the story about the "No Hab" at the O'Club. Along toward the end of the month, before the food deliveries would come to the base, you would go into the club to have dinner, get the menu, and order the steak. Waiter — No Hab steak! OK, I'll have the fish. Waiter — No Hab fish! If you were there, you know just what I mean! Just about everything on the menu was a No Hab. I do not remember just who it was, and it may have occurred just before I got there, but this guy would order the chili. (They got the chili in big cans and seemed to always have chili.) After a while, he would ask if they would just bring him a little rice along with the chili. They seemed to always have rice also, so that was no big deal. Then he got to asking for a few chopped up onions. That again was no big deal. Then he asked for a bit of shredded cheese. That again was no big deal. Pretty soon just about everyone was ordering the chili, asking for the extras (which they didn't charge for) and having a great time. It wasn't long before the club manager caught on and Chili, Rice, Onions, and Cheese was on the menu, AND you now got charged for the Rice, Cheese, and Onions!!

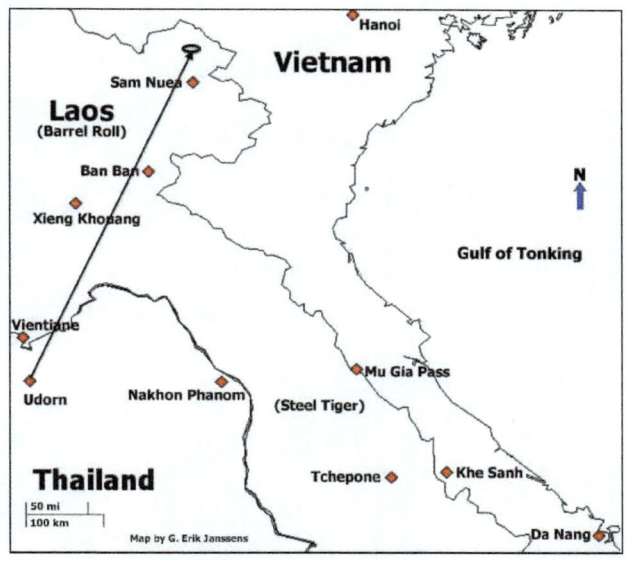

Second mission with Sandy Z.

Sometime during my tour, Udorn hosted the second RIVER RAT TACTICS CONFERENCE. Not much to say except guys from every base in Thailand attended and wore party suits. I have included some pictures (I have quite a few) of the event. Can't remember all the names so will just show the pictures without trying to put names with faces. At the time the guys who were "REAL" River Rats, that is, guys who had flown up over or by the Red River that flows through Hanoi, told us Sandy guys that we were included in this River Rat thing. They made us all River Rats. I only mention this because when I was at Nellis for the REAL FIRST River Rat Convention (after the POWs were back), a couple of the River Rats told me that IF I hadn't flown over the Red River, I wasn't a River Rat. Kinda pissed me off!

Just a few of the many pictures I took at the Second Red River Rats Practice Reunion/Party/ Meeting/Etc. It was hosted by the units at Udorn.

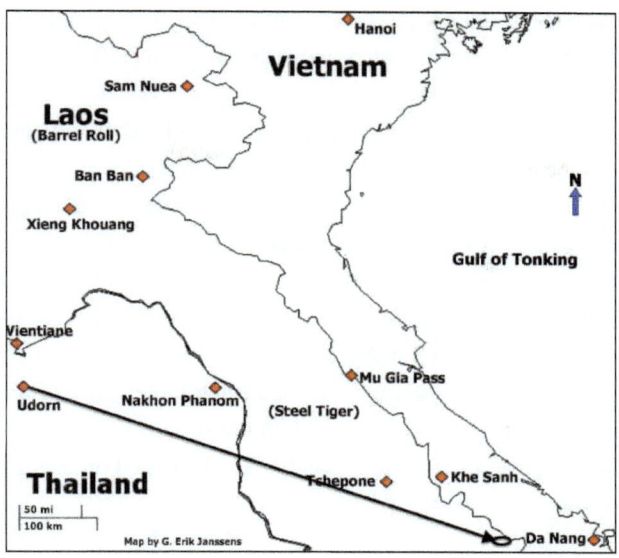

Destroy Helicopter mission with Sandy Z.

The flight log entry for 25 June in the Remarks column shows orbiting up in North Barrel Roll. We normally did this when the big Strike Force went into North Vietnam. This put us about an hour closer to where a possible SAR site might occur. We would orbit in the vicinity of North Station (aka Lima Site 85). I have included a story about Lima Site 85 as Attachment 6.

Anyway, the Sandys would hold in this vicinity while the Jolly Green Helicopters would normally sit on the ground at Lima Site 36. Lima Site 36 (Village/Air Strip Muong Hiem on a heading of about 220 degrees about 30 nm from North Station) was a forward outpost for General Vang Pao's Meo Army. As I understand it, this was also one of the places that Dr. Tom Dooley III did humanitarian work in the 1950's. The airstrip was about 1700 feet of dirt with very little or no taxiways. If you landed there, you stayed on the runway or just pulled it off the side so the runway could stay open. It really wasn't a place to land and take off unless you had a REAL emergency.

If we take another look at the flight log and the dates 2/3 July 1967, we find that I got to participate in my first successful SAR. It is a bit long, but here is how I remember what went on.

After reading the account of the rescue mission (Pintail 2) conducted on 2-3 July 1967 in the *Air Force Magazine*, May 1995 (Valor, page 124, written by John L. Frisbee), it set me to thinking about what really happened. The account as written is accurate but has left out a lot of what went on. I am sure it was condensed so it could fit on one page, but other things about this mission really make it interesting and should be recorded somewhere.

I was Larry Mehr's wingman on both the 2nd and 3rd of July, during the rescue. I'll record the events of the two days as I remember them.

It started off as a "normal" Sandy alert day. I believe Jack Cochran was Sandy 5, Don Miles was Sandy 6, Larry Mehr was Sandy 7, and I was Sandy 8. As the backup Sandys, we went to the briefing and then could go back to the BOQ, or wherever, because we were on 30-minute alert. It was Sunday (later I have a few words about Sandy Alert and Sunday!!), and after we went back to the BOQ side of the base I told Larry I was going to Mass. I think I even gave him my 38 pistol to hold for me. During Mass, I got tapped on the shoulder and told we needed to go to the shack because the first four Sandys had launched on orbit. Down to the squadron we went.

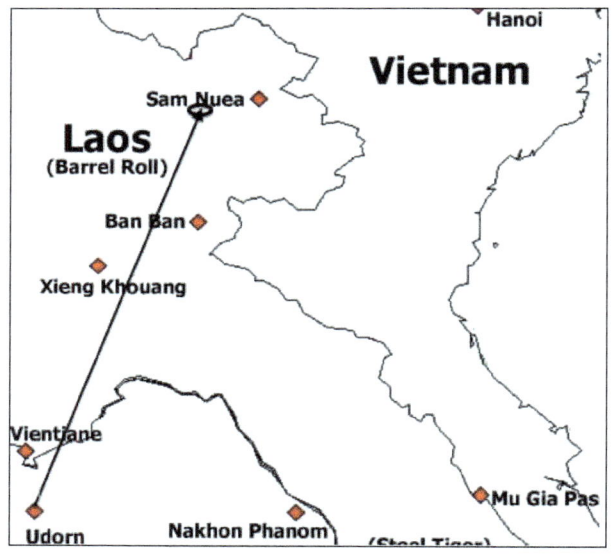

Sandy orbit point, vicinity of North Station

Now the long day of just sitting around started. Sandys 1-4 returned from orbit, and went on 30-minute alert while we held down the 15-minute alert slots. Somewhere around 16:30 (I don't remember the time exactly, but it was late enough that we thought all flights should have returned), I mentioned that I thought it a good idea if we checked to see if everyone was back across "the fence." Don't remember if it was Jack or Larry that said good idea, check with the Command Post. (NOTE: I had arrived at the 602nd in early June and I think this was about my 10th mission, so I was still an "FNG" and didn't do things like calling the Command Post on my own.)

I cranked the field phone and the Command Post answered. I asked if everyone was back across the fence, and if so, could the Sandys stand down from alert? The answer was, "I don't know but will check and call you right back." About one minute later the phone rang and all the Sandys were listening as I answered, hoping that we could go get that cold beer. The Command Post says, "LAUNCH THE SANDYS, GO EAST, WE'LL PASS THE DETAILS IN THE AIR!"

I was shocked to say the least and asked, "What, did you say launch the Sandys?" Of course I got a very sharp response to LAUNCH!! With everyone listening, it didn't take long to get running out to the aircraft.

We got started up and, about check-in time, Sandy 5 called Sandy 7 to tell him he was having flap problems and Sandy 7 and 8 should go ahead. (I think what happened was, Sandy 5 had put his checklist over on the left side console. The checklist hits the button on top of a T-Handle. When you depress the button and pull the T-Handle up, it cuts off all hydraulic pressure to the wings. The checklist hitting the button causes the T-Handle to pop up just enough to cut off the pressure and Sandy 5 couldn't get his flaps to retract. He discovered the problem and corrected it shortly after Sandy 7 and I got to the arming area.)

We took off and headed east as directed. The Command Post gave us a TACAN Distance and Radial to head toward and we contacted King. (King was the airborne Rescue Command Post.) We roared toward the point (now remember roaring in an A-1 is something like 160 knot!). When we got to the point, we set up an orbit and started looking. Sandys 5 and 6 were bringing the Jollys. We tried to contact the downed pilot but got nothing. We saw nothing and were starting to get nervous about where we were. After about 15 minutes in the area (again this is my best guess as I don't remember the exact amount of time we spent at this first site), the other F-105s of the flight (Pintail 2 was wingman to Karl Richter if memory serves me correctly) were now back from the tanker and one of them spotted Larry and me and hollered, "What the hell are you doing way up here?" Seems the location we were sent to is about 15-20 miles north of the actual location where Pintail 2 landed.

As a side note, we were told later we were orbiting over "Banana Valley." This didn't mean anything to me, but I found out later that this valley had a hell of a lot of guns and no one went in there just "trolling around!!"

We then went South and were directed to the correct location by the F-105s. I'll try to describe the site as best I can. Pintail 2 had landed on a ridge line of karst. The ridge had a gradual slope on both sides and wasn't one of those very steep karst ridges that exist all over Laos and Vietnam. To the east of this ridge was nothing but the flat farm land of North Vietnam. You could see the ocean on a clear day.

Coming down from the north was a road, very easy to see. The road ran along the east side of the ridge line and turned 90° to the west and crossed the ridge line. It went down the west side of the ridge and turned south. I think about 15 miles south it came to Mu Gia Pass.

On the west side of the ridge was a small valley about one-half to three-quarters of a mile wide. The valley had several small hills in it, and to the west, another small ridge line, and then the mountains. The ridge line ran north/south and kind of petered out about a mile to mile-and-a-half north of where the road crossed it.

Just to the west of the north end of the ridge line was a village. It sat at about the start of the little valley that ran north/south. The ridge line was probably 500-800 feet higher than the flat farm land to the east and had trees all over it, except for a clearing which was about a quarter mile wide. The clearing started about 200 yards north of where the road crossed the ridge and extended to the north, from the bottom of the ridge almost up to the top. It was just a rectangle of a clearing coming up from the flat land on the east.

The F-105 guys told us that they had seen a good chute and had seen Pintail 2 move away from the chute. I can't remember if they had talked to him before they left for the tanker. Anyway, we now started searching for the chute all the while calling for him on the radio. The entire area had a lot of flare chutes. The road crossing the ridge must have been a favorite target for night sorties. Larry once thought he had the chute spotted and asked me to check it out to confirm if I thought it was a personnel chute or a flare chute. I can remember just as plain as day flying about 500 feet above the trees in a left bank with the canopy open looking as hard as I could. [I mention this because later, and even today, I think how stupid this was!] All I saw were flare chutes and told this to Larry.

We finally went up to about 2000-3000 feet above the ridge and started an orbit elongated from north to south. The north end of the orbit was the end of the ridge and the south end was about a half-mile south of where the road crossed the ridge. We would fly just to the east of the ridge and just to the west on our north/south legs. This we kept up until it started getting dark.

Somewhere about this time a couple of Navy A-1s came into the area. They had their wing lights on and could be seen pretty easily. Larry and I decided to keep ours out and picked altitudes about 1000 feet apart, with him being at the lower altitude. We tried to keep on opposite sides of the orbit.

Just after it started getting dark, when flying the northbound leg of the orbit, you could look out to the flat ground on the east, and see "winks" of ground fire which increased in intensity as you flew north. By the time you got to the north end of the ridge to turn south, the flat land looked like a field of fireflies. There were a lot of people shooting at us that we could not see!

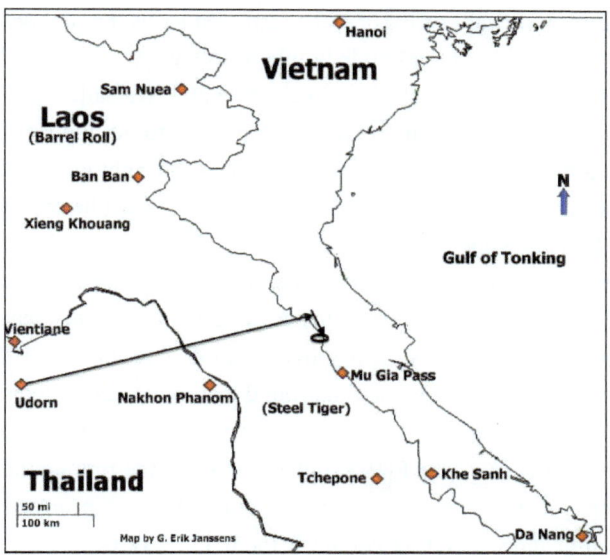

Rescue of Pintail 2

One time Larry's turn at the north end was a little wide and he got close to the village. I was coming north on the east side of the ridge and got my first look at "cherry popsicles." Again, being the FNG, this was the first time I had actually seen real bullets (tracers) being fired at me or my buddy. Boy, it was impressive! I told Larry about it and we never went close to that village again.

By now it had gotten a little darker. On one pass going north, I saw a bunch of "fireflies" blinking in the clearing on the east side of the ridge. I thought, "I'll show those bas——", and I rolled in and started strafing. NOT a good idea! All hell broke loose as they could now see a target to shoot at. I pulled out, very thankful that no one had hit me, and much smarter about doing such a trick again.

When it got real dark, we started getting a response from Pintail 2 on the radio. It wasn't very clear and the decision was made to have the Jollys come and fly in about the same type orbit we were in and to try to get a better fix as to just where he was. The short version of this is, the Jollys got shot at, hit, and had to beat feet back to NKP. We told Pintail 2 to find a hole and we'd be back at first light to get him out. Back to Udorn we went.

Somewhere between 20:00 and 21:00, we were back at Udorn. The four of us agreed that, rather than letting the Sandys scheduled for alert the next day go on the mission, we would go back. After settling that, we ate and went to bed. We were in the air on the way at 05:00 the next morning. As we approached the area, we got a call from a flight of F-105s, the same leader as the day before. He said that they had gotten rid of their 750 lb bombs a little way south (Mu Gia Pass) and had made a low pass over Pintail 2 to "wake him up." We called and Pintail 2 answered right away. (Note: You are always supposed to get the right response to several questions which you ask to make sure it is the right guy and that he isn't being held prisoner in a flak trap. We didn't do that! When he answered, we just knew it was him and he was OK.)

We started a search to pinpoint his location, got him located, and started putting in aircraft after aircraft of ordnance to silence the guns we had seen the night before.

Two things stand out very clearly in my mind. A flight of F-105s had some CBU and we had them put it in the flat ground just to the east of the ridge. Seeing all those little bomblets go off (being the first time I had seen such a thing in combat) was very impressive. The F-105 flight which was the first on the scene (with Richter leading) had gone to the tanker and returned. They informed us that they had some 20 mm and asked if we could use them. Larry directed them to run south to north and strafe just to the East of the road. (This was where we had seen a lot of "fireflies" the night before.)

Watching them strafe, I noticed during one of the passes a bright flash just to the east of the road. After a minute or so, a small column of smoke started up from where the flash was. As time went by, the column of smoke grew bigger and bigger. Pretty soon, it was obvious that it was a fuel dump and it was burning pretty good. It was one hell of a big fire before we left.

As the rescue progressed, Larry ran out of marking rockets and I marked. After I ran out, Sandys 3 and 4 took turns coming in and marking targets. (Note: Our call signs changed and we were then: Larry, Sandy 1, I was Sandy 2, Jack, Sandy 3, and Don, Sandy 4.)

I think it was after about one-and-a-half hours we finally decided to put down a curtain of smoke. We each had six 100 lb "Willy Pete" bombs. These were WW II, box fin type bombs. The four of us laid a string of the bombs from the bottom of the ridge up to as close to the top as the amount of bombs allowed. We did it in the form of a "V", the point of the V at the base of the ridge and the wide part at the top. The two legs of the V ran on a southeast to northwest heading and a northeast to southwest heading.

After the smoke started coming up pretty good, Larry called the Jollys in. Greg Etzel was flying the lead Jolly. He had been flying the Jolly the night before that was shot up so bad that they weren't sure they would make it back to NKP. They came from the west, avoiding the village, and flew down the ridge over Pintail 2's location from the top of the ridge toward the flat land to the east. It is very funny how four Sandys immediately shouted over the radio to the lead Jolly, "Don't fly out over that flat ground, there are a lot of guns out there!!!" Later we found out he was flying out that direction to determine if he could go into a hover with the external fuel tanks on or whether he would have to jettison them. He returned and went into a hover directly over Pintail 2.

It is almost "eerie" as I close my eyes and see that scene. Here was a helicopter, hovering with all that smoke around him, and the radio so quiet it was scary! After about a minute or two, we heard Jolly say, "We have him on board and moving out." (As I read back over this, I have to add this comment. Hearing that call on the radio gave me a bigger jolt of JOY than almost anything I have heard/tasted/felt or whatever. It was a feeling you have to experience to understand.)

Again he headed out over the flat ground, and again the Sandys yelled at him. He picked up speed, turned west and started climbing. The four Sandys got into a weave and covered the ground in front and to the sides.

About this time Larry called over FM that he only had about 5 minutes of gas left! We had made constant fuel checks so this came as a big surprise to the other Sandys. Larry told Sandy 3 and 4 to take the Jollys to NKP and told me to join on him to escort him to NKP.

As we leveled off, Larry was thinking about what to jettison. He was almost ready to jettison the centerline tank and had told me to stay clear when he said, "I don't remember if I ran that tank empty." (We didn't have gauges on the external tanks and would just run them dry, i.e., run them until the engine quit, or if you were quick enough to catch the drop in fuel pressure, you could get it before the engine quit.) He switched to the centerline tank and the engine kept running.

I don't remember how long it ran before it was truly empty, but it seems like about 10 minutes, then the tank was jettisoned. We were both praying that there would be enough to get him to NKP. We got to the river and let down below the scattered clouds to see the runway at NKP. Still running! Whew! Gear, flaps, and a good landing.

Later it was found that a 12.7 mm bullet had gone into the bottom of the fuselage tank (it was always a wonder how it had gotten past the external centerline tank!) and probably pushed the sealant up, allowing fuel to leak out. The sealant had finally sealed off the leak and Larry made it back. They fueled that A-1 with enough fuel that it was determined that there were only about 10 gallons of usable fuel left. I went on to Udorn, and Sandys 3 and 4 and the Jollys landed with Pintail 2 at NKP.

It was a very happy bunch of people that day. Prichard (Pintail 2) had money enough to buy a few drinks that day. Seems he had cashed his pay check and had all the cash with him when he jumped out. Laying there that day, with all the people shouting and firing in the air, he kept wondering if he should bury it. Knowing he wouldn't come back to get it if he hid it, he decided that he would just keep it.

I didn't get to talk to him directly, but understand from the other Sandys he had a hell of a story to tell. After he landed and got out of his chute, he turned off the beacon and beat feet away from the chute. He didn't go very far when he decided it was best to hide. He got down under a bushy-type tree and hugged it for all he was worth. He could look down the slope of the ridge and see a path. He saw several men with guns run by, an old lady and a young boy also. They would shoot the guns in the air and yell and then all of a sudden stop and listen. He stayed still. (We now know why he wasn't answering us on the radio.)

He got this funny feeling and turned his head to look up the slope. He said the path went off a bit to the right then turned back and came right past him just above. If anyone walking on the path above looked down, they would probably see him. He stayed still until dark when he started using his radio. That night he moved and waited until we arrived the next day.

Quite a story for the grandkids!!

A rather interesting finish to a mission that I do not have any notation of on the flight log. I was landing at Udorn after the mission, and I think it was just an orbit for possible SAR. I can't remember for the life of me all the details except the exciting landing. I was the last one in the flight to land. If I remember correctly the runway was east to west and we were landing to the west. We normally turned off at the mid-field taxiway. This day they had some EC-121's and C-130's parked on this taxiway and the tower told me to go to the end to taxi back. I did that and had moved just a little left of the center line. As I was approaching the end of the runway, I unlocked the tail wheel. It was at that point I became a passenger and not in control. The aircraft started a ground loop to the left the instant I unlocked the tail wheel. I used full right rudder, all the brake I could, and it would not straighten out. As I got turned 180 degrees, the right main gear went off the side of the runway and, as luck would have it, the gear hit a runway light that was set in a concrete block. The right main collapsed! The rocket pod on the outboard station of the right wing hit the ground just hard enough for the front cone to pop off but no other damage. The prop, still turning at idle was nicking the ground.

This is a picture I took when returning from a mission in the Barrel Roll area. Note, even with the glare, the airspeed is about 148 knots, heading 176 degrees, and altitude about 10,000 feet. Look at the "g" meter top right edge of the picture. Must have pulled 4 g's sometime during the flight.

[It was real funny at this point. A C-130 was sitting on the taxiway that I was going to turn onto waiting to take the runway for takeoff and saw me ground loop and the gear collapse. He called the tower and could hardly talk. He stuttered out that the A-1 had just run off the runway. I don't know why but him stuttering like that made me laugh. I guess he thought I was going to hit him.] Anyway, I shut down, and in just about two minutes I had a convention of people around me asking what happened. I told them that as I unlocked the tail wheel I became a passenger, and I had NO IDEA what caused it. If you remember when the gear retracted, it would rotate so the wheel was flat up in the wing. Well, the only damage to the aircraft (other than having to change the engine for sudden stoppage) was replacing that big ring on the gear. The maintenance guys had the aircraft on the schedule the next afternoon.

OK, time for another story about one of the missions from the flight log: the mission flown on 26 August 1967.

NKP, Nakhon Phanom, Thailand, "Naked Fanny", Channel 89, etc. NKP was about 45 minutes to an hour to the east of Udorn. It was right next to the Mekong River. To help if there was to be a SAR effort in southern North Vietnam (Route Package I) the Sandys would pull Alert at NKP. A flight of two would generally land just before sundown, refuel, and be on alert. We knew that we would never get launched at night because we had no night rescue capability. We were still considered "ON ALERT" during all the hours we were at NKP. I haven't looked at the calendar for this day (26 August 1967) but would bet that it was a Sunday. It (to me anyway) was the worst thing in the world to be on alert at NKP on a Sunday. Why? Well, it seemed that every Sunday the weather would be bad in Route Package V & VI, where the big strike packages of aircraft would go to strike targets around Hanoi and Haiphong. I could just see the pilots in the F-105s saying to themselves: "Whew, now we can go down to Route Pack I where the guns aren't so big." They would go down there and maybe get with a Misty FAC or hit just about anything that looked like a target, then, just for good measure, make a strafe pass or two. It was at this time that the "little guns" would shoot them down. Then we would have to go look for them. As I think more about it, this probably wasn't a Sunday because the SAR I went on was looking for a Misty FAC. Misty FACs were F-100Fs, had two pilots in them. One guy flew in the front one day then in the back seat the next mission. These guys were "fast mover FACs" that really knew their stuff! Did a great job.

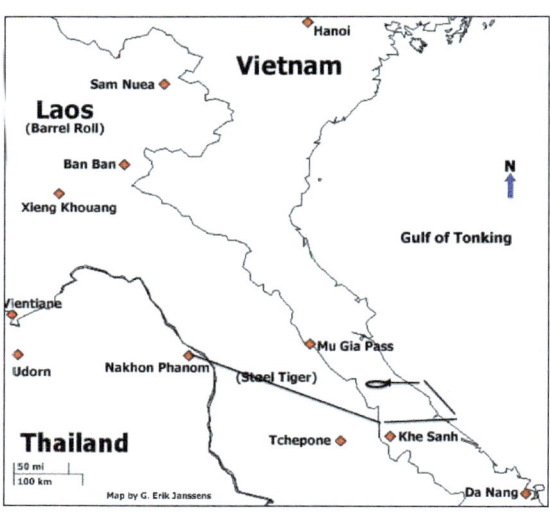

SAR effort for Misty One (Bud Day)

One got hit by something in the vicinity of "Fingers Lake" (17 12N, 106 40E), I think, but won't bet money on this location or that it was in the vicinity of Fingers Lake). It was mid-afternoon and we got scrambled. Since I had never been in Route Pack I, I decided to go down south till I was about straight west of Da Nang, go east until "feet wet," then north until I was abeam of the location. I did this and, as I was about to enter North Vietnam, I saw a couple of Navy A-1s coming out. I asked them what altitude was best going in since I didn't know the area. They said about 5,000 feet was OK. In we went. I think Jenks was my wingman that day. Arriving in the search area, I went into a left orbit calling for Misty and looking for a chute. King had said the chute had been seen earlier. I saw a bunch of flare chutes but no personnel chute. Had the canopy open and orbited at about 1,000 feet. After a while in a left orbit, Jenks called and said "Wouldn't it be a good idea to maybe orbit in the other direction?" All the while, and we were in there at least 45 minutes, I did not see a shot fired. Finally King told us to come out and go home. I went back out and home the same way I came. In Intel debrief, I really got scared! They kept pointing out the 37mm sites, possible SAM sites, 57mm sites, and all the reports of people getting the hell shot out of them in that area. Guess they were either tired of shooting that day or God had told them to take a break. Whatever, I was damn lucky!

I don't know why, but I had never thought of it until I wrote this. "WHY DID KING SEND US INTO AN AREA THAT HAD SO MUCH STUFF TO SHOOT YOU DOWN??" Something had to have shot down the F-100 Misty.

[NOTE: Just looked up 26 Aug 1967 and it was a Saturday.] [ANOTHER NOTE: *On August 26, 1967, Major Day was flying F-100F, AF Serial No. 56-3954, call sign "Misty 01", on his 26th Fast FAC sortie, directing a flight of F-105 Thunderchiefs in an air strike against a surface-to-air missile (SAM) site north of Thon Cam Son and west of Dong Hoi, 20 mi (32 km) north of the DMZ in North Vietnam. Day was on his 65th mission into North Vietnam and acting as check pilot for Captain Corwin M. "Kipp" Kippenhan, who was upgrading to aircraft commander. 37 mm antiaircraft fire crippled the aircraft, forcing the crew to eject. In the ejection, Day's right arm was broken in three places when he struck the side of the cockpit, and he also received eye and back injuries. Kippenhan was rescued by a USAF HH-3E, but Day was unable to contact the rescue helicopter by survival radio and was quickly captured by North Vietnamese local militia. On his fifth night, when he was still within 20 mi (32 km) of the DMZ, Day escaped from his initial captors despite his serious injuries. Although stripped of both his boots and*

PK at Chiang Mai

flight suit, Day crossed the Demilitarized Zone back into South Vietnam, becoming the only U.S. prisoner of war to escape from North Vietnam. Within 2 mi (3 km) of the U.S. Marine firebase at Con Thien and after 12–15 days of evading, he was captured again, this time by a Viet Cong patrol that wounded him in the leg and hand with gunfire. Taken back to his original camp, Day was tortured for escaping, breaking his right arm again. He then was moved to several prison camps near Hanoi, where he was periodically beaten, starved, and tortured. In December 1967, Day shared a cell with Navy Lieutenant Commander and future Senator and presidential candidate John McCain. Air Force Major Norris Overly nursed both back to health, and McCain later devised a makeshift splint of bamboo and rags that helped heal Day's seriously atrophied arm. On March 14, 1973, Day was released after five years and seven months as a North Vietnamese prisoner. Within three days Day was reunited with his wife, Doris Sorensen Day, and four children at March Air Force Base, California. On March 4, 1976, President Gerald Ford awarded Day the Medal of Honor for his personal bravery while a captive in North Vietnam. Day had been promoted to Colonel while a prisoner, and decided to remain in the Air Force in hopes of being promoted to Brigadier General. Although initially too weak to resume operational flying, he spent a year in physical rehabilitation and with 13 separate medical waivers, was returned to active flying status. He underwent conversion training to the F-4 Phantom II and was appointed vice commander of the 33rd Tactical Fighter Wing at Eglin Air Force Base, Florida. Day, in 2008, said of his imprisonment, "As awful as it sounds, no one could say we did not do well. ...[Being a POW] was a major issue in my life and one that I am extremely proud of. I was just living day to day. One bad cold and I would have been dead." [From Wikipedia, the free encyclopedia.]

    Another part of life in the 602nd was schedule. Notice, of course, that we flew several days in a row. When we had several days off, we were allowed to go just about wherever we wanted, just as long as we got back when schedule called for you. My roomy, Jack Cochran, and I took several trips together. One was to the old Thailand capital city of Chiang Mai. This was a very relaxing few days where we tried our best to drink all the Singha beer in the town. We did not accomplish that task. We even had a few days in Taiwan. We got to Taiwan via the C-121 AWACS which was stationed at Udorn also. They flew to Taiwan to have maintenance done on the aircraft. I don't remember if Jack and I went to Bangkok also, but probably did.

On the return flight from Taiwan, the C-121 we were scheduled in wasn't ready when it was supposed to be but after about an hour delay we loaded and taxied to the runway. They ran up the engines and checked the mags, then we took the runway. They sat for a while with the engines running at what seemed like full power and then released brakes. Fighter guys in the back of the big planes almost always look at the watch and see how long it is until we break ground. We hadn't rolled but about 40 seconds when the power comes off and they were braking. Jack and I looked at each other wondering what the hell. Well, they taxied back and tried again. They didn't roll; they must have seen something they didn't like, because we taxied back and got another aircraft. That flight went OK. As Jack and I got off the aircraft at Udorn, we both said NEVER AGAIN.

Jack Cochran in Chiang Mai.

Udorn also had a really good hobby shop where you could dub tapes and records to tapes. I think just about everyone bought a reel-to-reel tape recorder, or if they had one at home, they spent a lot of their free time dubbing tapes. I didn't notice it until I was home listening to the tapes, but it was really funny that when the big radar on base was operating, every time it came around you would get a real weak beep on your tape. You really had to listen for it, but it was there.

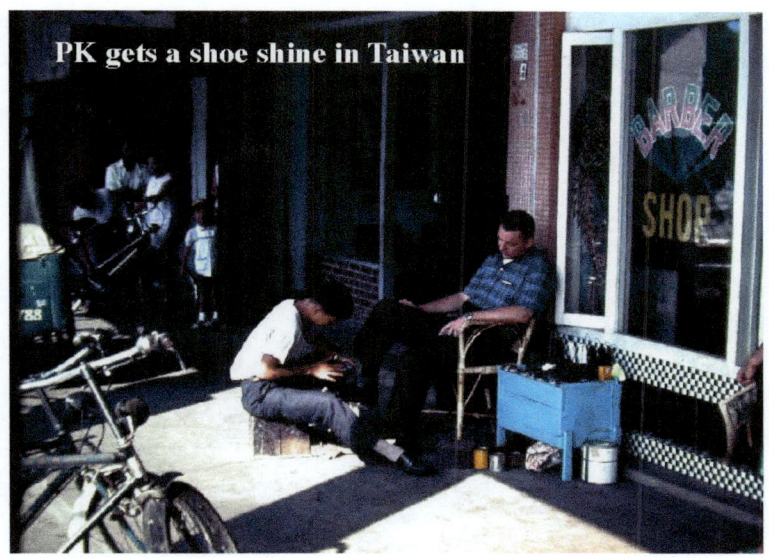
PK gets a shoe shine in Taiwan

The mission on 1 September 1967 is listed on the flight log as Knight Watch. This is the story about that day.

The Air America guy we had that briefed Barrel Roll targets was a really neat guy. I think he was actually an Air Force Lt. Col who didn't have an ID card and never wore a uniform but he really knew his stuff. Actually got information from "Road Watch Teams." This is a team of guys that would be put into the jungle way up north. The location would be close enough to a road/main infiltration route that they could see what was going on, but not be close enough to get discovered. Sometimes they would get discovered but high tail it out of Dodge and have to get picked up right away. Most of the time they would just stay in place until another team would replace them. If this guy briefed you that a certain target had trucks or stuff stored there, you could bank on it.

Before I got to the Squadron, a guy named Major Roy Knight was in the squadron and he got shot down and killed in the vicinity of Sam Neua. I think it was near a place we called "Poodle Karst" (20 27N, 104 11E) (obviously because it looked just like a French Poodle from the air). This place had some very big caves in it and it was loaded with stuff. At one time we thought that American prisoners held in Northern Laos were kept in these caves. I have never found out for sure.

One time we were going to run a rescue mission based on the fact that they had moved all the people out of the caves to a village just to the East of this location so they could hold a big meeting. We were told a lot of North Vietnamese Generals along with some Russians would be there. Weather got bad and this never came off.

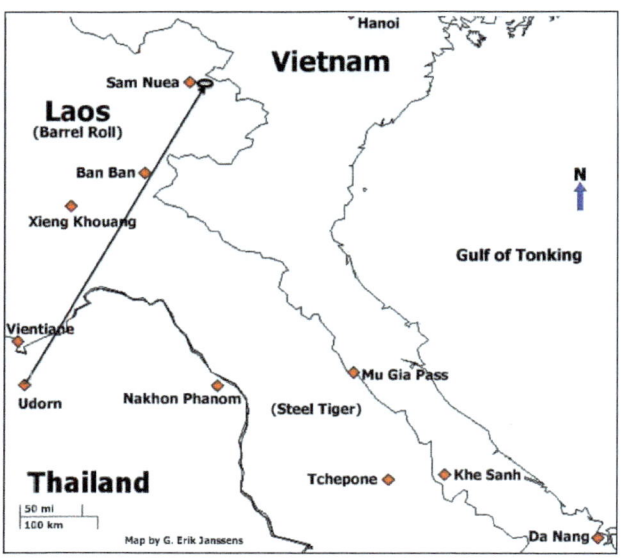

Knight Watch effort, Poodle Karst just East of Sam Nuea

With all the stuff that was in this area, it was decided to send a lot of aircraft to bomb the area and try to get as much of the stuff as we could. In honor of Maj. Knight, this effort was called "Knight Watch." [Several other times while I was in the squadron we hit places with a lot of aircraft and we would always call the effort Knight Watch.]

I don't remember how many sorties we put in that day, but it was a bunch. I held in an orbit about 15 miles south and Cricket would have the fighters check in with me. I was like an Air Traffic Controller. I just put them in a stack until the Firefly on scene would call and ask for more fighters. I did this until the Fireflys on scene ran out of marking rockets, then they came and replaced me and my wingman and I went up to FAC the fighters. The only real memorable thing about this was the amount of air we put in and how scared I got once. I marked for this F-4 flight (it was just about a broken layer at 3,500 feet) and the lead said he didn't have the mark. I said, OK, I'll mark again. As I rolled in, about wings level in the dive, the entire side of the mountain in front of me, where I was going to mark, just blew up! Seems just after he told me he didn't see the mark, he did see it, but failed to say anything to me about it. I thought they had a million guns and they were all firing at me at once! Scared hell out of me!! Of course that was to be expected from F-4 flights!!

I probably shouldn't be giving the F-4 guys such a hard time because I have a bunch of good friends who flew the F-4. However, I must tell the truth, and that is that for every flight of F-4's I controlled as a FAC that did a good job of delivering ordnance, I probably had eight that did a very poor job of getting stuff on target.

Here is the story about the mission on 11 September 1967, one I remember VERY well. That was one of those times when I should have really paid attention to the fact that once you arrived at NKP you were ON ALERT! I think it was Gould who was my Sandy 2. We got to NKP before sunset and went to the O'Club because that was the place to get something good to eat and Gould had a friend he wanted to visit with. We had dinner, then sat and talked and had a few drinks. It appeared to be one of those nights when you could sit there and just drink till the cows came home! Somewhere around 9 o'clock, I told Gould that I was going to bed. He decided to come along and I think by about 9:45 we were in bed. Somewhere around 2 o'clock in the morning, the airman on duty came and shook me awake saying, "They say to launch the Sandys!" I knew, of course that was stupid because we didn't launch at night. Oh Yea! I got on the phone after getting my boots and flight suit on. "Yes, launch and go east; we'll tell you just where when you get airborne." OK, off we went.

When we got into the aircraft and got them started, I found my radio wouldn't work. Just a side note, the weather was about 200 foot overcast and a light rain falling! I finally found out that it must be the mike button or something on the left side of the aircraft, because if I plugged into the radio cord on the right side of the aircraft, I could transmit and hear. Of course, to transmit I must use the mike button on the right throttle! Hell of a note, trying to fly using the stick and left throttle to fly, but having to reach over to the right side to transmit! I finally told Sandy 2 I'd go but he would have to lead.

When we got to the runway and started our run-up, we started sliding down the runway. Brakes were holding just fine, it was just too slick on the PSP for the tires to hold! About the time I got the gear up and started the flaps up, I was in the weather. If I had ever had any thoughts about anything else, I NOW STARTED TO FLY THE AIRCRAFT!! Weather, night, me a bit hung over, hell did I wake up or what?? Broke out on top about 1,500 feet with almost a full moon. We could see to the east and I swear I saw flares at what turned out to be the SAR area. It was over on the coast just north of Dong Hoi.

Decision time again. Do we go right east across North Vietnam or down south to cross to the coast over South Vietnam? We discussed it on FM and decided to go straight across! No problem. No ground fire. I'll tell you one thing, as long as you looked east and saw the water and moonlight on the water, you could fly VFR. Looking west, you saw nothing but jungle, and it looked like a deep dark ink well! Even with the moon, you couldn't tell sky from ground.

We got to the water and found out we were looking for a crew (2 guys) from a B-57. (The call sign I have is Redbird 44.) A couple Navy A-1s were in the area, as well as a Big Mother (Navy Helicopter). They had been in the area a bit, per my memory. Gould got contact with the resources in the area and we (he and I) thought we had control. How screwed up it was!

Sometime after orbiting out over the water and looking at the coast and seeing a lot of ground fire, with no contact with either Redbird guy on the ground, someone (and to this day I don't know who!) called for the one guy on the ground who had been using the radio to pop a flare. Well, it was like a magnet for all the ground fire in the area. Shortly after that, I think, the Navy people left.

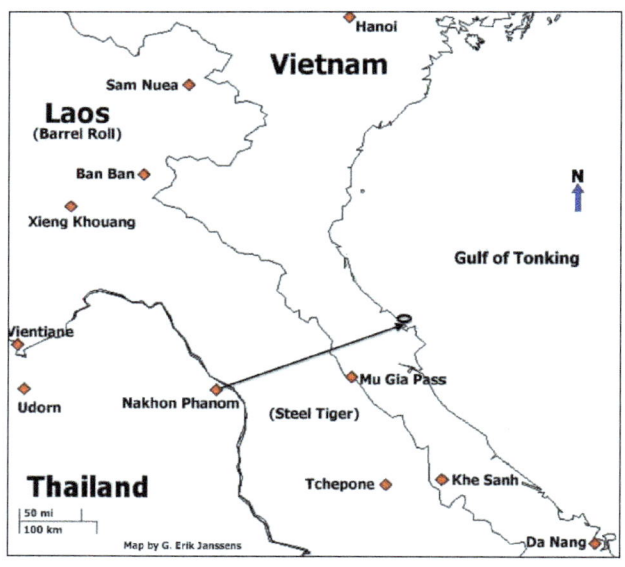

Night time SAR for Red Bird

I was in a left-hand orbit, going north out over the water, turning left, and staying just off the coast as I went back south in the orbit. In one of these turns I was about pointed straight west when the entire coast lit up with what looked like

122 | Paul "PK" Kimminau

gun fire! Man, I was scared and broke left, toward the water, and down. Then I heard this call, "That will teach those bastards." Well, it was years later that I found out that it was an F-4 (a flight of two from Da Nang which neither Gould or I knew were in the area!) who had just put in CBU!

After a few more orbits (I think we were in the area about 1 hour), we got word from King to RTB. Decisions again! Should we go back across North Vietnam or back to the south? It is much shorter to go straight across, so we did. I can't possibly describe just what this looked like, sort of like flying into a bowl of ink.

About halfway across North Vietnam, I looked down and saw a square of light on the ground. It looked just like those squares in the middle of a small southern city where the courthouse sits, about a block square and just lit up as bright as could be. I said to Gould, "Do you see that?" He said, "Yes." "What do you think it is?" "I don't have any idea." "Do you think it could be a SAM site?," I asked. "Well, we aren't going to strike it," he said. "No, you don't understand, do you think we should start a weave?" "Yea," he said. Hell, just imagine, here we were, a couple of A-1s going about 140-150 knots and I thought we should weave!

Again, a debrief in Intel has me shaking in my boots and drinking mission whiskey like water. All kinds of 57mm, 85mm, SAM sites, etc, just where we were crossing! Intelligence had no idea what we may have seen and to this day I have never heard anything it might have been. I also think if any North Vietnamese were awake and saw on radar a couple targets going about 140 or so knots they probably thought it was a flight of ducks that were lost, not a couple of dumb American A-1 pilots crossing their country in the middle of the night! I never want to do something like that again.

Now the story about the mission on 12 September. This was just a regular strike mission up into the Barrel Roll area. Somewhere after we crossed the fence (the Mekong River was called the fence) either I or my wingman started noticing the oil temperature going up. We decided that we wouldn't be able to make our scheduled mission—but we could dump some ordnance on the "Ziggies." The Ziggies to us is where Route 7 goes into Laos from North Vietnam. I think every fighter pilot in SEA called it the "Fish's Mouth." I had some CBU that I didn't want to take home, so at about 11-12,000 feet straight and level I started pickling them off. I don't remember the CBU number but they were the kind that had those little spring-loaded fingers that popped out and about a softball size bomblet attached. I think I made about two large orbits before these things started hitting the ground. I was pretty lucky that they were hitting right down the road. I have always wondered, if there were any enemies down there, what they thought. Here were a couple of airplanes flying straight and level way up there doing nothing (it is highly likely that, if there was anyone down there, they might not have noticed or heard us), and the next thing you know, here are these bomblets hitting the ground. Probably did nothing, but I felt good.

The mission on 13 September is a good example of how the people in higher headquarters have no idea of what goes on down at squadron level. This was the time that the project "Harvest Reaper" was going on. "Grim Reaper" we called it. It was the first introduction of the F-111 into combat. They were flying night low-level missions into North Vietnam. Single ship. After they lost a couple and had no idea of what might be happening, we were tasked to spend some time after each mission searching over the probable exit route to see if maybe they somehow made it back into Laos. I have shown a call sign of "Butt" but I have no idea of what call sign they were using. I know we never saw any sign of them or ever had one of them answer. The squadron spent a lot of hours searching for these guys. As I am now writing this, I also remember doing a lot of searching for some lost B-26s that flew night missions out of NKP. After I left the squadron and went to Hq 7th, the guys spent a hell of a lot of time searching for the lost F-111's.

The Sandy mission on 16 September was somewhat unusual. We normally did not divert to a Strike mission from a SAR Orbit since we had a "Sandy Load" and not a Strike Load. (I think this is the mission. Even if it isn't the exact mission, the event took place on one of my missions as I returned from orbit.) We got a call from Cricket. This was a C-130 that kept track of all Air Force strike sorties going out country. They told me that they had a Raven FAC who needed a strike. I got in touch with the FAC. He was to the north of the Plains de Jars; when we reached the area we found that he had a village he wanted hit. Now we were told NOT to hit villages. Of course, if in the process of a rescue, they shot at you from a village, that village was no longer a village but a military target. There was no shooting from this village. Now one other reason to hit a village was confirmation by a "brown body" that the village was "bad guy" country. In this case the Raven FAC confirmed that he had a brown body in his aircraft, and there was a regiment of Civil Engineers (North Vietnamese Regulars) in that village. Well, I and my wingman used the 100# "Willy Pete" bombs and when we left, the village was a huge funeral pyre. Not something to be really proud of, but it was the ONE AND ONLY mission where I hit a village.

Later on that same day, we were on the 30 minute alert, and had gone to the club for lunch. I don't remember if we had finished eating but we got a call to get back ASAP and launch. It was the only time I remember actually calling the tower and driving across the runway to get back quickly. We launched, and Sandy 2 and I went north, and I mean really far north! The log shows we searched for Resale 2, and although that call sign doesn't seem correct, what we were searching for was an RF-101 guy who had been hit and made it to about 30-40 miles southwest of Yen Bai, and King said there was a beeper. We got up there and orbited, looking and calling for this guy, and every once in a while we could hear his beeper, but never got voice contact. I could see the Black River and there were some villages in the area. We never had to fly over any of those, and we searched for 30-45 minutes. Finally we told King we just weren't going to be able to do anything about getting this guy out. About this time they started giving some warnings that Migs were getting airborne down around Hanoi. We did have some F-4's capping us so we headed back home. We were at about 11,000 feet and just above an undercast. The F-4 guys said we were really easy to see against the clouds and they recommended that we get below the clouds. We did. Returned to Udorn after an unsuccessful try at a SAR.

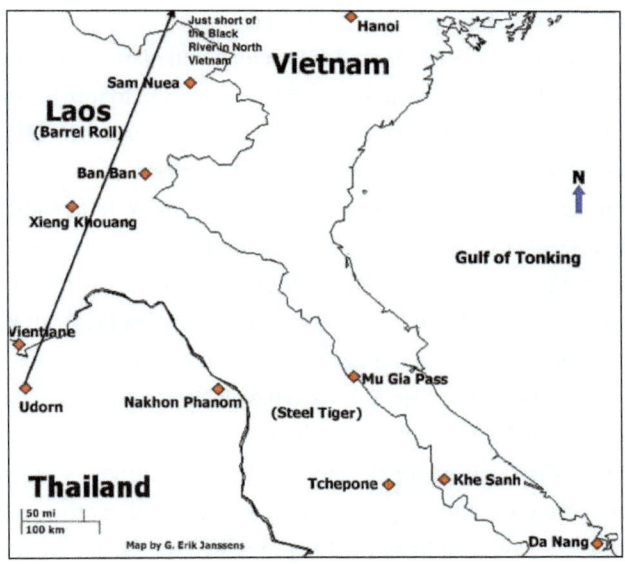

SAR Effort for RF-101, Resale 02

Somewhere about this time in my tour (September or October) something happened on one of my missions that wasn't exactly what you would like to happen. We had this one fellow in the squadron who had actually had some flying time in an F-86 in Korea. (I think he had at least one Mig kill.) He seemed to know just about everything there was to know about flying. (He took every chance he had to tell you that also!) Anyway he was leading a Firefly mission (just a regular strike mission) and part way to our target we got this call to divert to a SAR mission that was in progress down by Mu Gia Pass. [*The Mu Gia Pass is a mountain pass in the Annamite Range between northern Vietnam and Laos, located 90 km northwest of Đồng Hới, Vietnam. The pass is 418 m above sea level and connects Route 15 from Tân Ấp in Vietnam to Route 12 in Khammouane Province in Laos. (From Wikipedia, the free encyclopedia)*]

The two A-1s on scene were running short on fuel and needed replacing soon. Since we were already airborne, we were directed to go to the scene. The weather was about 3,500 ft broken which made it difficult to join up with the A-1's already there. This all-knowing lead I had was on the radio constantly trying to find out where the other guys were. As we were approaching the area, we were also letting down to get below the clouds. Just as we popped out of the clouds, I looked over to the 2:30 position and saw one of the other A-1's. I called to lead the position and got no answer. I called again and still got no answer, so I called on FM again. Now Lead said, "Two shut up!"

I was on his left side back about 7:00 o'clock and started a right turn to keep the other A-1 in sight. Again I called lead trying to get him to turn and see the other aircraft. To no avail—he just kept pressing on. In fact, he was headed right toward Mu Gia Pass, which I think was only about 10-12 miles away.

I lost sight of lead, but I did keep the other orbiting A-1s in sight. Eventually the other flight lead saw me and called to my lead to turn around and come back 180 degrees from the heading he was on. He finally did that; by then I was in orbit with the other two A-1's. When I was able to talk to my lead and tell him I was up there with the other two aircraft, he just about exploded. It settled into us getting a very quick briefing from the other A-1's and they beat feet home, almost out of gas.

I had a pretty good idea where the guys on the ground were, and the Jollys were on their way in. I called for the guy on the ground (there were actually two of them—an F-4 crew—and they were fairly close together) to fire his pen gun flare. He did, and I saw it right away. I kept my eye on the spot and directed the Jolly to their location. Very soon I heard the guys on the ground saying they had the Jolly in sight. They got picked up OK.

When we got back home, all hell broke loose. My lead came unglued on me and wondered why the hell I didn't stay with him down there. I tried my best to tell him if he had just shut up for only a little while and listened to me giving him the position of the other A-1's, everything would have been just fine. He would have none of that. He vowed that he never wanted to fly with me again. I said that would be just fine with me because, if he was that kind of lead, I wanted no part of him. This was the only time I flew with someone that I never wanted to fly with again. [NOTE: I must say to anyone reading this: I know how important it is for a wingman to stay with his leader. It is your job as a wingman to keep leads six o'clock clear. However, if lead never shuts up long enough for you to tell him there is something he should know, what the hell good is it for you to stay with him??]

This is "Motor" Carr's aircraft leaking oil. I know for those who have flown the A-1 oil all over the aircraft was pretty normal; however, this was really a lot of oil.

The mission on 7 October was unusual in that my wingman had to land on a dirt strip in Laos. I can't for the life of me remember his first name. Since his last name was Carr it was only natural he got a "handle" of Motor. This guy could sleep more than any person I have ever met. He would get to the squadron after a good night's sleep, brief, and if he was on 15 or 30 minute alert and didn't launch, he would be lying on a couch sleeping within minutes. You would have to wake him to go to lunch and after returning to the squadron, back to sleep! Wake him up to get his gear out of the aircraft, up to the room, over to the Club for dinner and back to his room to sleep. There were probably days he didn't sleep this much but I really remember him because he slept so much.

On this day, he was my wingman and we were going on a strike mission up in the Barrel Roll. Getting to the target area, we found that we would be unable to deliver ordnance because of weather. Now, this normally meant that you would go without a "Counter" on that mission. We contacted Cricket to see if there was any place else we could go, but to no avail. Finally I decided we would go to the "Ziggies" (described earlier as the Fish's Mouth) and just drop on the "Fords" and the road. We were still in the weather (and if we stayed in the weather we weren't going to get to drop even there), but we headed toward the target.

As if by magic, and I am not lying, we broke into the clear and right in front of us was the target. I told Carr to take spacing and I armed my bombs and rolled in. The instant my wing dropped for the roll in, the guns started to fire. Now for me this was something NEW! At the Ziggies I had dropped stuff a lot of times and had NEVER been shot at. There were four guns and the little white flashes were all in a row. I dropped my bombs and pulled out rather high and told Carr that there were guns in the target area. I saw him on his pass and the guns were firing. I really can't remember making a second pass so it must have been on his first pass that, after dropping his bombs, he pressed on with strafe. I had an Intelligence Officer in the right seat with a camera. We would take these guys along so they could get a combat mission and we could get some BDA (Bomb Damage Assessment) on the same mission. He and I were both yelling over the radio for Carr to pull out. Somewhere in the pass, I saw a puff of smoke come from his aircraft. He pulled out and announced that he thought he took a hit. I told him to head for home and I'd join on him.

When we came up on the right side of the aircraft, we saw it was covered with oil. Since he was still climbing (of course there was a high mountain right on track for home), he had the power up and oil was still coming out. Once he got leveled off, and pulled the power back, you couldn't see any more oil coming out. He never reported any instrument readings that would indicate the engine quitting. We declared an emergency and flew toward Udorn. Right in our path toward home was the village/air strip of Pak Sane. This is a dirt strip just to the north of the Mekong River in Laos. I thought it best we get him on the ground, so I made a pass over the runway, it looked OK, and he landed.

I was still talking to him and went back to altitude to talk to the Command Post at Udorn. I got the word that I was to tell him to find some paint and paint out the US Air Force markings on the aircraft. I asked in a very nice manner just where the hell he was going to find paint? They told me maybe he could get some mud and cover the markings. You see, we dumb Americans were still living by the rules and there was to be NO American military presence in Laos. Some guy that could speak

English met Carr and he seemed to be in friendly hands so we went home. It turned out that one bullet hit one of the tubes that covers the valve stem going to the cylinder and this had allowed some oil to come out. After replacing this tube and adding oil, the aircraft was flown out of Pak Sane the next day and back to Udorn.

Another interesting thing during my time with the 602nd was aircraft losses. The first one I remember was an A-1E with Russell and Raush shot down over the Fish's Mouth ("The Ziggies"). [I remember for sure Russell was one of the guys and am pretty sure Raush was the other, but it may have been someone else.] They were both picked up and seemed to have no injuries. We lost another A-1E at the same location and unfortunately we also lost the pilot. That was Cherry, but I can't remember his first name. (Dan, I think.) The speculation on his loss was that he rolled in and maybe pulled a few negative "g's", which threw the chute in the right seat forward, which then prevented him being able to pull the stick back to recover. I guess we'll never know for sure.

The mission on 12 October is of interest if only because I got a glimpse of a place in history. That would be the place where the beginning of the end of France's presence in Southeast Asia occurred (May 1954): Dien Bien Phu. Earlier I told about how the project Knight Watch got started. Well, on this day I got about 4 flights of 4 F-105s to strike a "truck park" that was just over the border in Laos on the road south out of Dien Bien Phu. This is quite a way North for an A-1. The Air America guy that briefed this mission wanted it to be a part of Knight Watch. There is really nothing unusual about this mission except I did get a look into the valley and actually see Dien Bien Phu. After reading all about the French and what took place there, it was kind of neat to be able to see the area. We hit the truck park and got a bunch of secondary explosions, so it was a good mission in that respect.

As noted earlier, I probably should not give the F-4 guys a hard time, but the mission I FAC'd on 12 October really was the one which I remembered the most about their ability to hit the target. I guess the only reason I mention this story is because flying around Ban Ban could be so different depending on what time you were there. During the time I flew, June 67-Nov 67, there did not seem to be any guns there. You could fly over the valley at about 3,000 feet and even go down and look at targets at a lower altitude, and no one paid any attention to you. Even a bit east in the valley, toward the Fish's Mouth, around "Pickle Mountain," there wasn't much shooting. Pickle Mountain was called that because it looked just like a big dill pickle laying on the ground. It was karst and had a lot of caves in it.

A good friend of mine tells about a mission he was on when the other guy in the flight of 2 F-105s shooting Bull Pup missiles put one right in the entrance and saw the entire mountain start smoking. All the air passages they had up in the mountain started pouring smoke so he must have really caused havoc inside the cave.

The mission I wanted to tell about was trying to get a radio tower which was in an open field about 3-4 kilometers west of the village of Ban Ban. The Air America intel guy had spotted it in a photo; it was very hard to see. He briefed me and I found it and called in a flight of F-4s to hit it. I'll never forget after contacting the F-4s, I asked them if they had me in sight. They responded, "Yes," so I said I would mark the area. I really didn't expect them to see the tower from the altitude they would be rolling in from. I put down a couple of rockets and had the tower pretty well bracketed. They said they saw the marks, so I cleared them in.

One called in and then called off. I was watching the target and didn't see the F-4; after a bit, when I really should have seen the bombs go off, I didn't see any ordnance going off. I told Two he was cleared, but I did not see lead's bombs. Two called in, and about that time I happened to look about 5 miles east of where I put the marks and saw the smoke of some bombs. I now saw Two diving for the same spot. He pulled off (it was too late for me to call him off) and called off. I now told the flight to hold high and dry. I asked just what mark were they dropping on??

To this day I can't remember if the other two in the flight came up to the real target or not. I think they did but we were unsuccessful in dropping the radio tower. I have to say at this point that this was what we A-1 FACs came to expect from F-4 flights.

The F-105s would normally come in flights of two. I was told that the first ten missions a new guy flew, he got to fly in a low-threat area. Barrel Roll was a favorite place for this slow introduction to combat. The lead on these flights was also normally a guy who had 90 counters and he was getting his last ten in a low-threat area. It was easy to tell who was the most experienced when you watched them drop bombs. I don't remember having an F-105 ever miss a target by very much, even the new guys could really drop bombs accurately.

Another interesting but sad note about Ban Ban Valley. My assignment out of Southeast Asia was to the Fighter Weapons School at Nellis AFB, NV. I was an instructor in the F-100. If my memory is not way off, sometime during 1969 a F-105 got shot down in Ban Ban Valley by a 57mm gun. The guy flying that F-105 had been an instructor in the F-105 Weapons School when I had attended the F-100 school in 1965. When I heard where he had been shot down, I couldn't believe it! As I said before, during my period with the 602nd we could fly through Ban Ban Valley at just about any altitude and not get shot at.

I remember one of the guys in the squadron telling a story about F-105s and bombs. Seems this guy (the guy in our A-1 squadron) had a favorite site he always saved one bomb for, if he could. [Note: This was not Larry Mehr's target.] It was a gun site on the road south out of Sam Neua toward Ban Ban valley. Route 67, I think. Seems one day when this guy was hitting a target close to this site, they shot at him. Kind of made him mad and he would always try to get that gun site if he could. Well, he had finished his mission this one day and was on his way home when Cricket called him and asked if he could use a couple of F-105s. He said, "Yea", and headed for his site. He directed Cricket to send the 105s to him.

Once in contact, the A-1 at about 10,000 feet asked if the F-105s (at about 18,000 feet) could see him. They answered, "Yes." He then briefed them that as soon as he dipped his wing, as if he were rolling in, they should watch this one spot and they would probably see this gun start to shoot. Sure enough, he dipped his wing to roll in and this guy started firing. The 105 guys said, "Get out of the way, we see him." Well, each of the 105s had two 3,000# bombs. They were spares for the Alpha Strike that day and weren't needed. As soon as the lead F-105 rolled in, the gunner started firing at him. No way could he have hit him at that altitude (it was probably a 12.7 or 14.5, NOT a 37mm), but he was trying. The A-1 guy watched the F-105 roll in, saw the bombs come off, and watched as they proceeded to hit the gunner in the forehead! One big ball of fire, and no more gun! That is the kind of guys we liked to FAC!!

The 12 November mission is one I also remember well. This is rather a sad story because we never got the survivor out. AWOL 1 was an F-4 out of Da Nang, I think. I believe the guy in the front seat was either the Squadron Commander or Ops Officer, and the back seater was Lance Peter Sijan. [What I remember about this is the front seater had gone to West Point and his "call sign" was Army. Of course Sijan was an Air Force Academy graduate.]

It was late in the afternoon when we got called. I was Sandy 2 that day and can't remember who Sandy 1 was. We were probably the third flight (maybe the fourth) of A-1s to get to the scene. The original call about this did not provide any information about how long they had been down and just how bad the area they went down in was. The first A-1 flights into the area found out it was a very hostile area. In fact it may be that the F-4 was down from the night before, I don't remember for sure. It, after the fact of course, appeared that the North Vietnamese knew just exactly where the survivors were and did not capture them so they could use them as bait for a flak trap.

Hoggate and Griffith were one of the Firefly flights to be diverted to the SAR. I think they were first in, and they weren't there very long before Griffith got shot down. Hoggate didn't see him eject, but a Jolly Green was in the area and called Hoggatt that his wingman had just ejected. Griffith didn't have a chance to make a call. He told me about it later when I visited him in the hospital. I think it was a right turn and he was in just behind Hoggate when he took a hit and the aircraft kept turning right. He couldn't control it and it was going down. They weren't very high at the time, about 1,000 feet I think. He extracted, the chute opened, and he was in the trees. He was caught up and never got to the ground. Since the Jolly saw him, they went directly to him. They lowered the penetrator, but Griffith couldn't reach it because of the trees hanging in the way. They pulled it up and the PJ (a highly trained Pararescue Enlisted man) got on it and they lowered him. He got to the same height as Griffith, but couldn't reach him. He took his M-16 by the barrel and got Griffith to grab the stock. They both pulled and the PJ strapped Griffith onto the penetrator, unhooked the parachute risers, and signaled them to raise away.

[A couple of things happened, but I think Griffith should tell you if you should ever meet and get to talk to him.]

Anyway this digresses from the search for AWOL 1. I believe Ed Leonard was also in a Firefly flight that went in that day. I remember he told me about a hit he took that came into the cockpit and hit his boot. I believe when we got on scene there wasn't much action or maybe I just don't remember what happened.

I do know that they planned a SAR for early the next morning in which they were going to have a couple A-1s with CS (a riot control gas, such as tear gas, which will partially incapacitate a person but not cause permanent harm) gas standing by at Pleiku. I led the Sandy flight the next morning that went into the area and searched for AWOL 1. Nothing to relate about that flight except I did not see one gun fired at me. I think the North Vietnamese had gotten as much value out of the survivors as they could and just called it off. I have never heard anything about what happened to AWOL 1A, but AWOL 1B was Lance Peter Sijan, and his is another story all by itself.

On the flight log you will notice a gap/lack of flying of about 12 days from 25 October to 11 November. This is the time period in which I did get some time off. It is described later (first part of Chapter 8).

I think it was also during this time that the Squadron got notification that they were going to have to send someone to Hq 7th AF for duty as a Frag Officer. When this word came out, I told John Carlson (Operations Officer) that I WAS NOT a volunteer BUT if it turned out that no one else would volunteer and would kick and scream all the way if sent, I would go. He did not want to send anyone and told me he did not want me to go. I said OK, but remember if no one volunteers I am still willing to go without screaming.

Also on the flight log you'll notice a flight on 17 November where the squadron provided me means of transportation to my new PCS station.

DATE 1967	CALL SIGN A/C Type	AREA MISSION	FLYING TIME	REMARKS
10 June	Firefly 17/A-1E	*Barrel Roll - Strike [O-1.2]	3+25	Right Seat "Dollar Ride"
13 June	Firefly 12/A-1E	Barrel Roll - Strike [O-1.37]	4+00	Left seat check-out
14 June	Firefly 18/A-1E	Barrel Roll - Strike [O-1.37]	2+10	No remarks in my log
15 June	Firefly 16/A-1E	Barrel Roll - Strike [O-1]	0+35	Air Abort-Sump Lite -First Solo ride
15 June	Firefly 16/A-1E	Steel Tiger - Strike [O-1.37]	2+35	First time into Steel Tiger
17 June	Dragon Fly 12/A-1E	S. Vietnam-Escort [O-1.37]	3+35	NW Da Nang-Destroy Huey
17 June	Dragon Fly 12/A-1E	S. Vietnam-Escort [O-1.37]	2+00	Return from Da Nang Greg Etzel passenger
18 June	Firefly 18/A-1E	Barrel Roll - Strike [O-1.37]	3+15	Strike-Target not noted in log
19 June	Firefly 16/A-1E	Barrel Roll - Strike [O-1]	0+20	Air Abort-Reason not noted in log
20 June	Firefly 16/A-1E	Barrel Roll - Strike [O-1.37]	3+25	Strike-Target not noted in log
22 June	Firefly 18/A-1E	Barrel Roll - Strike [O-1.37]	3+30	Strike-Target not noted in log
23 June	Firefly 16/A-1E	*Route Pack V-Strike [O-1.2]	3+45	Strike-Target not noted in log
25 June	Sandy 8/A-1E	Barrel Roll - Orbit [O-1.23]	3+15	Normal Orbit for possible SAR
26 June	Sandy 2/A-1E	Barrel Roll - Orbit [O-1.23]	3+25	Normal Orbit for possible SAR
26 June	Sandy 2/A-1E	Barrel Roll - Orbit [O-1.23]	2+00	Orbit for possible SAR with Sandy 7
1 July	Sandy 2/A-1E	Barrel Roll - Orbit [O-1.23]	3+25	Normal Orbit for possible SAR
2 July	Sandy 8/A-1E	*Route Pack 1 SAR [O-1.22]	3+30	First search for Pintail 2
3 July	Sandy 2/A-1E	*Route Pack 1 SAR [O-1.22]	5+00	Successful pick up of Pintail 2
4 July	Firefly 18/A-1E	Barrel Roll - Strike [O-1.37]	1+30	Air Abort-Reason not noted in log
6 July	Sandy 8/A-1E	Barrel Roll - Orbit [O-1.23]	3+10	Normal Orbit for possible SAR
10 July	Firefly 14/A-1E	*Barrel Roll - SAR [O-1.2]	3+55	Divert from Strike to SAR
11 July	Firefly 12/A-1E	*Barrel Roll - Strike [O-1.2]	3+20	First Lead Qual Ride (Mehr)
12 July	Firefly 18/A-1E	*Barrel Roll - Strike [O-1.2]	2+00	Also went to Route Pack III
13 July	Firefly 11/A-1E	Barrel Roll - Strike [O-1.37]	2+00	Lead Qual Ride (IP not noted in log)
13 July	Firefly 11/A-1E	*Barrel Roll - Strike [O-1.2]	3+10	Lead Qual Ride (Gould)
14 July	Firefly 14/A-1E	*Route Pack III - Strike [O-1.2]	2+50	Strike-Target not noted in log
16 July	Sandy 4/A-1E	Barrel Roll - Orbit [O-1.23]	2+50	Normal Orbit for possible SAR
17 July	Sandy 2/A-1E	*Barrel Roll - Orbit [O-1.22]	5+05	Normal Orbit for possible SAR
18 July	Sandy 8/A-1E	*Barrel Roll - SAR [O-1.22]	3+30	No note in log where SAR took place
18 July	Sandy 8/A-1E	*Barrel Roll - Orbit [O-1.22]	2+30	No note in log where SAR took place
28 July	Firefly 12/A-1E	*Barrel Roll - Strike [O-1.2]	3+25	Strike-Target not noted in log
29 July	Sandy 4/A-1E	Barrel Roll - Orbit [O-1.23]	2+40	Normal Orbit for possible SAR
29 July	Sandy 4/A-1E	*Barrel Roll - SAR [O-1.2]	4+20	Orbit with divert to Cricket
31 July	Sandy 8/A-1E	*Barrel Roll - Orbit [O-1.2]	4+40	Orbit with divert to Cricket
4 Aug	Firefly 13/A-1E	*Barrel Roll - Strike [O-1.2]	3+10	Lead Qual Ride (Bronczyk)
5 Aug	Firefly 11/A-1E	*Barrel Roll - Strike [O-1.2]	3+30	Lead Qual Ride (Solo)
6 Aug	Firefly 17/A-1E	*Barrel Roll - Strike [O-1.2]	2+15	Lead Qual Ride
7 Aug	Sandy 2/A-1E	*Barrel Roll - SAR [O-1.2]	3+25	Successful SAR (No note who/where)
9 Aug	Firefly 11/A-1E	*Barrel Roll - Strike [O-1.2]	2+25	Lead Qualification Check Ride
10 Aug	Sandy 3/A-1E	*Barrel Roll - Orbit [O-1.2]	3+35	Orbit with divert to Cricket
11 Aug	Sandy 2/A-1E	Barrel Roll - Orbit [O-1.37]	2+50	Normal Orbit
13 Aug	Firefly 11/A-1E	*Barrel Roll - Strike [O-1.2]	3+10	Strike-Target not noted in log
16 Aug	Firefly 13/A-1E	*Barrel Roll - Strike [O-1.2]	2+25	Strike-Target not noted in log (Wx)
18 Aug	Firefly 17/A-1E	*Barrel Roll - Strike [O-1.0]	3+05	Strike-Target not noted in log
24 Aug	Firefly 17/A-1E	*Barrel Roll - Strike [O-1.2]	3+45	Strike-Target not noted in log
25 Aug	Sandy 5/A-1E	Barrel Roll - Orbit [O-1.0]	0+20	Air Abort Sump Light
25 Aug	Sandy 5/A-1E	In-Country Ferry [O-1.0]	1+05	Flew to NKP for Alert
26 Aug	Sandy 7/A-1E	*Route Pack 1 - SAR [O-1.2]	3+05	NKP Scramble Search for Misty
27 Aug	Firefly 15/A-1E	*Steel Tiger - Strike [O-1.2]	2+30	Strike-Target not noted in log
28 Aug	Firefly 17/A-1E	*Barrel Roll - Strike [O-1.2]	3+35	Strike + search for F-111 "Butt 42"
29 Aug	Sandy 5/A-1E	*Barrel Roll - SAR [O-1.22]	2+35	SAR search-no note for who/where
30 Aug	Sandy 7/A-1E	In-Country Ferry [O-1.0]	0+45	Return from NKP Alert
31 Aug	Sandy 2/A-1E	Barrel Roll - Orbit [O-1.37]	3+00	Normal Orbit for possible SAR
1 Sept	Firefly 17/A-1E	*Barrel Roll - Strike[O-1.2]	5+15	KNIGHT WATCH
2 Sept	Firefly 12/A-1E	*Barrel Roll - Strike[O-1.2]	3+00	Strike-Target not noted in log
4 Sept	Firefly 18/A-1E	Barrel Roll - Strike [O-1.37]	2+50	Normal Orbit (Flew for Jack)
5 Sept	Sandy 8/A-1E	*Barrel Roll - Strike [O-1.2]	2+30	Strike-Target not noted in log
10 Sept	Sandy 6/A-1E	In-Country Ferry [O-1.0]	0+50	Flew to NKP for Alert
11 Sept	Sandy 1/A-1E	*Route Pack III - SAR [O-1.22]	3+50	Unsuccessful SAR for Redbird 44
11 Sept	Sandy 8/A-1E	In-Country Ferry [O-1.0]	0+50	Return from NKP Alert

DATE 1967	CALL SIGN A/C Type	AREA MISSION	FLYING TIME	REMARKS
12 Sept	Firefly 16/A-1E	*Barrel Roll - Strike [O-1,2]	2+00	Actually Air Abort due to Oil Temp
13 Sept	Firefly 1/A-1E	*Barrel Roll - Strike [O-1,2]	3+50	Strike + search for F-111 "Butt 44"
14 Sept	Firefly 12/A-1E	*Barrel Roll - Strike [O-1,2]	3+15	Log shows Weather on this mission
16 Sept	Sandy 1/A-1E	*Barrel Roll - Orbit [O-1,23]	2+25	Normal Orbit + divert to Raven
16 Sept	Sandy 1/A-1E	*Barrel Roll - SAR [O-1,22]	4+20	SAR search for "Resale 02"
17 Sept	Sandy 3/A-1E	*Barrel Roll - Orbit [O-1,37]	4+30	Normal Orbit for possible SAR
18 Sept	Sandy 5/A-1E	In-Country Ferry [O-1]	1+35	Flew to NKP for Alert
19 Sept	Sandy 7/A-1E	In-Country Ferry [O-1]	0+45	Return from NKP Alert
28 Sept	Firefly 16/A-1E	*Barrel Roll - Strike [O-1,2]	3+45	Strike-Target not noted in log
29 Sept	Firefly 17/A-1E	*Barrel Roll - Strike [O-1,2]	2+50	Strike-Target not noted in log
3 Oct	Firefly 18/A-1E	*Barrel Roll - Strike [O-1,2]	3+05	Strike-Target not noted in log
6 Oct	Sandy 2/A-1E	*Barrel Roll - Strike [O-1,23]	3+15	Normal Orbit for possible SAR
7 Oct	Firefly 18/A-1E	*Barrel Roll - Strike [O-1,2]	3+25	"Motor Carr" into Pak Sane
8 Oct	Burly 32/A-1E	In-Country - Local [O-8]	0+25	Test Hop
8 Oct	Sandy 6/A-1E	In-Country Ferry [O-1]	1+10	Flew to NKP for Alert
9 Oct	Sandy 8/A-1E	In-Country Ferry [O-1]	0+45	Return from NKP Alert
10 Oct	Firefly 15/A-1E	In Country - Strike [O-1]	0+35	Air Abort
12 Oct	Firefly 11/A-1E	*Route Pack V- Strike [O-1,2]	3+15	FAC/Strike by Điện Biên Phủ
13 Oct	Firefly 13/A-1E	*Barrel Roll - Strike [O-1,2]	3+15	FAC/Strike radio tower @ Ban Ban
17 Oct	Sandy 7/A-1E	In-Country Ferry [O-1]	0+50	Flew to NKP for Alert
18 Oct	Sandy 7/A-1E	In-Country Ferry [O-1]	0+45	Return from NKP Alert
18 Oct	Firefly 15/A-1E	In Country - Strike [O-1,37]	1+10	Air Abort
19 Oct	Firefly 17/A-1E	*Barrel Roll - Strike [O-1,2]	4+40	Log shows "917 Knight Watch"
20 Oct	Sandy 6/A-1E	In-Country Ferry [O-1]	0+50	Flew to NKP for Alert
21 Oct	Firefly 8/A-1E	In-Country Ferry [O-1]	0+45	Return from NKP Alert
22 Oct	Firefly 16/A-1E	*Barrel Roll - Strike [O-1,2]	4+15	Strike-Target not noted in log
23 Oct	Firefly 18/A-1E	*Barrel Roll - Strike [O-1,2]	4+10	Strike-Target not noted in log
24 Oct	Firefly 11/A-1E	*Barrel Roll - Strike [O-1,2]	3+15	Strike-Target not noted in log
24 Oct	Cabot 36/A-1H	In Country - Local [T-3]	0+45	First A-1H ride
25 Oct	Cabot 33/A-1H	In Country - Local [T-3]	0+30	Second A-1H ride
11 Nov	Sandy 2/A-1E	*Steel Tiger - SAR [O-1,22]	4+00	Search for AWOL 1 (Lance Peter Sijan)
11 Nov	Sandy 2/A-1E	In-Country Ferry [O-1]	1+05	Return from NKP
12 Nov	Sandy 3/A-1E	*Steel Tiger- SAR [O-1,22]	4+30	Search for AWOL 1
14 Nov	Firefly 13/A-1E	*Route Pack V - Strike [O-1,2]	3+15	Strike-Target not noted in log
15 Nov	Firefly 15/A-1E	*Route Pack III - Strike [O-1,2]	3+00	Strike-Target not noted in log
16 Nov	Firefly 17/A-1E	*Route Pack III - Strike [O-1,2]	2+50	Strike-Target not noted in log
17 Nov	VCSL/A-1E	Cross Country - Ferry [O-1]	3+35	A-1E to Siagon for IRAN (PCS to Hq 7th)
		1968		
11 Feb	Firefly 15/A-1E	Barrel Roll - Strike [O-1,2]	2+55	CBU on Xieng Khoung (S of PDJ) Recurrency
12 Feb	Firefly 14/A-1H	Barrel Roll - Strike [O-1,2]	2+15	SHOT DOWN SE of Lima Site 85
14 Feb	Firefly 16/A-1H	Barrel Roll - Strike [O-1,2]	3+00	Strike just E of Lima Site 85
15 Feb	Firefly 14/A-1H	Barrel Roll - Strike [O-1,2]	2+55	Dive Bomb Napalm E of Lima Site 85

NOTE:

In the Area/Mission column, those that have an "*" were "out country" counters. NKP= Nakhon Phanom Royal Thailand Air Force Base [Some times referred to as "Naked Fanny"]

Chapter 8

Frag Officer at Headquarters Seventh Air Force

Even though I was in Saigon, my connection to the 602nd was still strong. For example, one of the things we never could understand was Hq 7th having the bomb load on the F-105's they sent to us for targets in Barrel Roll as four 750# bombs with instantaneous fuse and two with long delay fuses. It seemed to us that when the instantaneous fuse went off, it would pretty well make the delayed bombs useless.

The first setback came when I found out that there was no BOQ room for me on base. I don't remember just how it happened, but I ended up in an apartment building off base with one of the guys that worked in the same office. I never saw a map of the Saigon/Tan San Nhut area when I was there, so am unsure of directions. Looking today at a map someone has put together of the 1968 time frame, it appears you would go out the main gate and turn right, go down this pretty big road about a mile and the US Army Third Field Hospital was there. Turn right on this smaller street and go about a half block and turn right again on a really small street that went for about a block to a dead end. Our building, three stories, was on the left just about the last one.

The first day I was at the job in Hq 7th, the old fellow (he told me a story of his getting shot down in WW II) was filling out the frag for the aircraft going into Barrel Roll. I asked him who determined the bomb load. He said, he did. I asked why he put that funny load on the F-105"s? He just got up from the desk and said, "Well, why don't you sit down there and put whatever load you like on them!" I did and then got in touch with Carlson up at the 602nd and told him he now had a guy in Hq that would listen to whatever request the squadron had. I can tell you it made for a lot better work done by the 602nd.

One of the things (if my memory is still good) was the fact that we were always carrying 250# bombs and wanted something bigger. I started fragging the

A-1's with 500# bombs but soon found out that they were actually for someone else and when they started running short, I had to quit giving them to the A-1's.

I am not sure about the timing but it must have been in December or very early January that Carlson at the 602nd and I discussed the building of a road out of Sam Nuea and the possibility of getting maybe a couple more guys for the radar bomb site at Lima Site 85. They were manned so they could direct missions only during the day. The Air America guy that briefed the 602nd thought that if we could run some radar missions at night against the guys building the road it would help. If my memory isn't really screwed up, I think they did increase the manning some so as to conduct some night missions.

Amusing aside about this same event: the Ops Officer of the F-4 squadron that was at Udorn had talked to Carlson, and he had called me asking if we could put a couple of two ships of F-4s doing some of the night missions. I thought that was a great idea, so I included them on the frag. That only lasted about a week when I got a call from the BOSS of the F-4s asking me what the hell I thought I was doing? Besides using up flying time and ordnance, the guys were going to get counters, and if they got to go home earlier than they had things scheduled, they would be short of pilots. The funny thing about it was, the BOSS who called was a Colonel Bartolf, the same man who was my Squadron Commander at Woodbridge in 1964. He gave me a real chewing out. I told him since the Ops Officer had called, I thought it must have been cleared up the chain. It wasn't, it was just an idea of the Ops Officer to get his guys some more sorties.

Other than that, I don't remember anything very exciting about the job until 30 January 1968. It was the start of the Tet Offensive. There was supposed to be a two-day cease fire agreement, but the Viet Cong broke it by attacking early in the morning of the 31st. The night before, I, my roommate, and just about everyone who lived in the building were up on the roof (big flat roof that people used to sunbathe) watching the fireworks. There was about a thousand foot overcast and with all the fireworks and smoke, it made it seem unreal. Almost like it was a movie.

I went to bed around midnight, and it wasn't but about three hours until my buddy shook me awake and said I should come up on the roof. I told him I had seen all the fireworks I wanted, and he said, "This ain't fireworks!" I went up there, and what I heard was gun fire.

Looking toward Tan San Nhut, we saw tracers going in and out and a big fire in the middle of the base. (Turned out the fire was the base chapel.) We stayed up on the roof watching all that was going on (I have a tape recording of the sounds). There was a Huey helicopter orbiting right overhead, and had been for about an hour. It got to be daylight and, looking over to the big street coming down from the base, we saw tanks and fully armed combat troops. One of the young guys was saying something like "maybe we should try to get out of here and go to the base." I told him, "What are you thinking? Look at those guys fully armed with helmets and all and you want to try to get to the base in a 1505 uniform??" Of course there was NO one with any kind of weapon so we were really helpless.

A gun captured during TET.

After about an hour in orbit, the Huey rolled in and started firing rockets. It looked like his target was just a few blocks past where the Third Field Hospital was. We found out later it was one of the police headquarters that the VC had taken over and they were blasting them out.

About mid-afternoon the Colonel from our office showed up in a staff car. He told us to bring some stuff for a couple of days because we weren't coming back to this place anytime soon. We got our drop kits and headed to the base.

There was NO place for us to sleep, so we ended up each getting a set of sheets and a mattress which we put on our desk, and that is where we slept the next seven or eight nights. One of the Colonels had a BOQ room right across the street, so when we got up in the morning we got to go shave and take a shower, putting on the same clothes we wore when we came on base. After a couple days, we went to the clothing sales store and got new underwear and a new uniform so we wouldn't look and smell really bad.

A rocket launcher captured during TET.

We went to the O-Club for breakfast, lunch, and dinner. Every once in a while, most days, we would jump under our desk, as the VC were launching rockets on to the base and they were hitting everywhere.

We finally got to go back to our room off base and it seemed pretty safe to go back and forth. Anyway after things had settled down a little bit, I got this call from CBPO telling me that I still had my 5 days of R & R coming. (This was in the first week of Feb.) Well, I was certainly getting tired of trying to get some sleep with all those rockets coming into the base and the area I lived in just outside the base, so I called the 602nd to see if I could come up to Udorn and fly some more missions.

I wrote this part as a separate story some time back and called it "A Most Memorable R&R." There might be a little bit of repeat information; however, I am going to keep the story as I have written it.

To explain why this was such a memorable R&R, I must give you just a little background. As a member of the 602nd A-1 "Sandy" Squadron in 1967, I was stationed at Udorn AB, Thailand. I arrived in very early June and during my stay at Udorn I had the opportunity to take several trips (the Squadron did a good job scheduling and allowing us to take a trip if we had free time) which did not count as R&R. One trip was to Chiang Mai, the old capital of Thailand and another was a few days in Taiwan. So I had mixed in a few good days off with all the flying and standing alert and had never officially taken R & R. I was officially reassigned to Headquarters Saigon in November 1967.

A picture taken from our off base quarters of the Base Chapel burning!

[NOTE: I will add here, since this isn't going to get published in a widely circulated publication, this fact. In late September and early October, I managed to get my leave paper fixed up so I could take leave back to the States to visit my family. This wasn't strictly legal because we weren't supposed to go to the States on leave, but our Squadron Commander had a policy of not asking and if we were late in getting back, it was automatically AWOL! I hitched a ride on a C-141 from Udorn to Clark AB, Phillippines, where I got stuck for several hours until another C-141 got me to Yokota, then McChord AFB in Washington; commercial airlines to Wichita, KS, and about a week with the family. Commercial airlines back to McChord and a contract flight to Yokota. I then had to take a C-54 to Naha AB, Okinawa, where I was able to catch a C-130 back to Udorn. Gone about 12 days with 7 at home! Pretty good, huh??]

This time period (early 1968) was also the time when "Harvest Reaper," the introduction of the F-111A low level night bombing up North, was being carried out. There had been several unexplained losses of F-111s, so after the A-1s of the 602nd would finish their normal mission, if they had fuel, they would search for several hours along the last known flight path of the lost F-111s. One of the guys

I replaced by flying these sorties had logged a hell of a lot of hours in a six-week period! The pilots were getting "punch drunk" from all the duties so the Squadron was only too happy to get another pilot to relieve the strain. I left Saigon via "Scat Back" (a T-39 courier that daily made a circuit of all the fighter bases and Saigon) on Sunday the 11th of February.

Not much detail, but this is a picture of The Plain of Jars.

I arrived at Udorn as planned on the 11th, was met at the aircraft, and taken directly to the Squadron. Since I was already in my flying gear, I went directly to the briefing. My personal equipment such as the harness, Survival Vest, pistol, etc. I checked out after the briefing at Personal Equipment. I would be flying in an A-1E with the Squadron Operations Officer (John Carlson). This was going to be a bombing mission to the southern part of the Plain de Jars. Actually we delivered CBU on a large troop concentration close to the village of Xieng Khouang. The landing after the mission was my recurrency, so I was now ready to fly some missions.

[*From Wikipedia, the free encyclopedia: Plain of Jars: Site 1 Coordinates: 19.46°N 103.18°E The Plain of Jars is a megalithic archaeological landscape in Laos. Scattered in the landscape of the Xieng Khouang plateau Xieng Khouang, Lao PDR, are thousands of megalithic jars. These stone jars appear in clusters, ranging from a single or a few to several hundred jars at lower foothills surrounding the central plain and upland valleys.*]

The mission on Monday morning was to be an escort mission. This involved meeting a helicopter (or several) and escorting it (them) to the point where they would drop off some "people." These "people" were a road watch team which would hide in the jungle next to a main road and log the traffic going along that road. If they could, they would identify where this traffic parked and would call in air strikes. I was going to lead a flight of two A-1s, me in an A-1H and the Squadron Operations Officer with a "new" guy in an A-1E. We would be going up to North Station to meet the first set of Helo's and escort them to a point along Route 67 running North out of Sam Nuea (the Pathet Lao Headquarters in Laos).

Once we had escorted these Helo's on their insertion mission, we were to meet up with another set of Helo's at Lima Site 36 (LS 36). Lima Site 36 was also a friendly site located about 32 nautical miles southwest of North Station (215 degree radial at 32 nm). This was the Meo Tribal village of Muohg Hiem with a dirt airstrip of 1500-2000 feet. This site was surrounded by Pathet Lao and North Vietnamese Regulars. The Helo's out of LS 36 were to insert their "road watch team" along Route 65, which runs South out of Sam Nuea. This of course we found out during the briefing. Out of the briefing, down to PE, and off to fly.

Wait a minute, not so fast. Another bit of information you should have: I hadn't flown the A-1H in combat before. I did get a couple of check-out rides in September when the 602nd was first getting A-1Hs. You got two flights with a "clean" aircraft to fly around the local area getting used to landing this single seat version of the A-1. The A-1E is just an A-1H with the cockpit area enlarged to hold two pilots side by side and a "blue room" behind that was large enough to hold 5-6 troops. It was called the blue room because of the blue canopy over that part of the aircraft. (Bernard Fisher was flying an A-1E when he won his Medal of Honor.)

When I flew the A-1H in late September for my checkout, it was not equipped with the "Yankee Seat." The Yankee Seat is an extraction system which works somewhat like an ejection seat. This of course allows you to bail-out without having to unstrap and crawl out like they did before the ejection seat. All the A-1Es had the Yankee Seat and the A-1Hs had them installed after they arrived at Udorn. Since the strap-in procedure was different for the A-1H than for the A-1E, I asked the Personal Equipment specialist to go with me to show me the proper strap-in procedure. Once I was strapped in, the Start Up, Taxi out, and Take Off were Ops Normal.

Our call sign for the mission was Firefly 15 (me) and 16 (my wingman). We flew North out of Udorn at about 10,000 ft MSL. After crossing the Mekong River into Laos, we entered a thin layer of clouds. We could see each other out to about a mile separation but could not see the ground. As we approached North Station, we established radio contact with the ground party that was to board the helo's. They informed us that the helo's had not arrived and probably would not try because the weather was so bad (the mountain was up in the clouds!). They suggested that we scrub the mission. We agreed and told the controller that we were proceeding to Lima Site 36 to complete the second part of the mission. Just before we left his frequency, the controller said that if for some reason we did not get to complete our other mission, or if we had fuel and ordnance left, we could come back because he had a target that he wanted us to strike. Flying back to Lima Site 36 was uneventful except we did start seeing the ground as we approached Lima Site 36.

Upon arriving at Lima Site 36 we were in the clear and could see the ground. Around Lima Site 36 we could see patches of clouds right down on the jungle. The controller at Lima Site 36 asked us to proceed out to the insertion site to see if the weather out there was going to allow them to complete the mission. We flew out to the proposed insertion site and found the clouds covering the ground. We returned to Lima Site 36 and informed the controller that we thought the weather too bad to complete the mission. We agreed that the mission was canceled.

I then asked the Operations Officer in Firefly 16 if he wanted to return to North Station to see about striking the target that was mentioned earlier. He replied, "Yes!" [Note: The first ride for a new guy is referred to as a "nickel ride." To be considered "checked-out" the new guy must deliver some ordnance. The Ops Officer wanted to get this guy checked out!]

When we got to the vicinity of North Station and made radio contact, the controller said the target was a road extension the Pathet Lao were building from Sam Nuea westward toward North Station. He directed us to the 101 degree radial at about 10 nm from North Station. "Anything you find in that area is fair game, hit it!"

We were back in the clouds and could not see the ground. We descended to about 8,500 feet when we got to the target area but were still in the clouds and had no sight of the ground. Some of the hills/mountains were pretty high in the area, so we decided not to go any lower. I informed the controller that we were in the target area and could not see the ground so we were going to RTB (Return to Base). We turned South and after flying only about two minutes we broke into the clear. (Looking at the map later and trying to remember where it was we came out of the clouds, I think it was on the 130 degree radial at about 15 nm.) I have described this many times, when we came out of the clouds into the clear, it was like flying into an inverted bowl. We were in this big dome of clear space and you could see the jungle very clearly. We descended and when we got to about 2,000 feet above the jungle we could see under the clouds as far as the eye could see!

On normal Strike missions, like this one, it was Squadron Policy not to attack any targets if you had to descend below 3,000 feet AGL. Knowing this, I asked the Operations Officer if he wanted to return to the target area below the clouds. He wanted to get the new guy checked out and I wanted to deliver ordnance myself, so we decided to go back. Flying about 1,500 ft above the jungle we went back to the 101 radial. As we approached what we thought the area was, I saw the road being built going in a westerly direction on this ridge line. I made a left turn and was heading about West when I spotted something that appeared to be a truck. Turning hard left to keep the area in sight, I heard Firefly 16 say they had lost sight of me. They had gone back up into the clouds. I called to them that I was rolling in on a rocket pass on what I thought was the truck. Firefly 16 said he would be with me shortly. I fired five of the seven 2.5 inch rockets that were in the pod. As I pulled off the target I got a good look and discovered that it wasn't a truck. In fact it was a load of logs. If you have ever seen one of those logging trucks that pulls a load of logs on a set of wheels, that is what it looked like. I called to Firefly 16 that what I had called a truck was just a bunch of logs and then, and to this day I don't know why, I told Firefly 16 I was going to make one more pass and then go back to the clear area South of the target.

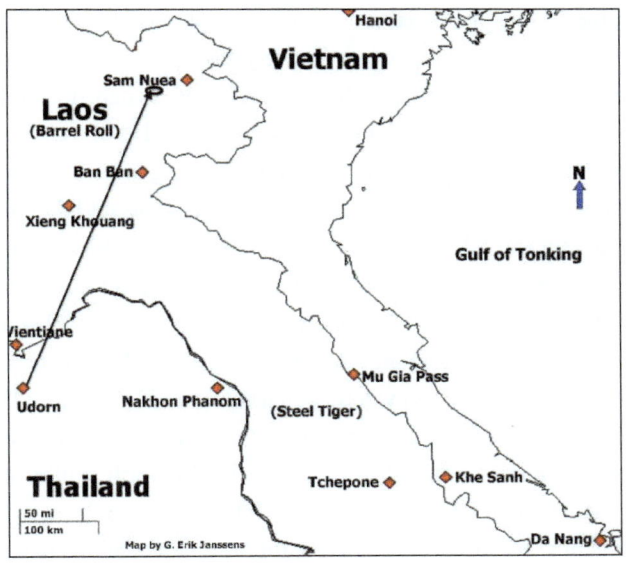

Location of my extraction and pick-up

Firefly 16 called to say he was back out of the clouds and would also make a pass on the target and come join up in the clear area. After I had rolled in on my second pass, I remembered that I hadn't changed my switches, so I would only have two rockets to fire. I pressed on, fired the two rockets and strafed with the six twenty millimeter cannons. You need to have flown the A-1 to understand just how slow those cannons fire!! Anyway, as I pulled off, I felt a "thump" in the aircraft. I thought it might be a hit, although I did not see anyone shooting at me. I checked over all the gauges and everything appeared normal. [NOTE: If any of you reading this have flown the F-100 with 450 gallon drop tanks, the thump felt just like when the 450's would go dry and the valve would close.] I continued my right turn and climbed back into the clouds to return to the clearing down South. I called to Firefly 16 that I was off and climbing on a heading of South. As I was passing through 8,000 feet, in the clouds again, I thought I saw something passing by the canopy; looking out, I saw nothing but clouds. (Thinking about it later I think this "thing" I saw was probably a puff of smoke.) As I returned my eyes to the gauges, I noted the oil pressure gauge going to "ZERO"!! (Again, you had to have flown the A-1 to know it, but the A-1 would fly with all kinds of major battle damage and get you home; it however WOULD NOT FLY LONG WITHOUT OIL!) I immediately pulled the power back a bit, leveled off, and called to Firefly 16 that I must have taken a hit and my oil pressure was going to zero. He asked my position and I looked at the TACAN to see that I was on the 125 degree radial at 12 nm. Calling my position to him, I also told him I was level at 8,500 feet and was going to jettison all my remaining ordnance. We agreed to go to Guard Channel on the radio. After we switched radio frequencies, I checked in and Firefly 16 asked for a hold down. We had UHF/ADF capability, so he wanted to get a bearing on me. I told him I was turning toward North Station and maybe we should call for the Jolly Green rescue helo's. He said they were already on their way to orbit and asked for another hold down. About this time another voice came over the radio and asked for a position report. I had no idea who it was but looked at my TACAN, saw it had broken lock, so called out that it had broken lock but I had turned Northwest from the 125 degree radial at 12 nm just a minute or so before. The voice came back, "Why don't you head toward Lima Site 223??" (I don't remember for sure if that is the correct Lima Site number, but think it is.) I replied, "I don't know where that Lima Site is, I am heading for North Station and if the engine is still running when I get there, I will try for Lima Site 36".

About this time the aircraft shuddered, the sump light came on and the torque meter went spinning up and down. The engine went back to running smooth. I told Firefly 16 what happened and added that I didn't think it would run much longer.

He asked for another hold down. After just a short while, the engine started a very high RPM type scream. I pulled the throttle back and everything got very quiet! I have no idea what the instrument readings were at this time. I have been asked if the prop was still on the aircraft and was the engine still running. I don't know. I got this big sinking feeling. It felt just like the bottom had dropped out. I called to Firefly 16 that the engine had quit and I was ejecting.

I reached down and pulled the nylon loop in front of the seat. The canopy left immediately. I can remember sitting in the seat looking out to my left, realizing that the canopy was gone and thinking I should be going pretty soon. OUT I WENT!! I found out from Firefly 16 that just as I came out of the aircraft I was also just coming down out of the clouds. They (Firefly 16) were right behind me and saw me come out of the aircraft. I was tumbling and thought that the chute should open soon. It did. I was exactly upside down and saw the chute stream out of the seat pack and open. Since I was head down, it snapped me pretty hard upright. After that I checked for a good canopy and saw I had a good chute. I then let go of the nylon ejection handle. To this day I can clearly see that thing floating away and me thinking, "I wanted to keep that for a souvenir." I got rid of my oxygen mask and started looking around. I saw Firefly 16 and waved to them to let them know I was OK. (They later said they never saw me waving.)

I saw a large hill to my five o'clock position so I turned the chute around so I was facing the hill. Once I was facing the hill, I grabbed the front two risers and started pulling for all I was worth. (If I had just looked, this chute had the "four line cut" thing and I could have used that to slip the chute.) I wanted to slip the chute so I would land on the highest hill I could find.

As I swung back due to my slipping, I looked down and saw that I was directly over a village! I admit it, NOW I WAS SCARED! I then put all the energy I could into slipping away from that village. No matter what I did, I did not move a foot away from the center of the village. When I got down to what I think was a couple hundred feet, I decided that I was going to land in the village, so I might as well get ready. I remember seeing some kids running around in the village pointing up at me. I saw a dog running around barking. Coming down the path from the big hill was a little old man with a big bundle of sticks on his shoulders.

As soon as I quit trying to slip the chute, I drifted in a southeasterly direction away from the village. The big hill I was trying to get to was now off to my left; directly in front of me was another hill, not quite as high as the first one. Between the two hills was kind of a gully or wash that came down right past the southeast side of the village. I saw I was going to land on the opposite side of this gully and also that I was headed for a tree. Again, it is funny what you think about at a time like this, but I remember thinking it was a cottonwood tree just like I had seen in Kansas when I was growing up.

I prepared for a tree landing. Now the first real lucky thing that happened was drifting away from the village and the second lucky thing was the tree! It was just exactly the right height to catch the chute and I had my feet on the ground with my knees slightly flexed. I did not even fall down!

I unhooked the chute and took off running up the hill away from the village. I had only run a few steps when I realized that all the covering from the seat pack chute and survival kit was hitting the back of my legs. This bothered me so I stopped behind a tree and unhooked the chute harness and took it off. As I was doing this I looked up and saw a helicopter. I know I didn't care what kind or whose it was, I was just glad it was there. It wasn't a Jolly Green so I made the assumption it was an Air America helo.

It turned out that the "voice" that had asked for my position and told me to come to Lima Site 223 was this helicopter pilot. He was at Lima Site 223 just getting ready to take off for a mission when they heard my call. Once he heard my position he knew that I was only a couple miles north of him. He took off and, keeping just below the clouds and going up a valley through the mountains, in just a couple minutes saw my aircraft come down and crash. He looked up and saw me in the chute, so it was just a matter of waiting until I landed.

After seeing the helo, I looked back over my left shoulder and saw through the trees a couple men running up the path on the other side of the gully. They must have had to go up a ways to cross the gully because they didn't come directly across after me. I took the 38 pistol out of the holster on the survival vest I was wearing fired off a couple rounds, not at anyone, just in the direction to let them know I had a gun. After many times telling this story someone asked me if THEY had guns. I never really thought about it. I suppose if they had and I had made them mad they would probably have shot me the first chance they got. I know I felt they were "bad guys," and if they had tried to capture me, I would have shot as many as possible.

I then took off running up the hill directly in front of me, directly away from the village. The hill was covered with trees but there was absolutely no underbrush there! It was as clear as a park. The hill was steep and I really had to chug to get up that hill. (It was fairly cool, and later I found I had a sore throat from sucking in all that air as I ran up the hill.) About halfway to the top, I intersected a path running to the top of the hill, coming up from my left and on up to the right. I looked and the path was clear in both directions as far as I could see. I got on the path and looked over in the direction of the village again. I saw through the trees a little boy and a dog running up the path, in the same direction the men were running earlier. [Note: Firefly 16 was in radio contact with the Air America helo and had asked if the village was friendly. They did not know for sure but thought it "might be." Firefly 16 told him he was going to watch and if anyone got close to me he would strafe them.]

I fired off a couple more shots in the general direction of the village. Then thinking, "This isn't the Westerns, I had better reload this gun!," I reached down to my top left pocket in the survival vest and opened it for more bullets. There was a compass! That's what you get for not making sure what and where everything is in your vest BEFORE you need it. I had always carried the bullets in that pocket when I flew regularly. I decided that I would not shoot any more until I really had to shoot at something.

I then took off running as hard as I could up the path toward the top of the hill. The helo was in a hover up there. As I came around a curve in the path at the top of the hill, the ground leveled off and I could see the helo, a guy in the door, and the "horse collar" hanging down on a cable. I was standing by a big tree and the guy in the door waved to me to come out into the opening. I looked around and didn't see anyone, so I ran out under the helo, put my gun away, donned the "horse collar," and got lifted into the helo. I lay on the floor of that helo gasping for breath. I couldn't do one other thing at the moment except try to catch my breath. I have often wondered if the helo hadn't picked me up at that moment if I would have had any more energy to run away from the people coming after me.

Before I had fully gotten my breath the guy in the helo asked if I wanted to see my aircraft burning. I had enough breath to say, "NO, just take me home!" After I had my breath back, I got up and sat on one of the seats along the side of the helo. I looked around and saw an old, old, man and a little boy. Probably his grandson. They just stared at me. I have no idea what they were doing on the helo, and to this day do not care. I then looked into every pocket on the vest and found the bullets under my right arm. I reloaded the gun. All this time the helo was headed toward North Station.

I asked the American guy in the helo for a drink. I carried a couple canteens in the aircraft but did not put one of them in my g-suit before ejecting. I was VERY, VERY thirsty. No water except some the old man had and the guy advised me not to drink that. OK, I'd wait.

Of course the weather was still so bad at North Station that we could not get in there. The Air America pilot had by then invited me up front with him, and I was riding and enjoying the view as we headed toward Lima Site 36.

When we got there, I immediately asked for a drink. All they had was some Welch's Grape-ade. I hate that stuff!! This time, however, I drank it so fast I did not even taste it. The only other thing they had to drink in cans was a couple cans of Japanese beer. I drank those so fast I can hardly remember the taste. Then I was just about satisfied so was able to drink some more a little bit slower.

The helo had to refuel and, after a few minutes, left to continue their mission. The people on the ground at Lima Site 36 said that an Air America Caribou would be there in just a few minutes and I could ride with them to Long Tieng (also spelled *Long Chieng, Long Cheng, or Long Chen, that is a Laotian military base located in Xiangkhouang Province. During the Laotian Civil War, it served as a town and airbase operated by the Central Intelligence Agency of the United States. During this time, it was also referred to as Lima Site 98 (LS 98) or Lima Site 20A (LS 20A). At the height of its significance in the late 1960s, the "secret city" of Long Tieng maintained a population of 40,000 inhabitants, making it the second largest city in Laos at the time, although it never appeared on maps throughout this period. Copied from Wikipedia, the free encyclopedia).*

This was General Vang Pao's Headquarters and Air America had a good air strip there. The Jolly Green Helo's would also land there sometimes if they had a reason. They would today, because I was the reason. About 16:00 a Jolly picked me up and returned me to Udorn. The entire Squadron was out to greet me with Champagne. The copy of the report I got later showed that I had ejected at 14:44L and was picked up at 14:49L. I agree with that; I felt I was probably on the ground about 5 to 10 minutes.

Another picture of Lima Site 20 A. It is a bit difficult to see it in the upper picture, but the village and runway complex sit in a "bowl".

After going to the hospital for the mandatory physical (which found I had suffered no injuries except pretty good bruises on my legs from the opening shock), I was off to the club to drink, drink, and drink!! I told the squadron that I probably wouldn't be able to make my sortie on Tuesday because of my sore legs, but I did make the Wednesday and Thursday sorties. The T-39 took me back to Saigon on Friday.

As an interesting aside. The Operations Officer in Firefly 16, after I ejected, was on the radio to the Squadron telling them to get the paperwork ready showing that I was actually at the 602nd and legal to fly with them. When he saw me get picked up, he called them again telling them to cancel the paperwork. You see, I was only there on my R&R. Ha Ha.

I can tell you one thing, it is the most memorable flight, or should I say half of a flight, I have ever had. Even the Viet Cong attack down at Saigon in early May of 1968, which drove me out of my apartment onto the base once again, wasn't enough to get my heart beating like it did that day!!!

On the 15th of February, a couple of days after I got shot down, the mission wasn't anything out of the ordinary except how I reacted to something that happened. I was in an A-1H again, and my flight had some finned Napalm that we were going to dive bomb on to a cave entrance on Phu Din Din Mountain. This was the supposed site of a 105 Howitzer that was shelling North Station at night.

I Was Lucky | 149

It was also just a few miles to the West of the place I got hit on the 12th, and just a few miles North of where I landed after jumping out.

Everything went just as planned. I rolled in and just as I got the wings level and dropped the Napalm, the aircraft started to "whistle." I can't describe it any other way, it just started to whistle. I at first thought it must be the air flow through the cowl flaps. So after I leveled out, I adjusted the cowl flaps. Nothing, it still whistled. I looked at all the gauges, nothing, everything was normal. I just didn't know what to think. Of course I got jumpy and thought back about having to jump out a couple days ago, so I called my wingman and asked him to look me over. He replied that he saw nothing but I decided that it would be best to go home. Enroute to Udorn, we were at about 14,000 feet when I happened to pull the throttle back a bit and noticed the manifold pressure drop. No big deal, that is the way it is supposed to work. However, I pushed the throttle back up and the manifold pressure did NOT go back up! I told my wingman this and started to think something was going to happen for sure.

I didn't move the throttle again until we were about over the Mekong River. As we let down into Udorn I moved the throttle and the manifold pressure responded normally. It was then I remembered that everything was probably normal because when you were up at altitude there was a feature which prevented you from "over boosting" the engine. It was just a jumpy reaction I had which I shouldn't have. This was my last combat mission in an A-1.

When I returned from my five days R&R at Udorn, it was back to writing the FRAG for Barrel Roll/Steel Tiger. It was pretty much routine except for a couple things. As I mentioned earlier, it was about this time that the squadron had the opportunity to send some guys [I was lucky enough to be one of them!] up to visit Vang Pao at Lima Site 20A. I don't remember the date, but it was after I got shot down, so it must have been in late February or the first week of March. (Remember now I was stationed at Hq 7th AF in Saigon, so I must have come up from there to go with the guys from the squadron.) We left out of Udorn in a Goony Bird, went to Vientian, got "sheep dipped," then flew into Lima Site 20A. I don't remember just how long we stayed, but we got to visit with Vang Pao in his home and went into the village of Long Tieng. I have included several pictures of that visit.

A picture of Lima Site 20A, home of General Vang Pao and home base of the Raven FACs. At one end of the runway (I think the north end) was a large Karst hill. Made a great way to stop an aircraft but you wouldn't get to fly it again. It made the decision on what direction to take off and land very easy!

A couple of interesting things happened while we were there. Vang Pao really liked his Scotch (Johnnie Walker Black Label, I believe). We were sitting around talking, and when he decided to have a drink, he would just "Shoot" his drink and you were expected to do the same. No sooner would the empty glass hit the table, bam, it would be full again because he had several guys going around filling them. In just a bit, he would take another shot, again you were expected to do it also. We had quite a few shots before we got up to go to the village.

That was some experience! We saw some of the women with a lot of silver necklaces, very heavy and expensive, and raw opium (solid and liquid) for sale. (No, the women weren't for sale, just the silver and opium.) It was not something you see every day, I'll tell you that.

Another interesting thing happened. While we were sitting and having the drinks, a man went walking by outside his house. Vang Pao saw him and started to give instructions to one of his guards. This guard got up and ran out to check on something and came back a few minutes later. Seems Vang Pao saw this guy was missing some fingers or something, anyway he thought that maybe the guy had leprosy and, while there were some of those around, they were NOT supposed to be in his compound. This guy did have some parts missing but he was a wounded Hmong fighter.

I Was Lucky | 151

General Vang Pao relaxes in his house at Lima Site 20A. Note we must have just charged our shot glasses!

PK & Vang Pao

A couple pictures of us and General Vang Pao. In the picyure below left to right: PK, Westbrook, Vang Pao, Stark, Jenks, and for the life of me I cannot remember the name of the guy in the red shirt. Note each of us is holding a rifle which Vang Pao gave to us. I did not get to bring it home with me. They were very rustic to say the least.

This picture was taken in the village. On the table can be seen large blocks of raw opium. The bottles contain liquid opium.

Then I was again back at Hq 7th and the March attack on North Station (LS 85) took place. (See Attachment 6.)

Remember earlier I talked about the North Vietnamese overrunning the place and eleven of our men not making it out. Makes me pretty sad that maybe I had something to do with them being in the wrong place at the wrong time. One other thing it got me to thinking about was the location of my shoot down on 12 February. In that book (*One day too long*) it describes how the North was building up forces around Lima site 85 for quite a while before the attack on 11 March. After reading that book, I realized I was a hell of a lot luckier than I had originally thought. There were a lot of bad guys right where I was hit and where I jumped out.

Another side note about the loss of Lima Site 85. On the 13th of March, the 602nd had a couple of A-1s go to help with the evacuation of some of the guys still at LS 85. One of the guys was Don Westbrook. He actually had his bags packed and had orders in hand to go home. He volunteered for the mission and of course got shot down. Very sad. (Westbrook is in several of the pictures I have of the River Rat party we had at Udorn and also he was with us on the visit to Vang Pao.)

Another pretty lively time I have already mentioned was the Viet Cong attack in Saigon in May. My roommate and I were awakened by gun fire and knew right away what we were going to do. We packed our shaving kit and a small bag each with an extra uniform and some underwear and headed for the base. We knew where the mattresses and sheets were and where we could get a shower, so we didn't miss a step.

Getting from our room off base to the base that morning was really exciting. When I said earlier we headed to the base, I should have said we jumped on my roommate's motor scooter and went to the base. It was kind of scary. There was not one person on the street by the Third Field Hospital or that big road leading to the base. Most mornings these streets were crowded with people and vehicles.

There was a big crowd at the traffic circle in front of the main gate. Seems all the Vietnamese who had a job on base wanted to go to work. There was this Vietnamese policeman standing in the middle of the circle and he was telling everyone (at least I think he was telling them) that there was a problem and no one could go on base. For whatever reason, he started shooting his AR-15 (had it on his hip and pointing straight up) and he emptied the entire clip. We were sitting on the scooter right next to him trying to find a path through all the people to get to the gate. When he started shooting, my roommate hit the gas and we shot forward, spreading the crowd, and hit the main gate going about 20 miles per hour. The guards were hollering at us, but we didn't even slow down. Down the road we went. It was a bit funny to see cars pulled off the side of the road and people lying in the ditch.

We got down to the main compound, and all was quiet with everyone moving around normally. We found out later that the bad guys were in the cemetery, which is adjacent to the base and (of course) right next to the road we had just sped down. We were lucky that some VC out there in the cemetery didn't pick that time to be shooting.

I think it was the next day, but may in fact have been the same day, we were at the O-Club for lunch and standing in line when we heard a big explosion and felt the building shake. We were all on the floor wondering what the hell was going on. Pretty soon we heard another explosion and the building shook. Then someone came in and said we ought to go out and watch. We went out and saw this flight of four Vietnamese A-1s rolling in right over the club and dropping bombs on the cemetery. You could see the bombs come off and follow them until you lost sight of them going behind the buildings, then you could see the explosion. Watching war up close!

This was May—the month I got to go home. Earlier I had received orders to report to Ft. Hood, Texas, for an ALO/FAC job. This was not what I wanted!!! I wrote a letter to my friend at the Fighter Weapons School (My IP, Max Templin) asking if there was anything he might be able to do to get me to the Weapons School instead. He asked me to send him a copy of those orders, which I did, and he got the Wing Commander (I don't remember his first name but nickname was Buckshot) to talk to TAC Personnel. Sure enough, a couple weeks after I had sent him the copy of my orders, CBPO sent me a new set of orders assigning me to the F-100 Fighter Weapons School. Hot damn, just what I wanted!!

A funny coincidence: one day (after I had gotten the new orders) when I was still at Hq 7th at Tan San Nhut, I was coming down the stairs going to lunch and I saw this full colonel coming up the steps. I thought I had seen him before and saw from his name tag that his name was White. It was the very same "Buckshot" White who had gotten me my job at FWS! He was there on some kind of trip and did not have any scrip (we used scrip and not US money) and was looking for someone to exchange some money so he could get lunch. I was very happy to give him some scrip!!

Chapter 9

Instructor at the F-100 Fighter Weapons School

Back to Nellis AFB to the F100 Fighter Weapons School! I think it should go without saying that this is one of the finest assignments any fighter pilot can get. You fly a lot and fly with the best.

On one of the early flights when I was getting re-checked out in the F-100, a Basic Fighter Maneuvers (BFM) mission, I was the wingman. On these missions, right after takeoff, you completed what they called a rig check. You would go to a spread formation and porpoise the aircraft to check that the slats were working properly. We had just completed this check when we were jumped by a single F-4E aircraft. We couldn't have been more than 10 miles from the airfield but we got into a heck of a dog fight. It was one of the few times (maybe the ONLY time) that I saw the forward fuel tank so low that I had to come out of afterburner. This fight went on for about 15 minutes, till the F-4 guy called that he had a fuel emergency (meaning he had to land ASAP). Looking at our own fuel, we were at minimum fuel and had to land also. It was one of the shortest flights (other than an emergency) I ever had in the F-100.

I guess it would be safe to say that, while all the flying at the Weapons School was very enjoyable, there were a couple of events that really stand out in my mind.

The first was actually not directly flying on my part. I was selected as the pilot member of an accident board. The accident was a Thunderbird F-100. The Thunderbirds had gone to the Dallas/Fort Worth, Texas, area for a practice deployment. [Early in the year, when they were getting ready for the show season, they would practice two or three times a day at Nellis. When they were getting ready to go on the road, they would fly a practice deployment to make sure everything was ready.]

Coming back from Texas, one of the aircraft developed a problem and the pilot ejected. He was safe and the aircraft crashed in an area where nothing was damaged. The accident team, Board President, Safety Officer, and Pilot Member went to the crash site to observe the site for evidence of what might have caused the accident.

It was really a learning experience for me. It appeared that the aircraft was in a flat spin when it crashed. That is, it landed almost perfectly upright and, though it had burned, you could see all the parts. I really did not know what we were looking for until I saw the Safety Officer looking around the middle of the aircraft wreckage. I asked him what he was looking for. He said, "The starter and starter cartridge holder." I asked him "Why?" and he told me that when the Thunderbirds started up for their flight back to Nellis, they had used starter cartridges. [These were cartridges that, when you hit the starter button in the aircraft, it would burn like fireworks, and generate hot gases to turn a starter turbine wheel, which would turn the engine over so you could get it started.]

Evidently the aircraft that had the trouble and crashed was one on which the cartridge failed to fire. They had hooked up the normal starting unit and started the aircraft. I asked if they had removed the cartridge first, and he said they did not. I then told him about my experience with starter cartridge starts and sitting Nuclear Alert in USAFE. Flying with a live cartridge in the aircraft was NOT allowed. If you attempted a cartridge start and it didn't fire, you had to remove it before starting normally.

We did find the starter turbine wheel, which had come apart from spinning (centrifugal force) too fast. It was determined, with the description the pilot had given of what he saw when the problem started, and the turbine wheel came apart, the cartridge must have fired and caused the starter turbine to over-speed. From the location where the starter is on the engine and the description of the cockpit readings the pilot reported, it was pretty easy to determine that the starter turbine coming apart was the cause of the accident.

The second event that sticks out in my memory during my tour as an F-100 Fighter Weapons Instructor really does have to do with flying. I was the instructor for the Air-to-Air phase of the Weapons School. One day the Ops Officer, Max Templin, put me on the schedule with him leading. During the briefing he told me we would be going up to the restricted area [it is now unclassified but I still don't like to put a name to it—Area 51] and would be seeing an aircraft that I hadn't ever seen before and I was to keep it to myself. Sure enough, we arrived in Area 51 and had a MiG-17 join up on us. This was part of the Top Secret Project called Have Drill. I was really surprised at how small the MiG-17 was, also at how well it maneuvered. We did not do a lot of "dog fighting"; rather we did some acceleration tests and some turning maneuvers that were controlled to see just how the performance of the F-100D was when compared to the MiG-17. It was a REAL learning experience. I have included some words and a picture of Area 51 from *Wikipedia*, the free encyclopedia.

Groom Lake aka, Area 51

Area 51 (also known as Groom Lake, or Dreamland) is a remote detachment of Edwards Air Force Base. According to the Central Intelligence Agency (CIA), the correct names for the Area 51 facility are the Nevada Test and Training Range and Groom Lake, though the name Area 51 has been used in official CIA documentation. Other names used for the facility include Dreamland, Paradise Ranch, Home Base, Watertown Strip, and most recently Homey Airport. The area around the field is referred to as (R-4808N). It is located in the southern portion of Nevada in the western United States, 83 miles (133 km) north-northwest of Las Vegas. Situated at its center, on the southern shore of Groom Lake, is a large military airfield. The base's current primary purpose is officially undetermined; however, based on historical evidence, it most likely supports development and testing of experimental aircraft and weapons systems. The intense secrecy surrounding the base has made it the frequent subject of conspiracy theories and a central component to unidentified flying object (UFO) folklore. Everything that happens at Area 51 is classified Top Secret/Sensitive Compartmented Information (TS/SCI).

A month or so later, Max and the Squadron Commander called me into the Commander's office and asked me if I would like to go fly the MiG-17. Well, I guess you could have heard my answer of 'HELL YES' on the other side of the world.

It seems that the Department of Defense had acquired the Migs and had contracted for a bunch of sorties to conduct the Have Drill Project. Thinking of the in-commission rate of US aircraft, they based the contract sorties using the same rate. It turned out that the MiG-17 was a bunch more reliable than anyone thought and after completion of the Have Drill program, there were quite a few sorties still available. Tactical Air Command was asked if they would like to have some of the sorties for TAC pilots. The Commander of TAC, William Momyer, said NO. The Navy responded that they would take all they could get. If my memory is correct this situation lasted until the Air Force Chief of Staff (General John "Jack" Ryan) heard that the Navy would be getting all the remaining sorties. He called Momyer and told him that Tactical Air Command WOULD be using half of the sorties. Of course the Air-to-Air instructors of the Fighter Weapons School were the first to be asked if they would like to fly the aircraft.

It was quite an experience. Since there were no two-seat MiG-17 aircraft, the first time you flew it, you did it alone. I was given a "Dash One" (technical description of the aircraft and systems) which had been put together by the pilots from the Have Drill Project. Also an aircraft check list you could use to preflight the aircraft and use when flying it.

The first time I went to fly the aircraft I got to sit in it for quite a while just studying the cockpit. I was surprised at some of the procedures necessary because of the location. For example, the aircraft was always kept in the hangar during certain hours because Soviet satellites would be coming over and taking pictures of the area. (This was true for a lot of the other aircraft that one could see at Area 51.) Finally the aircraft was towed out of the hangar and one of the ground crew observed me starting up the engine.

This is a picture of one of the MiG-17's that I got to fly.
This picture is from Wikipedia, the free encyclopedia.

After checking the systems out, I taxied to the runway. That was an experience in itself!! On US aircraft, the brakes are on the rudder pedals, that is, you push on the tops which would rotate forward and apply braking. Also on US aircraft, if you wanted to turn, you pushed the rudder pedal just as if you were using rudder to fly the aircraft and power steering would turn the nose wheel. On the MiG-17, the braking was done with a lever on the control stick. You squeezed it and applied brakes. If you wanted to turn, you pushed the rudder pedal in and squeezed the brake lever, and it would apply braking to that wheel so you turned in that direction. It took a little practice to get used to that and the first time you taxied, it was a lot of s-turning. One thing you had to be aware of, and it was important, was the fact that all the braking used an air accumulator which was filled before flight and DID NOT get refilled by the aircraft systems. So, you started the flight with the accumulator full and used it for braking to steer while taxiing. You had better not use it all up, because you need brakes when you land, and to taxi back to the ramp after landing. It did not cause me any problems, but I think I heard that some of the guys that got to fly it did run out of air pressure after they landed and had to be towed back to the hangar.

Flying the MiG-17 was a real eye opener!! I know it is not right to describe it this way, but it really does describe one aspect of its capability. "It could turn up its own ass hole!!" I guess that would tell you it was a very maneuverable aircraft. If you have ever talked to a fighter pilot, you know that they can never describe just how a maneuver goes without using their hands. Well, I tell people the MiG-17 could maneuver just like your right hand (if you are right-handed).

My first flight I just went up and flew around a bit, getting used to how it felt. I didn't do any real hard turning or high speed maneuvering. Landing was very easy. The aircraft was easy to fly.

There were a couple of very interesting things about the aircraft. The construction of the aircraft was not like any aircraft built in the US. For example, all the rivets on the wing were not recessed (countersunk) like on US aircraft; rather the rivet heads were left exposed on the wing surface. Another example, the way you turned on the pressurization in the cockpit was a valve that reminded me of an outside water faucet. Remember those faucets with the red round handle to turn the water on? It looked just like that. If I remember correctly, the oxygen system had been changed, so it wasn't so foreign to use.

On the second flight (and these flights were not chased, so you were just up there all alone flying around), I got to turn the aircraft pretty hard and learned a few of its limitations. For example, if you put it into a dive and got it going over 400 knots, you could pull on the stick as hard as you wanted, but you could get only one "g" and it would not turn very well. (It may have been a bit more than one g, but it did not turn very well above 400 kts.) The beauty part about the aircraft was the fact that it had the speed brake activation as a button on the control stick. So if you were going over 400 kts, you just put the speed brake out for a little bit, get below 400 knots, and you could get 7, 8, 9 g's and turn up your own a…h…!! I really had fun flying the MiG-17.

In my log book it reflects the fact that I got six landings in the F-113/114 (the designation the USAF used for the MiG-17—there were actually two MiG-17's used and I didn't really know which was which) and 3.9 hours flying time. I believe three of the flights were for orientation, then I was lucky enough to get asked to fly it three more times while other pilots flew their US aircraft against me.

One of those flights really sticks out in my memory. It was against an F-101 test aircraft out of Edwards AFB, CA. They were testing the development of TISEO (Target ID System Electro Optical). This was a system to help identify aircraft at a greater distance than eyeball range. (It was later put on the F-4 aircraft and used to good effect if it was kept bore sighted to the radar.) Anyway, I was just flying along and they were using the TISEO to observe me. They called for me to make a turn. Heck, they did not say a hard turn so I just went into a shallow turn. They called something to the effect, "Is that all it will do?" Well, I then put about 8 g's on the aircraft and heard them exclaim, "Wow"! They were very impressed that it could turn that well.

There are only a couple of flights as an instructor that I'll relate. One was a flight where we were dropping inert full scale bombs. This flight the bombs were loaded on a TER (Triple ejector rack) on the inboard station. I had not flown this configuration before and had been told that sometimes the bombs wouldn't release as planned. Well, sure enough, I couldn't get them off the TER. Not wanting to jettison the TER with the bombs loaded, I returned to Nellis and flew a straight in approach. Coming down final, things just did not look right! As I got the airspeed down to approach speed, the nose of the aircraft was way too high and it was difficult to see the runway. I knew this wasn't right, so I kept the power up and the airspeed higher than normal, so that the attitude of the aircraft was more like what it should have been. I touched down (a lot faster than I thought I should have), pulled the drag chute and went to raise the flaps. WHAT, no flaps?? Yeah, I had forgotten to put the flaps down. Stupid mistake, but not fatal because of my experience of knowing what attitude the aircraft should be in for landing.

One other flight I remember very well. We were clean (no external tanks) and flying an air-to-air mission against F-4's. Everything was going as briefed and fuel checks made as necessary. Somewhere in there, a little bit before we should have been bingo (fuel state requiring us to return to Nellis), a fuel check showed my student well below bingo. We headed straight back to Nellis. I declared low fuel for my student and briefed him to land straight in. This would be the safest way to get him on the ground using minimum fuel. I flew his wing down to final approach and it looked like everything was OK, so I went around to fly my own pattern for landing. No sooner did I start my go-around than I heard my student saying he was going around. WHAT??? I was worried that he might not have enough fuel to complete the pattern. It turned out that he thought he was too fast on final and couldn't get it slowed down, so he decided to go around. He must have had more fuel that I thought, because he got on the ground and everything was just fine. I did chew him out in the debrief.

One other event I remember that should be told. My boys were in Cub Scouts and I was helping the Cub Master. He was a really good guy, a North Las Vegas Fireman I think. Anyway I got permission to bring him out to the base to tour the Fighter Weapons School facility. I also got him dressed up in a flight suit, g-suit, and helmet, got him strapped into the back seat of an F-100F and taxied out for take off. Ran up the engine and lit the afterburner like we were going to take off, and then just taxied back to the ramp. He was really impressed.

When I asked for and got the assignment to the F-100 Fighter Weapons Instructor School, I expected to be there for a good four-year assignment. That was what the normal assignment was. What a surprise I got one day while sitting at the duty desk in the squadron. (This was in late September or early October and I had been at Nellis for about 16 months.) A call came from Tactical Air Command Personnel saying something to the effect that the F-100 school would be closing down. Realize the F-100 had been in service quite a while and the Air National Guard was now flying more F-100s than the active Air Force.

I can tell you every guy we had assigned to the squadron was in a sweat as to what their next assignment might be. Most DID NOT want a "desk" job at some headquarters. There weren't a lot of good assignments available. For me, going to Luke AFB, AZ, as an F-100 Instructor Pilot (one of the options) was not something I wanted to do. (Being an instructor in the F-100F meant you were in the back seat with the student in the front. These students were pilots who had NOT flown the F-100 before, so it could get to be a scary thing.) One other option was to stay at Nellis and go down the ramp to an F-111 squadron. That did not appeal to me either since you were in an aircraft with another guy sitting right next to you.

The guy at TAC Personnel said something about an ALO/FAC job at Ft. Carson, CO. [Fort Carson is at the southwest edge of Colorado Springs.] At that time it was a TAC policy that if you went to an ALO/FAC job for 18 months, you could get your choice of assignments when your time was up. I really wanted to fly the A-7D which was coming into the TAC inventory, but it was still in the testing phase at this time and there were no assignments available. After a couple days of trying to decide, I was talking to the Personnel guy and he said it looked like I was going to be assigned to Luke. I said, "wait a minute, is that job at Ft. Carson still available?" He yelled across the room to this other guy who he said was walking out the door, and asked if the ALO/ FAC job was still available. He answered yes, and I said, "I'll take it!" He yelled to the guy that he had someone for the job, and I got the ALO/FAC job at Ft Carson.

When we (I and the family) got to Las Vegas in June 1968 we had rented a house until we could decide which part of town we would choose to buy a house. In July 1969 we bought a house. When we finally closed on the deal, I think we got to make one house payment before we had to sell for our PCS to Ft. Carson.

Chapter 10

ALO/FAC at Ft. Carson, Colorado

One of the good things about going to be an ALO/FAC with the Army was the fact that I had made Major while at Nellis. Being a Major vs. Captain sure made a difference. We got a house on base, a two-story (with basement) brick duplex. It was on a corner lot and we liked it.

One of the problems I faced was just which/what aircraft I would be flying to keep up my flying status. The Division ALO thought I should fly the U-6 Beaver since it was a tail dragger and I had time in the A-1, also a tail dragger. So that was the aircraft I would be flying.

The check-out was really something. The Army Major who checked me out made some assumptions, I guess, because the check-out was not anything like how the Air Force goes about checking someone out in a different aircraft. I don't remember ever looking at a Dash One, and his instructions about the aircraft were conducted while he showed me how to preflight the aircraft. We took off and flew around a bit and made three landings and he signed me off as qualified. I think he must have thought since I was a fighter pilot with quite a bit of experience, I would be OK to fly the U-6. I guess I felt the same way but I learned some things while flying the U-6 that I don't think I would have ever learned in any other aircraft.

The aircraft I really wanted to fly, of course, was the F-100. The Colorado Air National Guard at Buckley Air Field near Denver had the F-100 and supported one pilot from those assigned to Fort Carson. When I arrived at Fort Carson, one of the other ALO/FAC's was already flying with the Guard so I couldn't. I got checked out in the U-6 in November 1969. I don't remember just when it was, but I also got to check out in the T-39 Saber Liner at Peterson Field there in Colorado Springs. My experience in the T-39 was very short. I think I was just qualified to fly passengers when the other pilot assigned to Fort Carson flying with the Guard was reassigned and I could then fly the F-100 with the Guard. This was in April 1970. I went to Cannon AFB, NM, and got a recurrency check-out in the F-100 in April and started flying with the Guard right away.

Picture of a U-6 Beaver. This has the Golden Gate Bridge as background. I obviously never landed by the Golden Gate!!

There are a few things I really remember about my flying experiences while at Fort Carson. The first was in early 1970. The weather was really great one day and I asked Captain Thomas (a C-130 pilot assigned to the Air Force unit there at Fort Carson as the Air Lift expert) if he would like to go flying in the U-6. He accepted, and I thought it would be fun to fly down to Pueblo and land and get a cup of coffee and come back. One of the enlisted guys who took care of our jeeps and other equipment was in the office also and I decided why not take him too. Well, we took off out of Butts Army Air Field (that was the air facility at Fort Carson) and flew down to Pueblo Municipal Airport. Landed and had some coffee and then headed back to Fort Carson.

We flew over the ranges and maneuver areas on the way back and then checked in with the Butts Tower asking for landing instructions. That was when I got my first surprise. The wind was about 20 knots and from a direction that made it a crosswind to both the runways at Butts. This would be the FIRST time I would try landing the U-6 in a crosswind. To make a long story short, I made several attempts on the long runway (North/South) then decided maybe it was less of a crosswind on the shorter runway headed East/West. Finally after several attempts landing to the west, I was able to get it on the ground safely. I know Captain Thomas was a bit worried but don't think the enlisted guy ever imagined that I was really sweating getting back on the ground safely. Never did want to try landing the U-6 in a crosswind again.

Another memorable flight in the U-6. The Officers Club at Fort Carson was having a Casino Night and one of the other guys and I thought we could help them out. We took the U-6 and flew to Nellis AFB, which of course is by Las Vegas, NV. My idea was to go down to the casinos and get whatever we could get free. Napkins, cards, dice, etc., whatever they would give us. We went, flying out on Friday, planning on staying the weekend. Well, after Friday night we decided we would just go back to Fort Carson with what we had.

Saturday morning the wind was blowing so hard that when we went out to the airplane (it was tied down, thank heaven) it was just bouncing up and down. The wind was actually blowing so hard that the airplane was trying to fly. We decided that it was best if we wait until the weather got better. On Sunday the wind was not quite as bad but still way too much crosswind to use the runway. The tower allowed us to use the taxiway for take off, and, with the strong wind we had, it only took about 300 feet of roll for us to be airborne.

Then came the fun part. We flew east, and after we got about 100 miles out, the clouds met the ground. We did not want to fly IFR so we turned around, went back a ways, turned south, and then turned back east hoping we could get around the weather. Again, a long story short, we ended up flying just a couple hundred feet above the ground and a few feet below the clouds right along the north rim of the Grand Canyon. A couple of times we were actually in the weather but could still see the ground. When we got to the east end of the Grand Canyon, the weather was clear all the way to Colorado. After that flight I knew the reason a lot of private pilots kill themselves trying to fly in clouds when they are not instrument qualified.

My last experience with the U-6, the Division ALO had a relative getting married out in San Diego, CA. We worked it out that I would come out in the U-6 and bring him back because it would be the last flight for me in the U-6. My plan was to leave on Friday morning and fly to Luke AFB, AZ, and spend Friday night with fighter pilots at the Luke O'Club. I got it all planned, then the morning I went to the Operations Building at Butts to file the flight plan and leave, the Army Major who had checked me out in the U-6 asked me if I would take along a couple of Army Warrant Officers he wanted to get some experience flying. Since there would be plenty of room and I would be glad to have the company, I said "Sure, I would be happy to take them along." The Army gave me a credit card for gas and we loaded up and took off.

We flew south from Fort Carson until we were just east of the Sangre de Cristo Range and then turned west to fly over the mountains. Another LEARNING experience!! There must have been an easterly (tail) wind because as we approached the mountains we got a lift, and it was easy to climb up to an altitude to get over the mountain. As we passed just over the mountain that "Lift" turned into something like a downdraft and it took full power to keep the airplane level so we wouldn't go smashing into the ground. It was probably less than a minute but scary for what seemed like a LONG time.

We landed at Farmington, NM, and I decided to get some gas in the airplane. When he asked me how much, I just told him to fill it up. Later this turned out to have been a very wise thing!!

Once we got airborne and on course for Luke, the Warrant Officers asked me if we were going to be close to the Grand Canyon. I told them we would be going just to the east of the Canyon and then asked them if they wanted to fly over the Grand Canyon. Yes, that was what they wanted. I changed my flight plan and headed west for the Grand Canyon.

When we got to the east edge of the Grand Canyon, the clouds and the ground met. I mean there was no going any further west unless you wanted to fly IFR (Instrument Flight Rules). I did not want to fly in the weather, and anyway we would not be able to see much of the Grand Canyon if we were in clouds. I turned the aircraft south and saw that maybe we were going to have to file a flight plan using airways anyway.

I had one of the Warrant Officers fly the airplane holding the heading and altitude while I got the charts out to find which airways we would be using to get to Luke. I first wanted to know just where we were so I used the navigation aid in the airplane (TACAN) to see how far I was from Winslow, AZ. I found we had a heck of a head wind out of the west. I finally got the flight plan filed and had to pick either 11,000 feet or 13,000 feet as the altitude to fly. At 11,000 it looked like we would be in clouds but I couldn't keep up the airspeed and climb to 13,000. So I told Center I would be flying at 11,000 feet.

That took us into some clouds. I wasn't afraid, because I had done a lot of instrument flying and it did not look like we would be in the clouds for more than a couple minutes. We weren't in the weather for more that a couple seconds when the airplane started to climb. I pulled back on the power and pushed the stick forward to hold altitude. Man, it was just like being on an elevator. I had the power back almost to idle and the airplane still wanted to climb. In just about 30 seconds, the airplane started to go down. It was taking full power and I was still going down! It was scary for a while, and then we popped out of the clouds into the clear. Looking out at the wings I saw we had about 3 inches of rime ice on the leading edge of the wing. I made up my mind right then that I would NEVER fly the U-6 in weather again.

I knew we weren't a long way from Luke but decided that we were going to be a little close on gas. I leaned it out and we had an enjoyable 10-15 minutes looking at the scenery. Ahead were some more clouds but it looked like if we let down we would be able to stay clear of the clouds. I got clearance from Center to descend VFR, pulled the power back a little, and started a descent. It wasn't but just a minute or so and the engine quit!! The heart rate went way up!! I did everything you are supposed to do when this happens and the engine just started up and was running just fine. It was then I realized that I hadn't gone back to full rich with the mixture, and as I was letting down, the engine wasn't getting enough fuel to run.

Once I got the heart rate back to normal, I saw we were getting close to Luke, so I contacted Luke tower for landing instructions. Yeah, you guessed it. About a 40 degree crosswind of about 20 knots!! Luke has real wide runways so I asked if it would be possible to land across the runway. Luke also has the dirt between the main taxiways and the runway stabilized with blacktop so for a light airplane it is almost like runway. They told me it would be OK to just land across the runway and then just continue on the black top stuff because all the U-6's that Luke uses to go back and forth to the ranges do that all the time. Another day of experience completed and off to the club for a few beers.

The next day filing an IFR clearance to get to San Diego and flying to Marine Corps Air Station Miramar was another experience. I won't bore you with that because it was a lot like filing the flight plan in the air the day before. We got there in time to actually go to Disneyland for a little while Saturday afternoon and night.

Sunday we got ready and filed out of Miramar to Winslow, AZ, where we would make a refueling stop. That we did with no problems. After we filled it with gas at Winslow, we were faced with a decision about the aircraft heater. This is nothing really but a butterfly valve which you can either close to have the heat come into the cockpit or open, in which case you will not have any heat. The cable that you use to open and close the valve was broken so we had to decide before we took off to either have it open or closed. We chose to have the heat which made it a bit warm for the first part of the flight but that turned out to be very wise because of what took place later.

Off we went toward Fort Carson. We were flying directly to Farmington, then to Pueblo, Colorado, and then to Fort Carson, planning on landing at Butts. We got to Farmington no problem, but then the weather to the east and Pueblo wasn't good. We decided to go north to Durango, Colorado, and if the weather wasn't good, we would land at Durango and spend the night.

When we got to Durango, we were at about 11,000 feet, and the weather didn't look too bad to the east, so we headed to Pueblo. On that airway we had to go to 15,000 feet. It wasn't any problem getting to that altitude because the outside air temperature was minus 40 degrees F. (Now do you see why it was good that we had the heater ON?) We really should not be at this altitude without oxygen to breathe. I told the Division ALO to keep looking out and if he ever can't see the ground, we would turn around and land at Durango.

I flew instruments and pretty soon the navigation TACAN broke lock on the Durango Tacan and we were just flying a heading. There are some pretty high mountains around there so this was no fun not knowing exactly where we were!! Finally the TACAN locked on to Pueblo and everything was fine.

It was then getting dark. I hadn't really flown the U-6 at night and probably shouldn't be trying it then!! After we got over the mountains and were only about 30 minutes from Butts Air Field, the Center told us that Butts Field was closed because of ice on the runway. Well, how about that!! OK, we'd land at Peterson Field. When we got close enough, we contacted Peterson Field tower. They cleared us on the long runway (North/South), landing to the North. Then they gave us the wind, and of course we had a 25 knot crosswind from the North West. I remembered that they had a runway that goes North West so asked for that one. They cleared us for landing on the NW runway.

When we were about five minutes out, the tower called and said we should look out for large patches of ice on the runway. Since the North/South runway is about 11,000 feet long I decided that maybe I would try that one even with the crosswind. I turned on the landing lights and started the approach. When we got down to a couple hundred feet and over the runway, it suddenly went all white out and we couldn't see the runway!! Then in a couple seconds, there the runway was. It turned out that the wind was blowing snow across the runway every once in a while causing the white out.

We finally landed and everything was OK. I vowed that this sure enough was my last flight in the U-6. I don't remember for sure but I think I had to go over to Peterson Field the next day and fly the airplane back to Butts.

As far as my flying time in the T-39, there was nothing worth remembering except the fact that during one of the check-out flights the IP did some rolls, which he shouldn't have.

My experience as an ALO/FAC included some work in the field with my Army unit. The first was an exercise that had one of the battalions as the Red Force and my unit as the Blue Force. Since I was assigned to the Hq Company of the

Battalion, I worked for the S3. [*A definition from the internet: Within the U.S. Army's organizational tables for the unit called a battalion, made up of approximately 700 soldiers, the positions filled by the officers of the command staff have designations such as S1, S2 and so on, all the way to S6. The battalion S3, the officer in charge of operations and training, has a variety of responsibilities that extend from the lowest-ranking individual in the battalion to the battalion commander and beyond.*] On this exercise the S3 decided to have a Huey Helicopter insert me behind the Red Force lines with a back pack radio and call in air strikes. It worked our really well and for me it was a lot of fun.

One other incident which was kind of fun was a ride I got in an Observation Helicopter. We just went up and flew around for a while and the Army pilot tried to teach me to hover the helo. I got out of the helicopter after this flight wondering just how I was able to pilot a jet fighter. I just could not get the hang of putting the helicopter into a hover. The Army pilot had a good laugh at the expense of a humble Fighter Pilot

One other field exercise (these exercises took place in the large maneuver area within the Fort Carson complex) was held in the winter time. It snowed while we were in the field and I spent a couple nights in a very cold tent. That is about all I remember of this exercise, just that it was DARN COLD.

On one of our Field Exercises, I tried to Cross Country Ski. Notice there wasn't much snow. Also I did not do very well on the skis!

I got deployed with my unit to Fort Campbell, Kentucky, for a one week exercise. This was in the summer and quite hot. The area we were maneuvering in was very close to the main part of Ft. Campbell. I took advantage of this and would go into my quarters on base to sleep. (Did not have to stay in a tent.)

Another thing I remember is that we had C-Rations to eat and one of the items in this one C-Ration was a pecan cake in what looked like a soda can. The army guys told us that if you heated it up on the manifold of the jeep, it made it taste better. I was having lunch and decided to try it. Well, before I got to eat this cake we had a call and went to do some ALO/FAC work, of course driving our jeep. It was about two hours later that I remembered having put the cake on the manifold. I retrieved the cake, it was really hot, and after it cooled down some, I opened it. It was some of the best cake I have ever had.

The flying with the Guard at Buckley was not only fun but allowed me to gain confidence in my flying ability. One example. They would sometimes allow me to have an airplane to "go out and back." (This would be "single ship," meaning you went as a single aircraft, something you never did in the active Air Force!) This actually allowed them to get flying time on their aircraft while doing less maintenance work. You took off at Buckley and flew out to some other base and landed. That base's "Transit Alert" then refueled and readied the aircraft for the flight back. That way the aircraft, while getting "double" flying time, only had to be serviced at Buckley once. A lot of units used to do this.

One of those times I departed Buckley in mid-afternoon on a planned flight to Wichita, KS. I would normally visit with my Mother if I had enough time in Wichita. This particular day when I landed at Wichita I was given a message to call back to Buckley right away. It seems the ANG unit in Dallas (they flew the KC-97 tankers, an air-to-air refueling aircraft) had one of their boom operators that needed some hook-ups before the end of the year. I think this was the last week in December. What they wanted me to do was plan a mission where I would meet up with this KC-97 in a refueling area down in Texas and do some hook-ups with them. I had never planned a mission like this but thought, "What the heck, I'll give it a try." Not only would this be at night but it would be the first and only time I air-to-air refueled from a KC-97. The mission went like clock work. I found the tanker, joined up, refueled, and headed back to Buckley. Great experience which I would have NEVER gotten while flying in the active Air Force.

When the assignment to the Army became a reality, I was not looking forward to it. As time went by (and as noted earlier being a Major was really a Blessing), it turned out to be one of the best assignments I ever had. The Brigade Commander treated me extremely well. The guys I worked with were some of the best people I met while in the service. At the time, some of the things I had to do did not seem like fun, but, looking back, it was a great experience.

I checked out in the Army Flying Club at Butts Field. They had a Cessna 172 and I took a couple interesting flights in this aircraft. One was to Topeka, Kansas, in April 1973. Lois's sister's husband, Ronald Van Sickel, was killed in a car accident and Lois, Alex, and I flew to Topeka. It was a fun flight even though the event we were going to wasn't a fun event.

The other flight in the flying club aircraft was when I went to Cannon AFB, NM, to get recurrent in the F-100. On this trip, I took Brian along. As we were flying down to Cannon, I told Brian to fly the airplane. He said, "NO, I don't know how to fly an airplane." I finally just took my hands off the controls and said if he didn't take hold and try to fly it, we were going to crash. He finally did and actually did a pretty good job keeping us straight and level.

Beechcraft Musketeer

One other thing I was able to do while at this assignment was take flying instructions and obtain both my FAA Flight Instructor (CFIA) and Instrument Instructor certificate (CFII).

I used the GI Bill to take my flying instructor classes at Peterson Field just East of Colorado Springs. The Flight Instructor lessons were in a Beechcraft Musketeer. One memorable flight was in the early afternoon. We (my instructor and I) were flying just east of the airport and some big clouds were building up. The bottoms of these clouds were probably 3000 feet above the ground. The IP wanted to show me something so he flew the aircraft to a spot under one of the building clouds. He actually pulled the power to idle and told me to watch the rate of climb indicator. We started climbing at about 2,000 feet a minute! Just like going up in an elevator. (This reminded me of the experience in the U-6.) He finally had to turn the airplane up on a wing so we weren't pulled right up into the cloud. It was the up draft that was building the cloud that took the airplane up.

The instructions and check ride for my Instrument Instructors Certificate were in a Mooney Ranger. This is a single engine, low wing aircraft—really a good aircraft. The one flight I really remember in this aircraft was my FAA Check Ride. The Check Pilot wanted me to do a back course ILS into Peterson Field. I had done this during practice so it wasn't something new. However, I still think I made the procedure turn on the wrong side during the procedure. I must not have because I passed the check ride and I don't think the Check Pilot would have passed me if I had made that error.

Mooney Ranger

Chapter 11

A-7D Instructor Pilot at Davis-Monthan

In early 1971 I got the assignment I wanted, flying the A-7D. At that time, to check out in the A-7D, you went to 333rd Tactical Fighter Training Squadron at Luke AFB, AZ. I went TDY from Fort Carson for the check out at Luke. The first wing forming up was the 354th at Myrtle Beach, SC. The pilots came to Luke for check out and then went back to their home base. The word was out that the 333rd Squadron would be moving to Davis-Monthan AFB at Tucson, AZ. (The 355th Wing was reformed 1 July 1971 at Davis Monthan AFB in Tucson, AZ.) In April I went TDY to Luke for my A-7D check out, then returned to Fort Carson to pack up and move the family to Davis Monthan in July.

In somewhat of a quirk of fate, the Squadron Commander of the 333rd was Max Templin, my IP from the F-100 Weapons School. In a very unfortunate incident the day I arrived (in early July) at Tucson to start my assignment, one of the A-7D's that was being flown from Luke to DM crashed very near the air base. It was suspected that he ran out of fuel. As is the usual case, the Squadron Commander got the blame and Max was fired, so I never got to work for him.

Flying the A-7D was great fun. It was a very good aircraft with very advanced systems for its time. I don't remember just when but I was made the Flight Commander of the Academic Flight of the 333rd and enjoyed that job. A lot of the guys coming to check out in the A-7D were men I had flown with in the F-100. Several were being assigned to Nellis AFB, where it looked like an A-7D Fighter Weapons School would be formed. I let it be known that if such a thing were to come to pass, I surely wanted to be a part of it.

One of the guys going to Nellis who was checking out was John Lynch. One flight I had with him was kind of funny. It was to be a Basic Fighter Maneuvers mission. We were to practice a little about air-to-air combat. One of the first things I was going to show John was what to do when someone was attacking you. I would just fly along straight and level and he was to attack from a higher altitude from either side. As he was closing, I would start a shallow turn toward him, and increase the turn until I was turning real hard. He should keep attacking until he would overshoot, and I would reverse my turn and be right behind him. He, of course, had a lot of fighter time and he would just never overshoot. I kept trying to get him to overshoot and kept pulling a lot of g's hoping he would. Finally I had been pulling g's for such a long time that my neck got so tired that I couldn't hold my head up. We finally had to call it off.

This is the class picture of the guys that checked out at the same time I did.

There was a period of about three months that the A-7 was grounded due to engine problems. Seems a spacer between the turbine wheels in the burner section of the engine would come apart and destroy the turbine section and the engine. After they had solved the problem, it was taking some time to get all the aircraft back to flying. As the first few were flyable, the Instructor Pilots were allowed to go fly to keep up currency. This was very rare because there were no training missions where you would go single ship and just fly and do what you wanted. The aircraft was clean, i.e. it had no external pylons. This was also very rare because the three pylons on each wing were always there. I remember going out east of Tucson and just flying around doing acrobatics and chasing clouds, just like in pilot training. I recall getting up to around 30,000 feet and then diving with full power to see how fast I could get it going. I don't remember for sure but think I got close to 500 knots, which for the A-7D was pretty fast.

The other flight I remember was one to the Tactics Range with a full load of inert bombs. These were 500 lb. bombs filled with concrete. We had MER racks (Multiple Ejector Racks), one on each wing, that had six bombs each. We were at low level (probably 500-800 feet AGL), and the three students were flying in route formation (they were spread out a couple hundred feet). I pulled the aircraft nose up and did a very fast roll. As I got back to wings level and stopped the roll I could see the MER's really swaying on the wing. I never thought anything about it, just told the students the aircraft was very maneuverable even with a full bomb load. It was a lot later that, looking in the Dash One, I learned that you should not do something like that because of the danger of breaking the pylon.

The A-7D was a single seat, single engine aircraft. The first pilots that were checked out in the aircraft were pilots who had previously flown a fighter type aircraft. This of course made for an easier time as an Instructor because you knew the guy you were training had flown in an aircraft of the same type. After the first few classes of pilots were trained, we got ten pilots who were straight out of pilot training. Their only experience was in Air Training Command in a training environment. All the IPs were wondering just how this would turn out. I got one of these pilots as my student. His name was Mike Shira. It was a very pleasant surprise. These guys did great!! In fact on the first ride to the gunnery range to do dive bombing, Mike got all bulls eyes! The system on the A-7, when it was working properly, was a very accurate system. However, you still had to fly the aircraft and get the pipper on the target. If I remember correctly, when they went to the range they had probably 7 or 8 rides in the aircraft.

An event that did not really involve flying but I think is worth mentioning was an event that was held for every class. After all the students had flown the required number of flights (five, I think) and had their check ride, we would go to the O-Club and have a party. The aircraft builder (Ling-Temco-Vought) would give each student a model of the A-7. After one such event, about 16 of us IPs were standing around on the O-Club patio just telling stories. Billy Vinson went into the Class Six store (it was right there in the O-Club) and got a bottle of Jack Daniels to take home. He came out with the bottle in a paper sack and was just going to tell everyone good bye when one of the other IPs (I think it was Joe Ashy) asked Billy what he had in the paper bag. Billy, being the great guy he was, took it out and showed it to the crowd. Joe took the bottle from Billy and opened it and tasted it to make sure it really was Jack Daniels (at least that is what he told Billy). He then passed it to the next guy on the side away from Billy and he took a taste. Well, it went all around the circle and when it got back to Billy, it was empty. He just went in and bought another but was wise enough to go out the front door and not back on the patio.

I just remembered another flight I think is worth mentioning. It was the only cross-country I got to take during this tour at Davis Monthan. Tom Allbee and I planned a cross country that would take us to Buckley ANG base near Denver, Colorado, where we would refuel. We would then go to McConnell AFB at Wichita, Kansas, to spend the night. The next day I can't remember exactly where we went but we ended up at Peterson Field at Colorado Springs, CO. Returned to DM on Sunday.

The part about this journey that was really funny happened on our way to Wichita. After we left Buckley, about a hundred miles east, we cancelled our Instrument Flight Rule (IFR) flight plan and went VFR (Visual Flight Rules). This allowed us to proceed to Wichita going just about wherever we wanted, as long as we obeyed the rules. We let down over western Kansas and I flew over the town of Scott City, telling Tom that was where I went to high school. We then flew over the farm house of a really close friend from high school that lived about seven miles south of town. After that we climbed back to a medium altitude and headed east toward Wichita.

When we approached the town of Kingman, which is about 50 miles west of Wichita, we flew over the little town of Willowdale, which is about twenty or so miles southwest of Kingman. I told Tom that I had a lot of relatives who lived in Willowdale and I wanted to fly over so they could see what an A-7 looked liked.

The funny part of this story is really what happened after we got back to work on Monday. Tom couldn't stop talking about my comments all during the flight about this house, and that town, and that church, etc. While he thought it was funny, I was just trying to tell him about where I grew up.

Chapter 12

A-7D Fighter Weapons School

In either late August or early September 1972, it was announced that there would be an A-7D Fighter Weapons School forming at Nellis AFB. I got the word and accepted an assignment to be an IP in the A-7D FWS.

This entire process for the next six months was so messed up it isn't even funny. I signed out of Davis Monthan and with the family went to Las Vegas and signed into the FWS. I then got two weeks leave and took the family on a camping trip. We went to Sears and bought sleeping bags, a family tent, and a lot of other camping gear. I remember we were staying at the BOQ but over at the old Nuclear Storage Area to the northeast of the main base at Nellis. We set up the tent and sprayed it with water and then let it dry out. The instructions said to do this because this would make it water proof by having the holes where the seams were sewed together swell shut.

We went camping on the north rim of the Grand Canyon and to the Indian camp ground at Crescent Lake in Arizona. A lot of things happened on this camping trip but none about flying, so I'll just leave those stories for another time.

Since school was starting and we had not sold our house in Tucson, I went to Nellis and stayed in the BOQ and the family stayed in Tucson. I drove back and forth for some of the weekends to visit and see how things were going. The flying at Nellis was just routine and mostly writing the course material for the A-7D school.

One funny thing about that—we included "Departures" in the first couple flights the students were to fly. These would be aircraft handling missions, i.e. learning to fly the aircraft up to its limits. A "Departure" meant "To depart from controlled flight," which meant that the airplane would actually tumble through the sky for a short time and, if the pilot just did nothing, it would just come out of this and start flying normal again. We wanted to do this because a lot of A-7D pilots had never experienced this and we did not want the instructors to be surprised if it ever happened to them or to one of their students.

When we sent the course material to Tactical Air Command Headquarters at Langley for approval, they called us and wanted to know why we were including instrument departures for these first few missions. We, of course, told them that those weren't instrument departures but real aircraft departures. They told us not only NO but HELL NO!! We couldn't be teaching how to depart from controlled flight because it was dangerous. Long story short, we had to remove it from the course. However, that did not keep us from teaching it anyway. We found a way and taught every student who went through the course what a "Departure" really was.

Sometime in late November, I was at the duty desk in the Squadron when a call came in from the guy at Personnel at TAC Hq. He said something to me like, "I hope you haven't bought a house yet." I said something like "no, I am still trying to sell my house at Tucson." He said he really shouldn't be saying anything but it was looking a lot like there would NOT be an A-7D Fighter Weapons School.

It was very soon after this that I got a call from the base housing people at Nellis saying that my name had come up on the list to get a house on base. I either had to accept a house or go to the bottom of the list. The house I was to get was the one that the former F-100 Fighter Weapons School Squadron Commander was living in. He had a metal shed out in the backyard and he either had to remove it or I had to accept it (actually buy it from him). So I bought it.

Then, sometime during the second week of December, TAC Personnel called again and gave me additional information. They were still unsure about the fact of the actual starting up of the A-7D weapons school, but he had another very interesting proposal for me. Since it appeared (Personnel looking at my records) that I would be picked to go to an advanced school pretty soon and there was a slot to the Armed Forces Staff College (Norfolk, VA) in January available, did I want to just take that assignment? Thinking it over, I decided that would be a good thing to do.

This was a bit complicated because I had gone PCS from Davis Monthan to Nellis within the past year (therefore I should not have been eligible for another PCS within that fiscal year), but since I had not gotten "Dislocation Allowance" for moving the family (remember they were still at Tucson) I could actually get another PCS assignment. Remember I also had a house on base at Nellis!! That was pretty easy to solve. Housing gave me the name of the next guy on the list for a house and I got in touch with him and sold him the metal shed and just like that, I did not have a base house anymore.

Took my camera along one day when I was Range Officer. This flight is just about to break for right range, left traffic.

The range mission complete, they joined up and gave me a fly by for this picture.

One flight in late December was a fun flight, and one I won't forget. It was a two-ship to the Tactics Range. Charlie Parker and I were just going out to have a fun time at the range. We decided to try very high dive bombing. We would climb up to 25,000 feet and try to get 50 or more degrees of dive and release the bombs before 10,000 feet. The funny part of this mission relates to the systems in the aircraft. The Heads Up Display would show you a lot of things. The Flight Path Marker was a little circle with a short line on it that made it look like a small airplane. This would display just exactly where the aircraft was going. It also displayed a lot of other bombing information when you had the switches set to drop bombs.

This day, because we were going up to 25,000 feet, we were getting into the "Jet Stream." The direction we had to make our run-in gave us a 90 degree crosswind of 90 knot winds. This of course caused the displayed information to be almost off the wind screen. In normal dive bomb, you release the bombs around 3,000 feet AGL. With us trying to release at 10,000 feet, it was real difficult to get the displayed information back into the proper place and we were really guessing just where to release to try to hit the target. We never did get very close to the target, and it was so funny waiting such a long time to actually see the bomb hit the ground after you released it. The thing we learned from this mission was: don't try to dive bomb with that much crosswind or at that high of a release altitude.

I think that was my last mission, so it was time to sign out from the A-7D Fighter Weapons School at Nellis, go back to Tucson and pack up the family, and go to Norfolk, VA. Don't remember just exactly when but we did sell the house in Tucson.

The six months at the Armed Forces Staff College were OK, I guess. Probably the best of the staff schools to go to (less bull sh…!). Normally your assignment out of a school is a staff job at a Headquarters somewhere. Since I had gotten the school assignment so late, Air Force Personnel did not have a staff slot to put me in. They just gave me back to Tactical Air Command Personnel. When I was talking to them, it became obvious that they had only one place for me. It seems that there really was an A-7D Fighters Weapons School and they needed an instructor. So it was back to flying the A-7D at Nellis AFB, NV.

The school was up and running and I was assigned as the Air-to-Air platform instructor. The A-7D was not a real dog fight aircraft. Its primary role was Air-to-Ground. This of course meant that you were normally carrying a load of bombs to a target and getting the bombs ON TARGET was your mission. The Air-to-Air tactics we taught were defensive tactics. That is, you did your best to defeat any attack by enemy fighters while keeping your bombs and still getting to the target to deliver them. This was difficult to teach the students, because when a fighter pilot gets attacked by another fighter, it just seems the thing to do is get into a dog fight. More than once there were long discussions about Air-to-Air and just how we should do it in the A-7D.

Tactical Air Command had formed an Aggressor Squadron at Nellis (flying T-38 aircraft) which studied and flew Soviet Air-to-Air tactics. The Aggressors would go to a fighter base and fly missions against the pilots, teaching them just how to counter what they might see in the real world. As the A-7D Air-to-Air instructor, I went to the four bases that had an A-7D wing to help the pilots get ready to fly against the Aggressors. This was a really fun time.

I don't remember just which base I visited first so will start in the East and go West.

The 354th TFW was at Myrtle Beach in South Carolina. There was one thing that really stands out in my memory about the flights at Myrtle Beach. The area we used for Air-to-Air was out over the water. This was the first time I had flown air-to-air over water and it was a real learning experience. When you are over land, it is very easy to see the land/sky division. When you are over water, if there is the least bit of haze, seeing the horizon can sometimes be very difficult. It takes away your concentration of flying against the other aircraft, because you must also keep track of just where the sky and ocean are. Other than that, it was a fun TDY.

The memorable flight at England AFB, LA, was kind of a funny incident. While on one of the flights, the angle of attack vane on the side of the aircraft broke off. This is no big deal, except I had become so used to landing the A-7D using the flight path indicator and the angle of attack cue that I couldn't remember what airspeed to use for landing!! I am sure that I landed "Hot" because I did not want to be slow and land in the over run.

The trip to Davis Monthan AFB, AZ, for the A-7D spin up for the Aggressors was very interesting. There were a bunch of the pilots at DM that I had flown with, of course, and I got to ride in the T-38 aircraft that was flying against the A-7Ds. When we attacked the four-ship of A-7Ds, the guy leading had briefed his flight to all "break" in different directions. The one on the left went left, leader pulled up, #4 on the right broke to the right, and #3 did a "split S." The Aggressor pilot flying the aircraft I was riding in was dumbfounded as he had never seen anything like that before. Of course he just went after the easiest target and we had a great debrief.

One other funny thing about my TDY to DM for this mission. When briefing the entire wing on the tactics to use against the Aggressors, the Wing Commander (who had flown the F-86) could not quite accept the idea we should fly defensive tactics. As I said earlier, fighter pilots want to go after anyone attacking them and, having flown the very maneuverable F-86, the Wing Commander thought he should turn into the fight and turn with the Aggressor. Not the thing to do if you are at a big disadvantage in maneuverability.

In October 1973, I went TDY to Korat AB in Thailand to assist the A-7D units there in starting dissimilar Air-to-Air training. The A7-D's would fly against the F-4's that were stationed at Korat also. I don't remember exactly but think there were two Squadrons from the 354th Wing from Myrtle Beach and one Squadron that was stationed at Korat doing the Air Rescue (Sandy) mission.

The one really interesting flight that occurred during this TDY was actually funny. When I did the big briefing to all the pilots, one of the things I stressed was the fact that when you were out doing Air-to-Air against a similar aircraft (like A-7D against A-7D) it did not seem difficult to calmly call out the "bogie" when you saw it. I said that for some reason when it was a dissimilar aircraft you sometimes got a bit tongue-tied. For this reason, I told them to take just a second to think about what you were going to say BEFORE you started to transmit. Sure enough, on the first flight I was leading, one of the guys on my wing made just such a radio call. He spotted the F-4 coming in from our four o'clock position (my right side, and my wingman was on the left) and called for me to "BREAK." Well, when you make that call you HAVE to include a direction, either left or right. I heard the break call but nothing about where the bandit was. Finally I had to holler at the wingman, "Where is the bandit??" Everything worked out and it was a very good learning tool for the debrief. The wingman acknowledged his error and told all the other pilots about how different it was when the other aircraft was a dissimilar airplane.

If you have been paying attention, you will have noticed that none of my assignments were "normal." That is, for some reason they were never as long as they should have been. This assignment wasn't any different. Somewhere around April 1974 I got a call from TAC Personnel telling me that my Overseas Return Date (the last time you had a PCS assignment overseas) was reaching a point where they were going to have to send me for a one-year remote assignment. I asked just what they had in mind and they said something about going to Turkey. What kind of assignment would that be, I asked? A Command Post Duty Officer. This of course was a non-flying job. Not something I wanted to do for a year!! I asked if there weren't something or some place I could go where I would be flying. Sure enough, if I volunteered for an A-7D assignment to the Sandy Squadron at Korat, I would go as the Wing Weapons Officer and that was a flying job. Not much choice. I volunteered.

It was either late May or early June that I left Nellis and went TDY to England AFB for A-7D Search and Rescue training. This was some training for guys that had never done this type mission before and for me, it was just a fun flying TDY. Only flight I really remember was on one of the days we flew, the weather got real hazy at England AFB with the visibility down to about a half mile. The flight of four was three "students" and one IP. Since this was a "Training Course" they treated "Students" as if they were young pilots right out of pilot training. The three "students" in the flight all had a heck of a lot of flying time, including a lot of weather flying, and also had flown the A-7D for maybe a year or two. They were going to make the flight divert to Barksdale AFB where the weather was clear. Before we were actually ready to land, the weather cleared up enough and we did land at England AFB. All of us, including the IP had a big laugh at the debrief.

An interesting side note of this TDY: Lois went with me, and one of the weekends we were there we went to New Orleans and had a great time. We tried all the famous restaurants and ate ourselves sick (among other things).

Chapter 13

A year in Thailand flying the A-7D

Then it was off to Korat AB, Thailand, and another year of wishing my life away. The flying at Korat was really great. I have several flights that made this assignment one of the best.

One of the first things about an assignment to the A-7's at Korat that needs to be told is the introduction the guys in the squadron gave you about going to downtown Korat City. There was one place in particular where we would go to party. The first trip downtown, a couple of the guys would get you to come along with them in one of the local taxi cabs. These were some really old cars and were not kept in very good condition. They would have you sit in the front seat and keep asking the driver to go faster. On my first trip downtown I was about as scared as I have ever been! The guy was driving like a wild man, honking the horn at everyone on the road, passing and cutting in front of other cars, and just missing Sam Lars [*From the Internet: Sam lars are three-wheeled tricycles with a covered seat in the back that are powered by the individual driving them. Nowadays they tend to be a nuisance and very dangerous weaving in and out of modern day traffic. They should be avoided unless a photographic opportunity presents itself, or you are very sure of your destination. For those driving at night be aware that Sam lars are quite common and have no lights or reflective objects so they are extremely difficult to see.*] We made it and the guys in back were laughing like anything at me sitting "white knuckled" in the front. I think that was the only time I ever took a taxi cab into town.

One other interesting "event" the squadron had was getting downtown by using the local bus system. It was pretty good and VERY cheap. You, however, had to show up at the drinking place with the ticket you got when you boarded the bus. If you didn't, you had to buy a round of drinks. We did this one night and after a lot of beer, I decided to go back to the base. Seems no one else wanted to go at that time. Now we normally NEVER went to or from the base to downtown ALONE. We always went with at least one other guy. Well, I had had just enough to drink that I decided that I would go back by myself. I walked out of the place and started walking toward the bus stop. It was only a little over two blocks from where we were drinking.

PK with A-7D

As I got within about a block of the bus stop, I saw this green bus pull in. It was the one going back to the base. I started running and got there just in time to jump on the bus before it pulled out. On a normal trip back to the base, the bus would go from the bus stop about a block, make a left turn, go over some railroad tracks and proceed about a couple blocks, then make a right turn; Then it was a straight run back to the base gate.

On this night the bus sure enough made the left turn and went over the railroad tracks, but then it just kept going straight. I then looked around and found I was the ONLY non-Thai on the bus!! Oh boy, I wondered to myself, just where is this bus going??? I thought, well, I guess I can just stay on it until it gets back to the bus stop in town.

All the Thais on the bus were looking at me wondering just what I was doing on that bus. After about 20 minutes and several stops, it made a stop at the Thai

Gate into the base. (I had gone into and out of this gate several times when I was TDY to Korat doing the air-to-air training when I was at the Fighter Weapons School.) I knew where I was, got off the bus, and had quite a walk to get to the US side of the base. Never did such a stupid thing again.

Another incident about downtown Korat City: one night there were 10 of us at this one place having a few drinks when someone came up with the idea to go to another drinking place he knew. We went out and got three Sam Lars and decided to have a race to the other place. Last one there buys the drinks! Sam Lars normally only hold TWO people. We had four in one of them, and three in the other two. I was in the one with the four "big Americans" and we kept telling our driver/"Motor" that if he got us there first, he would get a BIG tip. He was really working hard and going as fast as he could. Gary Lape was sitting on the side of the Sam Lar on the same side I was sitting. For whatever reason, he tried to change positions to get more comfortable, and fell out of the Sam Lar!!! He went flat on his face and the driver put on the brakes. He never got to a full stop and Gary didn't suffer even a scrape. He was up and running and jumped back into the Sam Lar. It couldn't have been two seconds AFTER he was back in the Sam Lar that a bus went roaring right past us!! Had it been just a couple seconds earlier, no telling what would have happened. Don't even want to think about it!!!

Sam Lar with driver/motor standing by.

There are three flights during the year at Korat that really stand out in my memory.

Even though the air war in Vietnam was at a halt, we still had aircraft in Thailand that could be called upon to attack if necessary. We practiced flying a "Package" to the North. A package was a large number of aircraft, some flying with bombs and some flying air cover for the bombers. During one of these practice missions, F-4s from both Udorn and Ubon were flying over northern Thailand, and I was scheduled with a single clean A-7D to act as a MiG-17 aggressor. I was on a separate radio frequency being directed by radar to intercept the strike package. Just as I was getting in an AIM-9 firing position, the F-4s flying CAP (Combat Air Patrol) saw me and attacked. I observed them coming in at my four o'clock position and made a small turn into them. I was again lining up for a missile shot when I saw the attacking F-4s getting into my six o'clock position. I made a hard turn to the right, and it was TOO hard! The airplane departed. (As explained earlier, a departure means the aircraft snaps very hard into an out of control maneuver.) The normal thing was to put your hands up on the canopy, take your feet off the rudders, and let the aircraft just do what it was going to do. Again, the normal thing was, it would do whatever maneuver it was doing TWICE, and then you would be able to take control and start flying again. This time was different! The aircraft did whatever maneuver THREE times (something I had never seen before) and appeared that it might be going into the maneuver for the fourth time. I thought, "Wait a minute, it isn't supposed to be doing this!!" I was just moving my hands and feet to try to apply some corrective controls when the nose dropped and the airplane started flying again. I told the controller that I thought it best if I took the airplane back to Korat. I wasn't sure if I had over g'd or not.

Also, the lead of the F-4s that were attacking me was the Wing Commander at Udorn and he thought I had gone into a spin and probably wasn't going to recover. He was broadcasting this on his frequency for all the world to hear. When I landed back at Korat, I was met by a host of people, the Wing DO, my Squadron Commander, and several others, wanting to know WHAT HAPPENED?? When they told me about the F-4 guys thinking I was in a spin, I asked if any of them had ever seen an A-7D depart? I told them that is what happened, even though it was the most dramatic departure I had ever ridden through. Maintenance did a complete inspection of the aircraft and found nothing wrong. It was a fun ride and a learning moment for sure.

The next really memorable flight during this tour was when the United States decided to evacuate the Embassy in Phnom Penh, Cambodia, in April 1975.

[*Wikipedia: On New Year's Day 1975, Communist troops launched an offensive which, in 117 days of the hardest fighting of the war, collapsed the Khmer Republic. The Lon Nol government in Phnom Penh surrendered on April 17, 1975, just five (5) days after the US mission evacuated Cambodia.*]

It was on April 12 that we flew orbits over Phnom Penh while helicopters picked up the Americans from the Embassy. They actually used the tennis courts as landing pads. We never were asked to deliver any ordnance.

The part about this flight that I think is "funny" is how we loaded the aircraft. Since we were not going to be using any "heavy" stuff, like bombs, we decided that we would carry rockets. Normally we would carry four pods, two on each wing. As Wing Weapons Officer, I decided we would carry three on each wing for a total of six pods on each aircraft. We had to borrow extra launchers from the F-4 unit there at Korat but were able to do it. After the mission I researched the flight manual and discovered that they had never certified the A-7D to carry rocket pods on three stations on each wing. I guess no harm, no foul.

The next "incident" should have been a flight. Things were getting very dicey in South Vietnam as well as Cambodia. There was a contingency to evacuate the Embassy and all Americans out of Saigon when it became necessary. The plans for this were called "Operation Frequent Wind."

[*Wikipedia: Operation Frequent Wind was the evacuation by helicopter of American civilians and "at-risk" Vietnamese from Saigon, South Vietnam, on 29–30 April 1975 during the last days of the Vietnam War. More than 7,000 people were evacuated from various points in Saigon, and the airlift left a number of enduring images. Preparations for the airlift already existed as a standard procedure for American embassies. In the beginning of March, fixed-wing aircraft began evacuating civilians through neighboring countries. By mid-April, contingency plans were in place and preparations were underway for a possible helicopter evacuation. As the imminent collapse of Saigon became evident, Task Force 76 was assembled off the coast near Vung Tau to support a helicopter evacuation and provide air support if required. Air support was not needed as the North Vietnamese recognized that interfering with the evacuation could provoke a strong reaction from US forces.*

On 28 April, Tan Son Nhut Air Base came under artillery fire and attack from Vietnamese People's Air Force aircraft. The fixed-wing evacuation was terminated and Operation Frequent Wind commenced.]

The previous paragraphs from Wikipedia notes that Air Support was not required, but I am here to tell you that there WAS air support orbiting overhead as they were carrying out the evacuation.

Anyway, the wing at Korat got the word to prepare aircraft to support the operation. It was a very orderly plan and scheduled to start early in the day. At the time I did not know just what screwed it up, but after we briefed to go, we were told to hold. Some of the F-4 flights from Korat did get launched about noon and my flight was told to launch about 15:00 hours. We started up and were taxiing out, just about to the arming area, when we got a call from the Command Post to abort. I was somewhat upset about all the delay and decided that before I did abort, the Command Post would have to authenticate. (The guy on duty was a good friend and his reply to my request to authenticate was, "Aaah, come on, PK.") He did in fact authenticate and we taxied back. Later as I heard about all the weather over Saigon and all the confusion going on down there, I was really happy we DID NOT go!!

I am going to insert a short paragraph from the Wikipedia write-up that explains just WHY the operation did not go as planned. Earlier I talked about the book *One Day too Long* and the fact that a civilian (the Ambassador) got into the decision making process and screwed it up. The same thing happened concerning the evacuation of Saigon. [Wikipedia has a really good write-up of Operation Frequent Wind.]

[*At 07:00 on 29 April, Major General Smith advised Ambassador Martin that fixed wing evacuations should cease and that Operation Frequent Wind, the helicopter evacuation of US personnel and at-risk Vietnamese, should commence. Ambassador Martin refused to accept General Smith's recommendation and instead insisted on visiting Tan Son Nhut to survey the situation for himself. At 10:00 Ambassador Martin confirmed General Smith's assessment and at 10:48 he contacted Washington to recommend Option 4, the helicopter evacuation. Finally at 10:51 the order was given by CINCPAC to commence Option 4; however, due to confusion in the chain of command, General Carey did not receive the execute order until 12:15. At 08:00 Lieutenant General Minh, commander of the VNAF and 30 of his staff arrived at the DAO compound demanding evacuation, signifying the complete loss of VNAF command and control.*]

The last of the flights during my year at Korat was a really memorable one! The following paragraph from Wikipedia explains what occurred.

The Mayaguez incident, which took place between the Khmer Rouge and the United States from May 12–15, 1975, was the last official battle of the Vietnam War. The names of the Americans killed, as well as those of three U.S. Marines who were left behind on the island of Koh Tang after the battle and who were subsequently executed by the Khmer Rouge, are the last names on the Vietnam Veterans Memorial. The merchant ship's crew, whose seizure at sea had prompted the U.S. attack, had been released in good health, unknown to the U.S. Marines or the

U.S. command of the operation, before the Marines attacked. It was the only known engagement between U.S. ground forces and the Khmer Rouge.

The A-7D Squadron at Korat played a big part of the operation. Several of my good friends flew sorties during the first days of the operation and actually did sink a gunboat. [Go to Wikipedia and search for Mayaguez Incident. There is a really good write up about what happened.] We were all set to go on May 15th. After a mass briefing each flight briefed. (I must admit that I was really confused about some aspects of this operation after the briefing. For example, until I was airborne, I did not realize that the Marines would be coming in by helicopter; rather, I thought from the briefing they would assault the island from landing craft.)

I was leading a flight of four that would be carrying the riot control agent (tear gas). We all went to the aircraft, but before my flight could taxi, we were told to come back to the operations building and wait. About an hour later, we did arm and launch. Going toward Koh Tang Island and listening to the radio chatter, it was obvious that some of the helicopters had been shot down. We got overhead and were orbiting at about 20,000 feet observing the other A-7Ds trying to help the Marines who were being pinned down on the island.

The lead flight ran low on fuel and headed back to a tanker and my flight was called in to do the searching to try to pinpoint exactly where the Marines were. I only made a couple passes and was told to go back to altitude and hold. After we were back at altitude and in a holding pattern for about 10 minutes, we got a call to strafe the Mayaguez. WHAT??

After a call to make sure that was really what they wanted my flight to do, it was determined that we should descend and put the tear gas on the ship. During the flight briefing, we had discussed the fact that the munition we were carrying was designed to dispense the tear gas after it hit the ground. Well, this wouldn't work since the ship was sitting in water. I figured out an altitude at which we could deliver the tear gas and have the canisters open BEFORE they hit the water. We made our run in right down the ship and I had the other three aircraft in a loose wing-tip formation. I had briefed that I would call when to start the release. This we did and when we pulled up to see the results, there was a perfect box of tear gas all around the Mayaguez.

A few words from Wikipedia about the results: *At 06:13 on May 15, the first phase of the operation began with the transfer by three HH-53s of Marines to the Holt. As the Holt slowly came alongside, USAF A-7D aircraft saturated the Mayaguez with tear gas munitions. Equipped with gas masks, the Marines at 07:25 hours then conducted one of the few hostile ship-to-ship boardings by the U.S. Navy since the American Civil War, securing the vessel after an hour-long search, finding it empty.*

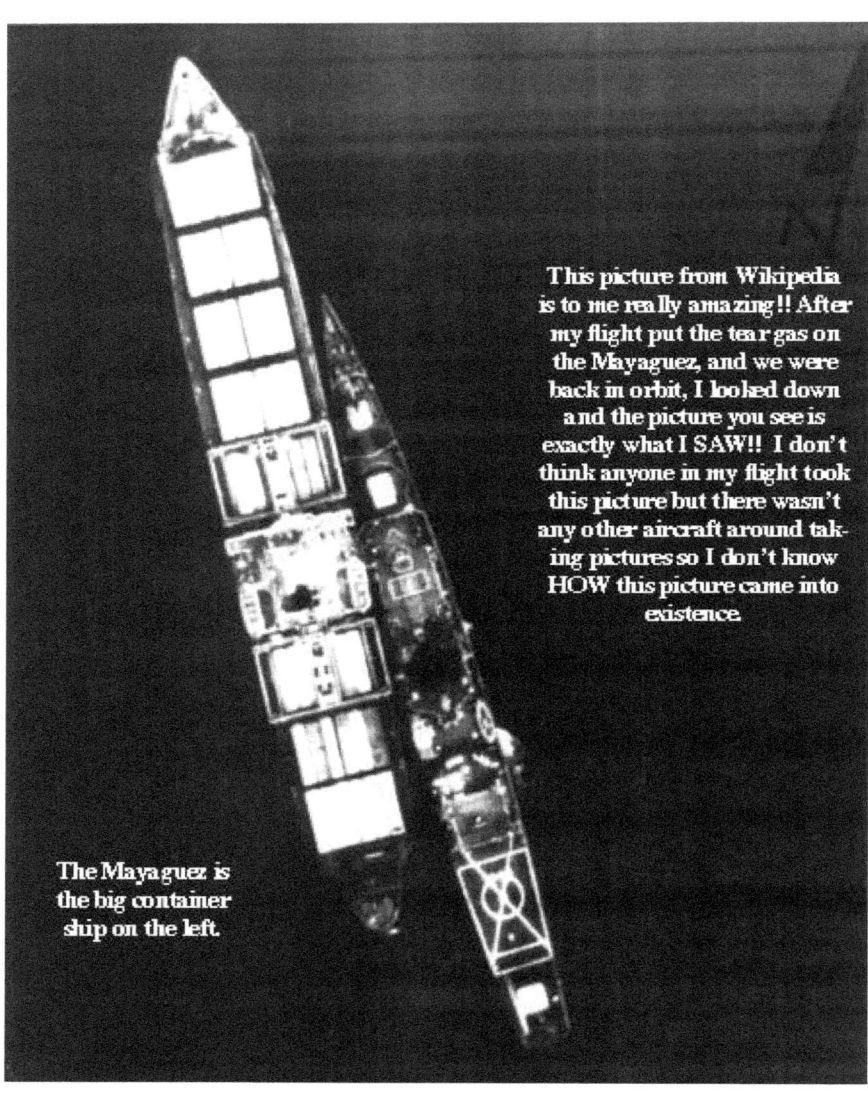

The Mayaguez is the big container ship on the left.

This picture from Wikipedia is to me really amazing!! After my flight put the tear gas on the Mayaguez, and we were back in orbit, I looked down and the picture you see is exactly what I SAW!! I don't think anyone in my flight took this picture but there wasn't any other aircraft around taking pictures so I don't know HOW this picture came into existence.

Although it doesn't say it in the Wikipedia report, we were told that the Marines did find warm meals sitting on tables in the galley of the Mayaguez.

After we delivered the tear gas, each aircraft jettisoned the empty pods, climbed to about 10,000 feet and started an orbit over the Mayaguez. I called for a fuel check and discovered that I had a fuel problem. The forward tank was really low and if something didn't happen real soon, I would flame out. (I say "Forward tank" but it was probably really the Sump Tank.)

Now to explain what happened: just before we descended to deliver the tear gas I called for the flight to go to "Combat Fuel." There was a lever just below the left canopy rail that had three positions. The one you always flew in was "Normal." If you went to Combat, you moved it to the first detent, which was the "Combat" position. This would depressurize some of the fuel lines, making it less hazardous if you took a hit. There was also another position called Alternate which was all the way forward. This position was used if you had a fuel transfer problem and it would allow fuel to gravity feed. You really only used this position if you had transfer problems. As IP's we always told the students, "LOOK at what you are doing because in a moment of stress you can screw up switch settings very easily." Well, I should have taken my own advice!! I had gone all the way forward.

When I discovered that the forward tank was really low, I declared an emergency, and I and my #2 started climbing toward Korat. I went through what emergency procedures I could remember (one thing I did do was move the fuel lever back to Normal) and tried to get the heart rate back from extremely fast. The forward tank seemed to stay at the same level all during the climb. When we leveled off at 20,000 feet and I pulled the throttle back, I watched the forward tank start to fill up. I got out the check list and started looking at fuel emergencies. Sure enough, I discover that if you fly around at high power settings and that fuel lever is in the forward position, you'll run the forward tank dry. (I remember very clearly sitting there in the cockpit, looking over at that lever, and saying to myself, "Did you put that thing all the way forward or did you stop in Combat?" It wasn't long before I convinced myself I had gone to the Alternate position!) DON'T DO THAT!!! I told my wingman that everything looks OK because I am pretty sure I had the fuel lever in the wrong position, called off the emergency, and we went back to Korat with my tail between my legs. A red-faced Wing Weapons Officer got up at the next pilot's meeting to enforce what we had taught: Make sure where you put the switches, LOOK to make sure.

What I am about to put in here (The third of August 2015) is a write up by the Editor of the *THE INTAKE*, the official Journal for the Super Saber Society. It will of course, contain a lot of what I have just written so will be a repeat. The difference, of course, is a bit of "just how I remembered it" and how others remember it is quite different. Here it is, with permission of the SSS Editor.

War is hell, isn't it?
By R. Medley Gatewood

As told in Issue 27's Part I and Issue 28's Part II of this series, our reason for publishing these articles was to rebut a claim that the A-7D pilots of the 353rd TFS made when they came home from Korat in 1973. They said that they had "... dropped the last bomb and made the last strafing pass of the war." (That "war" meaning the Vietnam War and its outliers in other parts of SEA.) Clearly, the content of both Parts I and II support the notion that the Mayaguez Incident was the last battle of the Vietnam hot war chapter of the much longer Cold War era. Having established the fact that the 353rd's claim was overcome by events, our purpose for Part III of this series is simply to close the series and make room for more Intake-quality articles on other subjects of interest.

But before we do that, we're going to share two additional recollections about the incident from three other SSS members. First we hear from PK Kimminau and Gary Lape who was in the thick of things in their SLUFs early in the morning of the 15th of May, the last day of combat; and then we'll hear from John Wagner, who was cooling his heels near the end of a four-year staff tour at USPACOM HQ in Hawaii working in the J-5 shop (Plans & Policy) when the Mayaguez Incident came down. Then, we'll close with the second half of the Time Magazine article titled The Captain's Log: A Tale of Terror, the first half of which we used to close Part II. Hang on, here we go! Ed.

15 May 1975: The Day of Chaos

Everyone I've talked to about the events of this day, who were there, has used the word chaos somewhere in their recollections. PK Kimminau, who was the 388th TFW Weapons Officer, led "Phil" Flight this day, with Gary Lape as his Element Lead. Together their inputs provide us with rare insight into that chaos in the form of a written account about Phil Flight. PK says he doesn't recall writing it himself and believes it's a copy of a report written by Intell folks who attended the extensive Phil Flight debriefing when they all got back to Korat. It's a fascinating read, and we deem it historic enough to use it in its entirety.

Be advised, it is indeed rich in detail, and filled with chaos, a frequent numerator of the "Fog of War"! To break up the sometimes chaotic narrative, we've inserted topical titles to help keep you oriented. Read on. Ed.

Phil Flight Debrief Phil 1 – Maj. Kimminau, Phil 2 – Lt. Col. Orf, Phil 3 – Maj. Lape, Phil 4 – Capt. Middagh

The Easy Part for Phil

Attended the 0200 mass briefing. Briefed the flight on procedures and tactics to be used in the target area in a normal flight briefing. The tactics briefed were those to be used to deliver CBU-30 [CS = Tear Gas], as this was the ordnance Phil Flight was fragged for. (2 CBU-30 per aircraft plus 20 mm) Proceeded to aircraft for a 0450 takeoff. At taxi time, Command Post advised Phil they were on at least a 1 hour hold. After proper authentication, the aircraft were shut down and topped off with fuel. At 0530, a launch ASAP call from the Command Post was relayed to Phil. At 0555, Phil Flight was airborne. Join-up, climb out, cruise was normal.

At 0615, at FL 250 and 30 NM from feet wet, calls by Karen Flight [A-7Ds], one calling Knife 23 and "May Day" survivors on the beach were heard. After several calls, Karen finally got "May Day" to relay his correct call sign which was Knife 31. As we proceeded to Koh Tang Island (after checking in with Cricket [Airborne Command and Control C-130] on secondary freq), Karen set up the SAR effort and suppressed ground fire. [Karen was responding to the instant mayhem going on at Koh Tang Island after the Marine's USAF helicopter assisted assault on the island at about 0600 turned into a really bad SNAFU!] At 0625, Phil Flight arrived overhead K.T. Island and went into prebriefed formations at 13.4 units AOA to conserve fuel and observe the events. (Formation was wing man in 2,000' fighting wing looking mainly for the other aircraft, and the second element in trail 6,000-8,000'.)

The scene was: One helo on the beach of a cove on the eastern side of the island burning, and another on the northern shore of the same cove with the tail rotor missing. Karen Flight was conducting a SAR and suppressing ground fire being directed at Knife 31. (Three survivors in the water using the burning helo for what cover they could.) During the first orbit, Phil 3 advised Phil 1 that a boat was approaching from the north and was about 20 miles out. Phil 3 was told to contact Cricket to find out if the boat was friendly.

The Pace Picks Up

At about 0640 – 0645, Phil advised Karen that he (Phil) was on scene and available if needed. Karen advised he still had 10–15 minutes fuel. Cricket advised Phil 1 to contact Bingo Shoes Golf-01 [B.S. Golf-01] and to work with him. Phil went to FM and after several calls established contact with B.S. Golf-01 [an element of the Marine Ground Security Force, Golf Company, 1st Platoon's Commander.] He and his troops were in place on the beach in a cove on the western side of K.T. Island. At this time, Karen Flight came up on Golf-01's frequency. Phil advised Karen of Golf-01's location, and Karen then proceeded to assist Golf-01, in addition to Knife 23 and 31. Two other helos came in to the beach in the western cove in an attempt to insert Golf-01's remaining troops. The helos called on guard that they were receiving ground fire. Karen Flight strafed the ground fire. At about this time, Karen advised Phil that he was at Bingo fuel and after as much briefing as possible, turned the on scene command over to Phil.

During the descent to take over on scene command, Phil 1 observed a boat coming from the north and only about five miles north of the [stationary] Mayaguez. Phil 1 asked 3 if this was the same boat he had checked out with Cricket and 3 advised Phil 1 that this was the same boat, which was friendly. This "boat" was the ship USS Holt, a Destroyer Escort, with Marines aboard. The Holt's mission was to get their Marines onboard the Mayaguez. The farewell briefings from Karen and the observations during the high orbiting, plus the news of the Holt and its mission, were more than enough data for Phil 1 to comfortably assume on scene command, which he did.

Phil 1 was aware of Knife 23 and 31's positions, but he was not sure of Golf-01's position. After three dry passes, Golf-01's position was positively identified. Just about then, Golf-01 called that he was taking heavy auto weapons fire. An attempt was made to establish the position of this fire. After a dry pass over Golf-01's position, the ground fire directed at G-01's position abated enough that Golf-01 felt no more immediate danger. At this time (about 0700 and only 8–10 minutes after taking on scene command of the SAR from Karen), another A-7D flight lead, Denis 1, contacted Phil and advised him that Cricket had a different mission for Phil Flight. Phil asked Denis his position. Denis was close enough to see Phil, so after pointing out Golf-01's position to Denis 1, Phil 1 turned the on scene command for the SAR over to Denis 1 and went up to 12,000 feet to hold at 13.4 units AOA. (Note: No attempt to point out Knife 23 or 31's positions to Denis was made because it was assumed that Denis knew those locations.)

The New Mission(s) for Phil
After holding for about 10 minutes, Cricket advised Phil that the new mission was to put his CBU-30 on the Mayaguez! Time was 0714. Phil 2 was put on the right wing 50' out, and a level pass at 500 feet, 450 KIAS, was made. The system was set up to dispense from both CBU-30 pods on each aircraft. Phil 1 and 2's CBU

30 went down the right center of the ship. Phil 3 and 4, about one minute behind, placed their CBU-30 smack in the middle of the ship. Cricket was advised that the CBU-30 passes were completed at 0716. The USS Holt was in position and moved in on the starboard side of the Mayaguez. After Phil had reported mission complete and jettison of the empty CBR-30 pods to Cricket, they told Phil to hold high over the Mayaguez, in case their strafe might be needed.

As the USS Holt pulled alongside the Mayaguez, Cricket advised Phil to strafe the Mayaguez. Phil 1 asked for confirmation/clarification about this astounding request, and after receiving it [they wanted the strafe to be in the water opposite the Holt for warning purposes] was rolling in from 8,000 feet when Denis 1 called, saying HE was "IN" for the warning strafe runs on the Mayaguez! On the heels of that transmission, Phil 3 asked Phil 1 to check with Cricket to see what part of the ship they were to strafe. Cricket said to hold off till he determined the answer to that question. Meanwhile, Phil observed Denis Flight (three aircraft) pass by the Mayaguez.

[*Break, Break! Keep in mind that this document is a transcript of the Phil Flight debriefing, some hours after the events, and may not be completely accurate—on the parts of all or some of the four pilots, or the recording Intell folks. Furthermore, keep in mind that Chaos was the word of the day; it applied to what was going on with the crew in the back end of the Cricket bird, as well as in and between multiple flights of multiple types of friendly airpower AND sea power. And as it played out, it was crystal clear that all players were NOT completely briefed in on what and when and who was doing all sorts of tactical things in a fast paced and continuously changing field of battle! The Intell Report continues...*]

[Almost like a "time out,"] Element Lead Phil 3 asked about fuel. After the flight fuel check, Phil 1 advised Cricket that Phil 3 and 4 were heading to the tankers. At about 0730, Phil 1 heard Denis 1 advise Cricket that he and Denis 3 were going to the tankers, and that Denis 2 was solo and acting as on scene commander.

Phil 1 and 2 checked in with Denis 2 on FM to advise him that they were at 8,000' holding and had 20 mm available. About two orbits later, Phil 1's Fuel Low warning light came on and he and 2 started a climb, headed via Direct toward U-Tapao RTAFB in southern Thailand for an emergency landing. En route, Phil 1 determined the cause for the Fuel Low light, fixed the problem, and he and Phil 2 skipped U-Tapao, RTBing to Korat.

[*Thus ended Phil 1 and 2's early morning mission. But, Phil 3 and 4 remained, on their way to the tankers—and subsequent bouts with Chaos in the K. T. Island battlefield that had turned into a full-fledged SAR and Extraction effort.*]

Phil 3 and 4 proceeded to their assigned tankers and on-loaded 4,000 lbs. apiece. While Phil 3 and 4 were on-loading, Denis 1 and 3 having departed, Denis 2 arrived at the tanker.

Meanwhile, Back at K. T. Island

En route to K.T. Island, Cricket advised that a SAR was in progress on UHF 282.8, but Phil 3 and 4 heard no activity on that freq and reported that to Cricket. They advised Phil 3 and 4 to contact Golf-02 on FM and provide him with needed support. Denis Flight was just departing the scene when Phil 3 contacted Golf-02, Golf Company's, 2nd Platoon's Commander, who had landed with his troops while Phil 3 and 4 were refueling.

Much time was wasted trying to accurately pinpoint Golf-02's position. He was taking fire and needed immediate support, but Phil 3 said he would not strafe until he could pinpoint the southern perimeter of Golf-02's positon (fire was coming at them from the south). No smoke, mirror or red panels were available to mark, so Phil 3 asked Golf-02 to put some automatic weapons tracer fire into the sea near his position, which they did. Phil saw that marking fire and made multiple dry passes to pinpoint Golf-02 before attempting defensive hot passes.

After 8 - 10 combined dry passes by Phil 3 and 4, the area for the needed strafing was agreed upon by Phil 3 and Golf-02. At this point, Cricket cut in and gave clearance to expend on the agreed upon area. Phil 3 and 4 armed their M-61 Gatling guns, and as Phil 3 turned base and rolled out on a long final, Bingo Shoes Golf (BSG-06, Lt. Col. Austin, the Commander of the HQ Element of the 2nd Battalion, 9th Marines, the last unit to land on K.T. Island in the first wave of the helicopter assault) cut in on the radio and said that the area Phil was flying over and was preparing to strafe was his location—another LZ to the south of Golf-02 and Golf-01. [*Good grief, more Chaos!*]

Phil 3 then went to work with BSG-06 and Golf-02 to try and determine how far apart they were, to see if Phil could strafe between them. It appeared to Phil that BSG-06 and Golf-02 were much closer together than they thought they were. (BSG-06 advised that he was taking automatic weapons fire from the north and had seen rounds hitting the sea water up that way: Phil 3 was convinced that these were the marking rounds fired by Golf-02!)

Phil 3 advised Cricket that he now had Golf-02's position identified fairly accurately, but was not sure of BSG-06's positon. Phil 3 further advised Cricket that he thought Golf-02 and BSG-06 were close enough that they might be engaged with each other, assuming each other activities to be enemy activity!

Cricket agreed that this might be the case and it was decided NOT to expend. [*Thank goodness, now we're facing fratricide!*] Phil 3 and 4 hit Bingo and RTBed. Denis 1 and 3 arrived back on the scene as Phil 3 and 4 were out-bound and there was no time available to brief them on the current situation at that point in time.

Official Lessons Learned
[*This is the end of the Intell gathered notes from the Phil Flight debriefing session after the flight reunited at Korat, except for a notation of four "Problems" as follows: 1) Tanker was too far away – over 100 NM. 2) Cricket didn't offer any type of situation briefing prior to passing Phil Flight over to the Marine GSFs. 3) No continuity in passing on scene command from flight-to-flight. Ground situation had to be re-established between each flight leader and the GSF Commander – much time wasted! 4) The on scene commander must be very careful when he passes the command to a new flight. NO assumptions should be made! The "old" on scene commander must ensure that the "new" on scene commander understands the situation fully.*]

So ended Phil Flight's four pilots' direct and collective knowledge of further events in the K.T. Island Theater of Operations that final day of the Mayaguez Incident. Our purpose here is not to give a full report on all the combat activities of that final day, but rather, by example, give an idea of the complexity of a slice of the operations and how difficult it was to provide adequate command and control, at all levels of authority, when the whole day is ruled by Chaos and unexpected, unwanted (or uncommunicated) developments. Thanks to PK and Gary Lape, and other Phil Flight and Denis Flight members who contributed to our report on these examples. [**This is the end of the part of the SSS Journal write-up that had to do with my part in the incident.**]

PK gets a drink of Champagne and a bucket of water!

The only other flight I'll mention from my time at Korat was my last, or as we called it, my "SAWADEE" flight. (This was on 16 June 1975.) It was an Air-to-Air mission with a good friend in the squadron. It was the custom that when you came in after your "Sawadee flight" you got a good soaking down and they met you with a bottle of champagne. Thinking ahead, before I took off for this flight, I borrowed a head set from one of the ground crew and put on a funny T-shirt and shorts under my flight suit. After we landed, I spent a little extra time in the de-arm area. I took off my g-suit, boots, flight suit, and helmet. I put on the head set and taxied back to the parking spot, where all the guys were waiting. They saw me taxi in with the head set and a sailor's hat on my head. After I shut down, I climbed out barefoot and dressed in my T-shirt and shorts. I only did this to be a little different, and to keep my boots and g-suit dry. It was fun. You'll see pictures of this event somewhere in here.

Another interesting couple of weeks while I was at Korat did not involve flying by me, but I was observing aircraft flying practice bombing missions. The USAF had a detachment of four enlisted men and one Officer assigned to the Air-to-Ground Gunnery Range operated by the Thailand Military. The US personnel would control the

US aircraft that came to the range. These personnel had a one year assignment, just like all the other Air Force personnel. I do not remember exactly the reason the Officer in command of this detachment was going back to the states for two weeks (maybe just taking leave), but they needed someone to take his place. I'm not sure if I volunteered for this but I did go to Chandy Range for a couple weeks. It was actually a very, very pleasant time. The enlisted guys did all the work and the Commander just made sure they did not get into any trouble. I got to play a lot of golf during the two weeks.

The front gate at Chandy Range.

One other interesting event that occurred during my year at Korat was a Wing party at the Officers Club. All the Squadrons had their own "Party Suits" and it was a very colorful party. I have included a picture to give you an idea of the "Party Suits."

I don't remember the exact time frame, but I got notice that I had been promoted to Lieutenant Colonel. Yea!!!! We had a great promotion party at the club.

While I was in this job the people who built the A-7 aircraft decided to build a two seater (the A-7K). Actually at the time I think they were calling it the YA-7E. They had the aircraft in the Washington, D.C., area and were taking some of the Air Force guys who had flown the A-7D for a flight to get data on the feasibility of producing a two-seat version. On December 3, 1977, I got to go fly in the two seat A-7. The company pilot was letting me fly it a bit when another Navy A-7E "jumped" us. He took control and we went round and round in aerial combat maneuvering for about 5 minutes. It was fun.

Since I mentioned the stuff about the OER system, I will tell you that by December 1977 I was really fed up with working in the Pentagon. The job I was in was normally a four-year tour, but I felt I could probably get the Generals to let me go if I found a flying job. I started calling everywhere looking for some kind of A-7D flying job. I really wanted the Air National Guard Advisors position at Tucson International Airport. The guy that was currently in that job was supposed to give it up in early 1978. He was/is a good friend of mine and I found out that he asked for and got an extension, something that was NOT normally done. I looked at a couple of other ANG Advisor jobs but did not like the locations. Finally I got a call from the Director of Operations of the 355th Wing at Davis Monthan in Tucson asking if I would take the Wing Training and Plans Officer's job. He would allow me to fly the A-7D if I took the job. I said YES!! So on February 12, 1978, I signed into the 355th Wing at Davis Monthan.

Chapter 14

Flying the A-7D and A-10 at Davis-Monthan

I think the first thing to tell about this assignment would be the fact that the guy I replaced as the Wing Training/Plans Officer was Dick Rutan. Yeah, the guy who flew around the world non-stop. He was retiring from the Air Force and going to work with his brother, Burt Rutan, out in California.

There was one interesting event, and although it isn't about flying, it sure sticks in my memory. When I checked in all my personal equipment, the knee board I had was one of the older models. Unknown to me, these had been replaced and new "softer" models issued. The Personal Equipment guys just took my old metal one and threw it in the trash. Dick Rutan was leaving the Air Force; he saw it that same day in the trash and asked the PE guys if he could have it. They said, sure. Later that same day, I went to the PE shop and discovered that they had thrown out my knee board. I raised hell and asked just where it was because it had some papers on it that were very important to me. (In fact, the line-up card for my flight over the Mayaguez was on the knee board.) The PE guys told me that Dick Rutan had taken the knee board. I called him at his house (he was actually moving his stuff that day) and told him I would be right out to get my knee board. I got it and the papers that were on it, and I still have it today.

It was at the very end of March 1978 that I went to Holloman AFB, New Mexico, to get my re-currency flights. This was rather funny to me because I was going to get my re-currency in a T-38 (which was used in Pilot Training and most of the current pilots had flown it during their training) which I had only flown ONCE as a passenger. I got five rides and returned to Davis Monthan the second week of April.

On the second of May I flew the A-7D again!! It was as if I had never been out of it. Everything came back and I felt right at home flying the "Sluf." After about eight flights, I was once again an Instructor Pilot in the A-7D. Somewhere during the year I was promoted to Chief of Stan Eval. This was a heck of a lot better deal than Training/Plans.

Hard at work as the Chief of Stan Eval

While all the flying was great, one flight really stands out. (Checking my log book I see this flight was on March 13, 1979.) I was number three in a flight of four that was led by a guy named Blatter. We went to the range over north of Holloman AFB, NM. He briefed it radio out and he had it cleared with all the control agencies, including the range. We started up, taxied out, took off, flew for about 45 minutes, and upon entry to the range, we finally broke radio silence. It was one of the most fun flights I ever had!! There was always talk about having to do some "radio out" missions during war time, but I had never practiced it until this flight.

Actually there are a couple more A-7D flights that I won't forget. One was a return of an airplane from Tinker AFB, Oklahoma. That was where the A-7D went for its Inspect and Repair As Necessary (IRAN) maintenance. When I got ready for take off at Tinker for the flight home, it was pretty crappy weather—raining, low ceiling and poor visibility. Just after I got airborne and had the gear up, the generator failed. Well, I was in the weather and didn't really want to return to Tinker, so I deployed the Ram Air Turbine (RAT), which provided essential electrical power. When the A-7D came into the Air Force inventory, most of the guys who checked out in it were former F-100 pilots. We all commented that if you ever had to fly it without all the fancy new avionics, it would be like flying the F-100 again. Well, that was just what it felt like when I climbed out from Tinker in the weather. Since I was really concentrating on flying in the weather, I did not try to re-set the generator right away. That was the emergency procedure if the generator failed. Once I got leveled off and kind of settled down a bit, I re-set the generator and it worked just fine. The rest of the flight was no problem. Maintenance at Davis Monthan never could find anything wrong with the aircraft.

The other flight I especially remember was returning an A-7D that was assigned to the Puerto Rico National Guard to Tinker for IRAN. I do not remember just why they didn't have someone to fly it to Tinker but I do remember saying I would do it. It was about as routine a flight as any could be. I flew down to Puerto Rico by commercial airlines and spent the night. The next morning I pre-flighted the aircraft and filed a flight plan to the Naval Air Station in Jacksonville, Florida. After refueling there, I completed the flight to Tinker and flew commercial airlines back home. It seemed just a normal old flight to me. Now, when I look at a map, I see just how much of that flight was over water, and I wonder if I had even thought about that at the time?

One other event I remember occurred when I got to go cross-country. This generally was a weekend and you could get some flying time and get to go to other A-7 bases. It was probably about 15:00 on Friday when we got airborne. It was just two of us and we were going to England AFB. We headed out northeast and were over Oklahoma; I was telling Stan Kwader (my wingman) that just down and to the right a little was Clinton Sherman Air Base. It was now a civilian field but at one time it was Clinton Sherman Air Force Base. [It was a Strategic Air Command base and my older brother had been stationed there. In fact, on my way to Lackland AFB for my entry into the Air Force, I had stopped and stayed one night with my brother at Clinton Sherman.]

As I was saying this, I looked over to my right wing where Stan should have been and could not see anything. (He had started a descent toward Clinton Sherman.) Then I heard him call on Guard that he was declaring an emergency and needed to land as soon as possible.

I joined up on him and we headed toward Clinton Sherman. Just about that same time someone in the control tower at Clinton Sherman came up on the radio and gave us permission to land. It was a very long and wide runway so there was no problem landing. I landed behind him. We had to get Air Force help from Altus Air Force Base, which was just about 50 miles south of Clinton Sherman. Although my aircraft was OK, the other aircraft was going to have to have the engine replaced before it could fly again.

We contacted the Command Post back at DM and they directed us to spend the night and have Stan come home the next day by commercial air. The guy that we talked to in the tower loaned us a car and we went into the town of Clinton to spend the night. The next morning Stan took a bus into Oklahoma City to get a commercial flight back to Tucson. I went back to Clinton Sherman and continued my cross-country.

On 30 May 1979 I flew the A-7D for the last time. The 355th Wing was down to just one squadron of A-7s and they would be gone pretty soon. The Director of Operations asked me to check out in the A-10 and remain as the Chief of Stan Eval. Boy, that was sure a good deal for me.

My last flight in the A-7D at D-M. I get soaked!

The Log Book reflects that it was the 11th of June 1979 for my first A-10 flight. My instructor was Steve McClain. On the second flight with McClain (the next day), we practiced a simulated single engine approach. This was June in Arizona. Naturally, it was really hot out, and of course the A-10 did not have engines with a heck of a lot of thrust. I was amazed at just how much rudder it took to keep the airplane flying straight and just how you had to really stay alert because you were right on the edge of going out of control.

After I got soaked, I got a drink of champagne!

I had always said BEFORE I ever flew the A-10 that I did not think it would be a very good aircraft to be flying in combat. While it did/does have pretty good armor around the cockpit and has two engines, you still were flying pretty slow. I did not change my opinion after flying it for a while. In fact, the only cross-country I got to fly in the A-10 was to Colorado Springs to visit the Air Force Academy. My son Jon was in the Academy and he asked if I could come give a briefing to his class.

I gave the briefing, and it was on the return flight that I got a big surprise. We flew south from Colorado Springs and were over Santa Fe, New Mexico, flying southwest. I looked out (it was a very clear day) and you could see Los Alamos to the west of Santa Fe. Someone in the flight mentioned Los Alamos as the place where they did the research for the Atomic Bomb. After we had flown for a couple minutes, I looked out and it seemed as if we hadn't moved because you could still see Los Alamos very clearly. It was some time before we had gone far enough that you finally lost sight of Los Alamos. We had about a 90 knot head wind and were

NOT making a very good ground speed. That convinced me of just how slow the A-10 was.

While it is a bit out of order, I think this is the place to put the following information. While working for Hughes Aircraft Company in Tucson after I retired from the Air Force, I was involved with the development of the Infrared Maverick Missile. When the Gulf War was fought, the A-10 was deeply involved. Its main ordnance was the IR Maverick. A lot of the guys flying over there I knew from having flown with them and having briefed them about the Maverick. It was a GREAT AIRPLANE to be flying in that war!! Currently, with the modifications it has, it is one of the best Close Air Support aircraft ever built.

Another flight from the memory banks. A good friend and I were selected to go to the plant (Hagerstown, Maryland) where the A-10 was built to pick up two new airplanes. This was in late February 1980. When we got ready to fly out of Hagerstown, I told my good buddy that this flight would be his "No Notice" Instrument Check. After we briefed, we went to the aircraft.

One of the airplanes was in a nice warm hangar and the other was outside on a very cold, ice-covered ramp. Being the good guy I am and the fact that I had surprised him with a no-notice check, I let him have the one in the hangar. It was the coldest weather I ever pre-flighted an aircraft. I mentioned it was cold and that really caused a surprise later. Having only flown the A-10 around Arizona where it was always pretty warm and the engines seemed to never give you much thrust, it was a big surprise at how much thrust they had in the cold weather. The take-off roll was really short and the join-up after take-off was really fast. I think this was the only time flying the A-10 that I thought it had plenty of thrust.

Another flight that made a big impression on me really taught me about the capabilities of the F-15. I was scheduled with a student to fly an Air Combat Mission against two F-15s that would come from Holloman AFB, NM. We briefed as a flight and then I briefed with the F-15 pilots over the phone. When we arrived in the training area, we discovered that only one of the F-15s would be coming. We got set up and sure enough it wasn't long before we saw the F-15 attack us. We made a hard turn, and I really expected the F-15 to go shooting past and climb away from us. Expecting the overshoot, I reversed and was super-surprised to see the F-15 doing a loop and getting into position to arrive at our six o'clock position. I had never flown against any aircraft that could do that. It was a REAL learning experience.

I need to tell a little about my experience as Chief of Stan Eval because of a couple flights. As the Chief, I told the other five pilots that worked for me that I would fly all the check rides with full Colonels and any Generals that might need a check ride. That leads me to relate the following two stories.

The first was a check ride for the Assistant Director of Operations. (This guy actually was the one who wrote my OER, even though the DO was my actual boss.) This was his check ride to qualify him to lead students to the range. The flight would be him leading with a student on his wing as number two. I would be number three in the flight with a student on my wing. The briefing and flight to the range were good and everything looked normal.

As we approached the range I could tell that maybe he did not know exactly where he was. He was offset to the right of the run-in line into the range by about a mile. If he had just looked to the left, I am sure he would have seen where he was and could have made a correction.

The rules are such that if the Check Pilot has to call a correction for flight safety, it is a failure. Well, I was on the right wing and could see the range and was just hoping he would see it also. I made up my mind that if he could call a correction and I could be sure he knew where he was, he could still pass the check ride. He never did, and as we passed the bombing circle and were still heading in the wrong direction, I had to make a call to turn left. I had to fail him on the ride. It was a difficult de-brief with his boss (Director of Operations) and him being the one writing my OER. He had never failed a check ride before.

There was one other check ride when I had to fail the guy. This was a one-star General that was getting the seven-ride check out. He was just going to learn the basics because he would be going to Nellis and get most of his training there. During the check ride he just could/would not get the correct airspeed going around final and on the final approach. He was about 10-20 knots fast on every pattern he flew. I even had him fly an extra pattern hoping he would do it right. Well, he never did, and I had to fail him. (At Davis-Monthan and at Nellis the runways are plenty long enough that this would not have been a dangerous airspeed. However, with the A-10 it is very likely that he could have been flying into some fields with a lot shorter runways and there the correct airspeed would be critical.) Again I had to de-brief him with the Director of Operations sitting in on the de-brief. I don't think I have ever seen anyone get quite as MAD as the General. He was VERY unhappy. The DO wanted to know if I couldn't pass him and maybe let the people at Nellis give some more training. I just couldn't do it but did say that if he flew with the check pilot at Nellis and they could pass him, I would then call it an OK ride. I don't really remember if I ever heard that he flew a good ride at Nellis.

The last flight I had in the A-10 was June 27, 1980. It was actually two flights. It was a flight of four with me leading. We went to Gila Bend Airfield and landed. This was a simulated scramble for a close air support mission on the South Tactical Range. I remember that it was very HOT at Davis Monthan when we pre-flighted and taxied out to take off. When we landed at Gila Bend and opened the canopies, it was HOTTER still!!! It seemed just like you opened an oven and climbed in. There was no wind and I am guessing it was over 140 degrees on the ramp. We flew our mission and I did a tactical pitch up for landing back at DM and my Air Force flying career came to an end.

I did get checked out in a light airplane with the Davis Monthan flying club. My log book shows it was a B24R, which would be a Beechcraft B24 Sierra. I really don't remember it being a Beech aircraft but will believe the log book. It shows I had only two flights in the B24R, the check-out ride in October 1980 and a flight to the Winchester Mountains in November.

I got a check-out in the Flying Club T-34 Mentor in January 1981 and took Alex for a flight on 8 February 1981.

I have had a lot of people ask me if I still fly. I tell them this story. Right after I retired, I checked out in light airplanes with the DM Aero Club and thought I would keep flying. It did not take long until I learned two things which made the decision about continuing flying very easy. The first thing I learned was that flying was very expensive. Even with the very good rates that you could get in the base Aero Club, it was still pretty expensive.

I get wet after my final A-10 flight.

I am all wet but still get a hand shake.

The second thing was the experience I had while giving Alex the ride in the T-34. In the Air Force during my assignments where I was flying regularly, I would get at least 20 hours flying time a month. When you got to fly that much, you get pretty proficient. This meant that most of the time you could just tell that everything was operating OK. You could tell by the sounds and the feel of the airplane that it was running and flying right. This allowed you to spend a good amount of time looking around and making sure there were no other airplanes around and seeing the outside world.

One of the things you have to do when doing aerobatics is to look outside the aircraft. For example, when Alex and I were out flying I showed him a Barrel Roll. To do this properly, you pick a point way out on the horizon, put the nose down to gain airspeed and turn about 30 or 40 degrees either left or right away from the point you have picked. As you roll out to get wings level, you also pull up so that you are level flight, wings level pointing about 30/40 degrees away from your point. You continue to pull up and roll so that when you are directly lined up with your point on the horizon, your wings will be 90 degrees to the horizon. You continue to roll and as your nose is pointing the 30/40 degrees to the other side of the point, you are upside down with your wings level to the horizon. Continuing the roll you will end up with the wings again 90 degrees to the horizon directly below the point on the horizon. You continue to recover and will end up wings level pointing the 30/40 degree off the point just like when you started the Barrel Roll. If you do it properly it is very gentle and smooth.

When I showed Alex the Barrel Roll I was spending way too much time looking in the cockpit making sure about my airspeed and other things that I really "Dished Out." What that means is that at the bottom I was pointing way too nose low and had too much airspeed and did not get back to level flight, wings level when I should have. This taught me that I wasn't proficient enough to fly keeping my eyes out of the cockpit like I should if I were going to do aerobatics. It convinced me that unless I got a lot more flying time I did not really want to fly and become dangerous to me and anyone else who might be with me. Hence my decision to just quit flying my own aircraft and just ride along with someone who was proficient.

I did fly in a USAF aircraft one more time. While working at Hughes Aircraft Company, one of the jobs I had was to brief Air Force/Air National Guard/Air Force Reserve fighter pilots on the use of the Maverick Missile. Once while briefing the Air National Guard at Homestead AFB, Florida, my buddy Ken Schanke and I got to ride in the back seat of their F-4's. It was a 2-ship low-level mission over water to the water range down by Key West. The weather was not suitable for the range work so they changed to an air-to-air mission and we had a great time. When we returned to Homestead, they let Ken and I fly the aircraft. We even flew some close formation. Ken had a camera and took a couple pictures which I have included here.

Attachment 1

T-33 Cocked Nose Wheel
by Lt. Col. (then Captain) John Larrison (USAF Ret)

One of the unique things about the T-33 Trainer used for Basic Pilot Training in the 1950s and early 1960s was the lack of nose wheel steering. The nose wheel was designed to freely swivel based on the use of the independent left and right main gear wheel brakes.

As with most aircraft the brakes were independently controlled by toe pressure on the left or right rudder pedals. During normal taxi, take-off, and landing speeds, this was not a problem. However, at very low speeds, when first starting to move or when almost stopped, brake steering could lead to a situation known as a "Cocked Nose Wheel." The most common cause was a student trying to make small changes in direction when pulling into a parking spot. These actions could lead to a cocked nose wheel where it flops over to a full left or right position of about 45°. In a congested area like the parking ramp, this would require a crew chief to straighten the nose wheel. However, this cocked nose wheel story did not occur on the parking ramp. It involved two key individuals: a solo student and an instructor pilot performing Senior Mobile Controller duties. During student training operations, control of the runway and traffic was performed by an instructor in a mobile control unit located at the landing end of the runway. This story is about a solo student who had been cleared onto the runway by mobile for take-off.

This requires the pilot to taxi onto the runway and lineup in a take-off position headed straight down the runway. He then performs the "Pre-Takeoff" checklist items prior to brake release, full power, and take-off.

A key portion of these pre-takeoff checks was a check of engine operation at 80% power. This required heavy brake pressure to hold the aircraft with the power at 80% while engine instruments were checked to insure they were all proper, "In-the-Green."

The student had taxied into position, abeam of the mobile unit and lined up straight down the runway. The brakes were pumped to hold the aircraft during checks; however, the brake pressure was not held strong enough to prevent one wheel from moving slightly during the student's prolonged engine instrument checks. While looking in the cockpit, he did not notice that this wheel creep led to an inevitable "Cocked Nose Wheel." Visualize a T-33 on the runway; student's head in the cockpit checking instruments, right wheel brake letting the right wheel slowly roll, resulting in a cocked nose wheel. The T-33 was now doing a slow 360° pivot around the left main gear.

With the student being the only aircraft on the runway, the senior mobile controller made a simple radio call to the student. "Warlock 58, the next time the runway comes by, you're cleared for take-off."

That call shall long be remembered by those at Vance and it was good for a laugh. Today I'm afraid the result would be different.

Attachment 2

After I finished the F-100 training at Luke AFB, AZ, it was off to Stead AFB near there for Survival Training. This entire remembrance will be "from the really gray" part of the brain!! Like I said, it was not something that was a pleasant time, so the memory cells probably did their best to forget. I called one of the guys that was on the trip with me so I think some of what I will relate is accurate. I think we got there on a weekend so the adventure started on Monday. One of the first things we found out was the fact that we would be the first group of the year doing the "Winter Trek." It was about mid September so the possibility of snow when we would be out in the woods was pretty good. This meant that we would be doing a much shorter distance for our Escape and Evasion course than the Summer course. As it turned out, we had great weather and were lucky to have the shorter E & E course.

    I think the first two-and-a-half days were classroom stuff. On Wednesday afternoon we got ready for an "obstacle course" which we would go through, ending up about daylight at a place where they would "capture" us and put us in a POW camp. I can't remember much about this night except it was just one of those things you go through knowing you'll make it and end up where "THEY" want you. Of course we did!

    I remember when they "captured" us, we were led to the camp and they made us take all of our clothes off. Then we had to lie down on this pad of concrete. It had some gravel on it and before I laid down I was sweeping with my foot this gravel off the spot where I was to lay down. BOY OH BOY!! This did not go over too well and I was told to get my ass down right NOW!! This was the start of it. We did get our flight suit back so we were not naked but for an hour or so.

    I really don't remember a hell of a lot about the time in the POW camp. I know we got a bunch of stuff that we were supposed to prepare for all of us to eat. They had it fixed up so that the only way we had to make use of the coffee they gave us was to put it into the stew we were making, then take the liquid off the top for our coffee. I do remember that it had been long enough since we had eaten that we did it and enjoyed the stew!!

Only one other thing sticks out in my mind about our time in the POW camp. One of the guys somehow got away for enough time to sneak into the Camp Commander's office and steal some files. I guess these were somewhat important because they called an "Academic Situation" to ask for the papers back. They finally got them but only after we got something, fresh fruit I think.

I don't remember too much about all the interrogation or the punishments they gave you. Some guys got put into these locker-type things which were very small; some got very claustrophobic and had to be let out. There was also a big hole, which looked about the size of a grave. It was filled with water and sawdust and some other stuff that made it look and smell like sewage. It was something you did NOT want to be put into, but some guys were. I don't remember any real bad punishment I got, but the over-all experience made it very clear to me that you NEVER wanted to become a POW.

I don't remember exactly when we got out of the POW camp but I think it was Saturday morning. We had the rest of Saturday and Sunday off; Monday morning early we were trucked off to the "woods." We were divided up into seven (again it may have been six or eight!) man teams and had an enlisted guy as an instructor. We were going to be taught about "camping" out!! For those of us who had done hunting/fishing or whatever, this was actually a fun time. For some of the guys from big cities or who had never been out in the wild, this was a real trying time for them.

Guys who had been through Survival Training before told us about this "field exercise" and the fact that if you could sneak some stuff to eat (like potatoes, onions, etc.) along with the stuff they gave you, you could get along pretty well. The first afternoon they gave us a live rabbit. All the other guys in the group I was with just stood around and wondered just what the heck we were going to do with a rabbit. In short order I showed them that I had a lot of experience with cleaning and cutting up a rabbit. That first night we had a GREAT meal.

There was also a stream that ran near where we were camped. We could see trout in the stream and we were told we COULD NOT catch any of the fish. I know some guys did and had a good fish dinner.

Again, if my memory is correct, it was Tuesday afternoon late that we broke camp and hiked for a couple miles. We were then told to rest because we would be walking all night doing night navigation. We stopped by this stream and one of the guys in our group saw a bunch of small holes in the bottom of the stream. It was very clear water. He thought that there might be clear water mussels in the bottom. Sure enough, he got in and got about two dozen mussels. Boy oh boy, we thought, tomorrow morning we are going to have a good breakfast. Well, we took turns carrying a sweatshirt full of those mussels all night long. They were heavy! Next morning we found a can, cleaned the mussels, put them in water we had boiling in the can and just waited for our great breakfast. Ha Ha!! They turned out to be almost inedible!!! Every time you bit down on them, it was like chewing on a rubber ball. You could not bite through them!! Well, we ate them anyway.

It was after we had breakfast that we were split up into two-man teams. As a two-man team, we were going to do the Escape and Evade part of Survival Training. We were given a map and on it were two designated check-in points. The first would require us to check in at midmorning the next day. Then you had to navigate to the second point, which was the final destination. The check in time at the final check point was the morning of the following day. We started out Wednesday afternoon, checked in to the first check point on Thursday morning, and the final check point on Friday morning. Then they would truck us back to Stead and Survival Training would be complete.

I believe it was about midafternoon when they sent the first wave of the two-man teams on there way. My partner for our two-man team was a guy named John "Jack" Redmond. We had gone through the F-100 training at Luke together. We were in the third wave to go out. I think it was about an hour after the first wave left. Jack and I discussed the fact that we felt pretty sure they wouldn't have the "bad guys" out looking for us until all the teams were underway for at least an hour, maybe two. (Bad Guys were actually our enlisted instructors dressed in "enemy" uniforms who tried to catch us doing something wrong. If they caught you, there was a card you had that they would punch or mark showing that you had done something wrong, like walking down a road or using a trail or just walking out in the open.)

If we were correct, and since it would be getting dark in a couple hours, when they let our wave get underway, we went really fast. There were a couple of places where there was a large open area to cross and if the "bad guys" were really out and looking for us we would have had to navigate around these areas. We actually ran some of the time and it wasn't long before we passed two-man teams from the second wave. In fact just after dark, we caught up with a team from the first wave. Now we did something we weren't supposed to do, and would have got a bunch of demerits if caught: we joined up as a four-man team.

Going in the direction that would take us to the first check-in point was a real nice road. Looking at the contour lines, it appeared that if we stayed on this road it would lead us to higher ground and pretty close to the checkpoint. Well, we walked on it for a while and instead of the mountains on both sides of us getting shorter, meaning we were going up hill like we thought we should, the hills on both sides kept getting higher. We decided that we should check the map and make sure we were where we thought we were. We got under a poncho in the middle of the road and had a flashlight on looking at the map, when we heard a jeep coming. It sounded just like it was right around a bend from us so we all just ran to the side of the road and jumped into a lower area with trees. As I jumped something hit my eye.

We remained very still until the jeep went past. If fact, it took several minutes before the jeep even got to us. It had been a lot further away originally than we thought. After it passed, I told the other guys that I had hit my eye on something and I could not see out of it very well. Well, they turned on the flashlight to look at me and one of them said something like, "MY GOD"! It kind of scared the hell out of me! We got a hankie out and got it wet and wiped my eye, it was bleeding pretty good. Just after we would wipe it, I could see OK. Then the blood would cover it again, and to see I had to wipe it again. The bleeding stopped pretty soon and I could see just fine so we continued on. We did finally find out exactly where we were and made it to the first checkpoint just fine.

When we checked in, they logged us as having completed the first part of the course. They gave each of us an orange. I didn't really ask for any medical attention because if they had taken me in for a check up, they might not have let me finish the rest of the course. In that case, I would have to stay over and go through the entire E & E course again. I DIDN'T WANT THAT!

Jack and I decided what we would do is just keep going, and if my eye started hurting too bad, we would then get the attention of some of the guys looking for us and they would take me somewhere to have it checked. Sure enough about midafternoon, when it was getting pretty warm, I started getting some sweat in the cut on my eye lid and it started to hurt and swell up a bit. We just got on a road and decided if we didn't get caught by the bad guys, we would make great time toward the final check point. If we got caught, we would just tell them we were looking for medical attention for my eye.

We had not been walking on the road for more than about 10 minutes when the bad guys jumped out of the woods and asked for our cards. I turned to the first guy and said, "I need some medical attention for my eye." The young guy really jumped and said, "OK." He had a radio and called for a jeep. It wasn't very long until the jeep showed up. We decided that I would leave my backpack with Jack and he would wait right where we were until I got back.

Off we went in the jeep to the final checkpoint campsite where all the staff were staying. They did not have a doctor but did have a medic take a look at my eye. Just about the time he was examining me, the enlisted guy who was our group instructor came over to me to ask what was wrong. When he saw my eye and the fact that the medic thought I might have scratched my eye ball and should be taken to Stead to have it checked out, he wondered how far we had gotten and how many demerits I had received. I was pretty upset at having to go back to Stead because I did not want to have to come back to complete the E & E course. My instructor said he felt since we had gone as far as we did and did not have any demerits, he thought they would call me complete. He couldn't say this for sure but he would recommend to the Commander that I would be complete. With that, it was decided that I would just wait at the camp until a little later when they had a truck going back to Stead. They went back up and got my backpack and Jack had to complete the rest of the course alone.

I got to Stead and went to the hospital to have a doctor check my eye. He put some dye in my eye and checked to see if the eyeball was scratched. Thank heaven, it wasn't. He did say he would have to put a couple of stitches in my eyelid. Then he said he would not be able to use any local anesthetic because of the swelling. Well, that was OK by me. He then used some sterile water to rinse the dye from my eye. That was the part that hurt the worst!! He kept pushing on my eye so hard I thought he was trying to push it out the back of my head. When he finally put the stitches in, I could feel him tugging on the string (or whatever he used) and pulling my eyelid. It is so funny, because I can close my eyes right now sitting here at the computer and still remember the feeling of him tugging on my eyelid.

When he finished, I asked what I was supposed to do then?? He had no idea, and there was no one else around who could tell me what to do, so I went to the Officers Club and had a couple of cold beers and a really good dinner. Boy, that cold Coors really tasted GOOD!

I knew that the next morning I was to report to the Commander's office in uniform to find out if he would call me complete or make me go do it all over. After having talked to my enlisted instructor, and asking me a few questions, he called me complete. Man, what a relief! I just waited for the other guys to come in from the field and enjoyed a few more beers with them.

Then it was back to Luke to pack up the family for the TDY to Nellis AFB for the final F-100 training.

NOTE: I am adding this in August of 2015. It should be noted that NOTHING we endured during our Survival Training could have helped prepare us for what the POWs in North Vietnam went through. There is no way they could simulate the amount and type of torture that the POWs suffered. I am really glad I never had to learn that the hard way.

Attachment 3

I can really only remember having two weekend trips in Turkey. OK, that is the way I wanted to start this but after going through all my pictures, I think I should have started it by saying: I know I went on ONE weekend trip and fully intended to go on another, but never found the time. The weekend trip I do remember, and that I have a lot of pictures of, was a trip we took to the north of Izmir (when I say "We," I cannot remember just who the other guy(s) might have been). Again, if memory serves me correctly, we just hired a guide who had a car and paid a flat rate for a full day's tour.

We went to the town of Bergama. The pictures reflect the fact that there were a LOT of Roman ruins in Turkey, and we visited some of them. The several pictures I have of the Red Basilica are in the old town. The following description is taken from Wikipedia: *Known for its cotton, gold, and fine carpets, the city was the ancient Greek and Roman cultural center of Pergamon; its wealth of ancient ruins continues to attract considerable tourist interest today. Located on a promontory north of the Bakırçay river, 26 km removed from the Aegean Sea, Bergama has a population of about 55,000. The ruins of the ancient city of Pergamon lie to the north and west of the modern city; Roman Pergamon is believed to have sustained a population of approximately 150,000 at its height in the 1st century AD. Among Bergama's notable ruins are the Sanctuary of Asclepius (or Asclepeion), a temple dedicated to an ancient Greek god of healing, and the "Red Basilica" complex ("Kızıl Avlu" in Turkish), a 2nd century AD construction of the Emperor Hadrian that straddles the Selinus River. The town also features an archaeological museum.*

The second trip I wanted to take would have been to the South of Izmir. It would have taken us to the city of Selcuk which has the ancient city of Ephesus very close by. The following description is taken from Wikipedia:

Ephesus, Greek: Ἔφεσος Ephesos; Turkish: Efes) was an ancient Greek city, and later a major Roman city, on the coast of Ionia, near present-day Selçuk, Izmir

Province, Turkey. It was one of the twelve cities of the Ionian League during the Classical Greek era.

In the Roman period, Ephesus had a population of more than 250,000 in the 1st century BC, which also made it one of the largest cities in the Mediterranean world. The city was famed for the Temple of Artemis (completed around 550 BC), one of the Seven Wonders of the Ancient World. Emperor Constantine I rebuilt much of the city and erected new public baths.

Following the Edict of Thessalonica from emperor Theodosius I, the temple was destroyed in 401 AD by a mob led by St. John Chrysostom. The town was partially destroyed by an earthquake in 614 AD. The city's importance as a commercial center declined as the harbor was slowly silted up by the Cayster River (Küçük Menderes).

Ephesus was one of the seven churches of Asia that are cited in the Book of Revelation. The Gospel of John may have been written here. The city was the site of several 5th century Christian Councils, (see Council of Ephesus). It is also the site of a large gladiators' graveyard. Today's archaeological site lies 3 kilometers southwest of the town of Selçuk, in the Selçuk district of İzmir Province, Turkey.

Since it has been almost fifty years, I am really at a loss as to just WHY I did not go to Ephesus. I actually may have but since I have NO pictures I can identify as having been taken at Ephesus, I am pretty sure I did not get to visit there.

I have included a few pictures taken in the town of Izmir during some of the trips sight-seeing the town and having dinner.

One of the first things we saw on our trip was this guy with a bear. Our guide/driver stopped and we watched him wrestle with the bear for a few minutes. If I remember correctly we tipped the guy and continued on our way.

There were several locations where we saw aqueduct ruins and theater ruins but I have included only these two pictures.

These five pictures of ruins were taken at several places along the way to the town of Bergama. A couple of the ruins looked to be old baths or places where healing/ medicine were practiced.

On this page are two pictures of the acropolis at the old city of Pergamon. The following is a definition of "acropolis": An acropolis (Greek: Ακρ⬜πολις; akros, akron, edge, extremity + polis, city; plural: acropoleis or acropolises) is a settlement, especially a citadel, built upon an area of elevated ground—frequently a hill with precipitous sides, chosen for purposes of defense. In many parts of the world, acropolises became the nuclei of large cities of classical antiquity, such as ancient Rome, which in more recent times grew up on the surrounding lower ground, such as modern Rome. The lower picture is of the Altar of Zeus in the Acropolis of Pergamon.

These three pictures were taken in downtown Izmir during one of our weekend visits. The guy in the center picture is Richard Head, a guy in the Squadron that was a joy to go touring with.

Red Basilica

Description and drawing below taken from Wikipedia, the free encyclopedia.

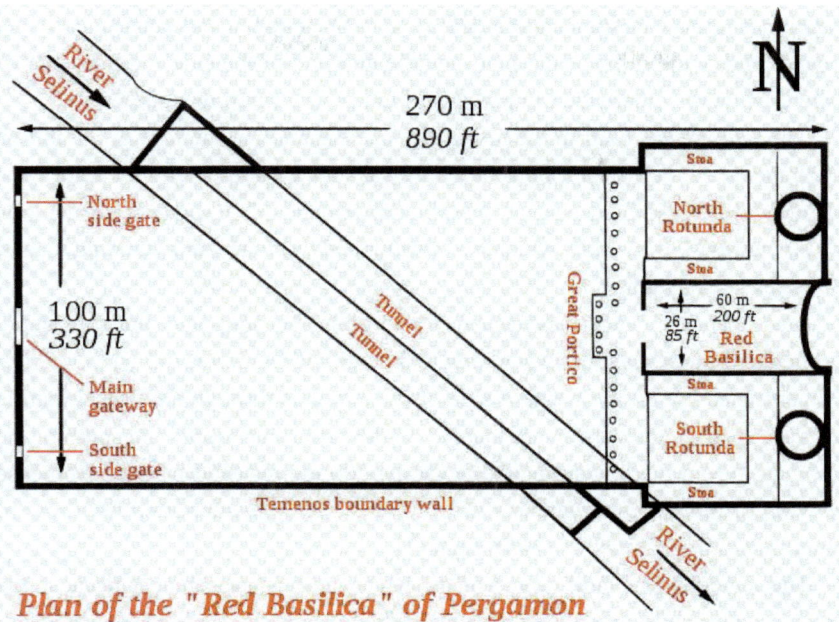

Plan of the "Red Basilica" of Pergamon

The "Red Basilica" (Turkish: Kızıl Avlu), also called variously the Red Hall and Red Courtyard, is a monumental ruined temple in the ancient city of Pergamon, now Bergama, in western Turkey. The temple was built by the Roman Empire, probably in the time of Hadrian and possibly on his orders. It is one of the largest Roman structures still surviving in the ancient Greek world. The temple is thought to have been used for the worship of the Egyptian gods – specifically Isis and/or Serapis, and possibly also Osiris, Harpocrates and other lesser gods, who may have been worshipped in a pair of drum-shaped rotundas, both of which are virtually intact, alongside the main temple.

Although the building itself is of an immense size, it was only one part of a much larger sacred complex, surrounded by high walls, that dwarfed even the colossal Temple of Jupiter in Baalbek. The entire complex was built directly over the River Selinus in a remarkable feat of engineering that involved the construction of an immense bridge 196 metres (643 ft) wide to channel the river through two channels under the temple. The Pergamon Bridge still stands today, supporting modern buildings and even vehicle traffic. A series of tunnels and chambers lies under the main temple, connecting it with the side rotundas and giving private access to different areas of the complex. Various drains, water channels, and basins are located in, around and under the main temple and may have been used for symbolic reenactments of the flooding of the Nile. The temple was converted by the Byzantines into a Christian church dedicated to St. John but was subsequently destroyed. Today the ruins of the main temple and one of the side rotundas can be visited, while the other side rotunda is still in use as a small mosque.

The temple was built in the lower city of Pergamon at the foot of the hill on which the ancient city's acropolis stood. It was located at the eastern end of what was originally an immense sacred precinct or temenos, 270 metres (890 ft) long by 100 metres (330 ft) wide, which was surrounded by stone walls standing at least 13 metres (43 ft) high.

Most of the temenos was destroyed and built over long ago, but substantial fragments of the walls remain standing to a height of 13 metres (43 ft) today. The main entrance lay on the western side of the temenos through a colossal marble gateway; smaller gateways were located on the same side, north and south of the main gate. From there, visitors walked some 200 metres (660 ft) to an immense propylon or monumental gateway in front of the temple, supported by a row of columns standing 14 metres (46 ft) high.[1]

The temenos was built on top of the River Selinus, presumably because the person who commissioned the complex wished it to be located in the city centre rather than in an outlying district. As the city was already substantially built up, the river bed offered an otherwise unused location for the temple complex and reduced the number of properties that would have to be demolished to make way for it. The river was channelled into two tunnels passing diagonally for a distance of about 150 metres (490 ft), northwest to southeast, under the temenos and temple. This structure, the Pergamon Bridge, still stands today and continues to drain the river underneath the complex.

These three pictures I took during the trip. The upper picture has the Red Basilica in the center of the picture and is a bit difficult to see. The picture was taken when we were on the acropolis.

The four pictures on this page are from Wikipedia, the free encyclopedia.

Attachment 4

My R & R trip to Greece (1964)

Lent and Easter Sunday were past, and it came up that I could take some time for R & R. This other guy (don't remember his first name, last name Gilchrist) and I decided to go to Greece and take a tour. One of the other guys in the squadron had gone over, flew military air into Athens, and had stayed at a hotel downtown. He said he had got to be good buddies with the concierge and he was pretty good at putting things together. OK, so off we go.

We got to Athens just fine, got to the hotel, and checked in. It was about the middle of the afternoon when we got the concierge to come up to our rooms. We had decided to take the five-day tour around Greece. (It has been a really long time since this all happened, but I am pretty sure I still remember most of this correctly.) We told the concierge what we were thinking about and he said yeah, sure enough, he knows just what we want. He asked us if we wanted to go first class, or the one in the middle, or the cheap class. We decided that going with the one in the middle was probably the smart way to go. It was cheaper than the first class, yet still had reasonable hotels where we would be staying. We gave him our money (CASH!); if my memory is correct, it was between $300-$400 US.

After he took off to get our tickets, Gilchrist and I looked at each other and wondered if we had just been scammed!! We had just met this guy and were taking the word of the other guy in the squadron that he was honest.

Well, just about an hour later, he showed up with our tickets and directions. We were to have our bags packed and with us, and go down about two blocks to where there would be some signs about bus loadings. I think we were to be at the place at about 8 o'clock in the morning. So that is what we did.

We got there a little early, and were standing there, all by ourselves, with our bags, thinking "I wonder if this is the scam?"

Nope, just a bit before eight, several big tour buses arrived.

We saw the sign on one of them that said it was the five-day tour. We moved our bags to that bus and right away the guy loading the bags on the bus tells us NO, that isn't the bus we were supposed to get on. He moved our bags to the bus that had a sign saying it is the week long tour. We show him our tickets and he shakes his head telling us this is the bus we belong on. OK, whatever you say.

As we went up the steps into the bus from the back of the bus comes this shout, "Good morning, Americanos." Looking around we saw a bunch of older people (actually there were couples from a lot of different countries) and in the back of the bus were these young girls (16/17 years old). There were thirteen girls and their chaperone! We found out later they were from a finishing school in Belgium. The girls were all from Central or South America (most from Colombia) attending the school in Belgium. They had just finished a week tour of the Greek Islands in the Mediterranean and were just starting the week tour of mainland Greece. (Gilchrist and I thought later that the concierge at the hotel must have set this up for us to get put on the bus with these girls.) Right off the bat, we thought "This is going to be one fine tour!"

A real small Greek church we visited in Athens before we started the tour.

I remember we went to the South of Athens visiting places along the way. I think the first place we stopped to view Roman Ruins was Megara.

Megara is an ancient city (pop. 28,591 in 2011) in Attica, Greece. It lies in the northern section of the Isthmus of Corinth opposite the island of Salamis, which belonged to Megara in archaic times, before being taken by Athens. Megara was one of the four districts of Attica, embodied in the four mythic sons of King Pandion II, of whom Nisos was the ruler of Megara. Megara was also a trade port, its people using their ships and wealth as a way to gain leverage on armies of neighboring poleis. Megara specialized in the exportation of wool and other animal products including livestock such as horses. It possessed two harbors, Pegae, to the west on the Corinthian Gulf and Nisaea, to the east on the Saronic Gulf of the Aegean Sea. (From Wikipedia, the free encyclopedia.)

I don't remember where we stayed the first night. The hotel was just fine and the dinner was pretty good. Up early and on the way again. We next stopped at Corinth. I guess it would be more accurate to say we stopped at the Canal of Corinth.

The Corinth Canal is a canal that connects the Gulf of Corinth with the Saronic Gulf in the Aegean Sea. It cuts through the narrow Isthmus of Corinth and separates the Peloponnesian peninsula from the Greek mainland, thus effectively making the former an island. The builders dug the canal through the Isthmus at sea level; no locks are employed. It is 6.4 kilometres (4.0 mi) in length and only 21.3 metres (70 ft) wide at its base, making it unpassable for most modern ships. It now has little economic importance.

The canal was mooted in classical times and an abortive effort was made to build it in the 1st century AD. Construction finally got underway in 1881 but was hampered by geological and financial problems that bankrupted the original builders. It was completed in 1893, but due to the canal's narrowness, navigational problems and periodic closures to repair landslips from its steep walls, it failed to attract the level of traffic anticipated by its operators. It is now used mainly for tourist traffic. (From Wikipedia, the free encyclopedia)

Just one of the many paintings on the ceiling of the first church we visited.

Corinth Canal picture from Wikipedia

Left: My picture of Corinth Canal looking East (1964)
Right: My picture of Corinth Canal looking West.

Hill top ruins near Megara. The first ruins we visited on the tour.

Amphitheatre in the hill top ruins near Megara.

One of the many Greek villages we drove thru.

Walking up to a hilltop ruins. The granary is on the left.

On either the first or second day, we saw this ruins.
It was a granary and very large.

Greek church in one of the villages we passed.

Two pictures of ruins at Corinth. The lower is the location where St. Paul gave his Sermons to the Corinthians.

PK enjoys a local wine at one of the stops on the tour.

One interesting thing while we were stopped at the Canal: There was one of those little "Food Carts" that had kabobs. I don't think I had ever had lamb before so we tried the lamb kabobs. They were really GOOD! I don't know what they were seasoned with but I remember it was really good. After our stop at the Canal, we visited the old part of Corinth and saw the place where St. Paul delivered his sermons to the Corinthians. Then it was off to see more ruins. Somewhere along the way we stopped at one of the many villages we passed through. Gilchrist was a real connoisseur of wine. I, on the other hand, did not like wine and had not even tasted any since high school. (One of my buddies in high school and I got a bottle of Mogan David wine [real sweet stuff] and had just enough to make us sick and never want wine again!) Gilchrist insisted that I try it. It tasted just like kerosene! Well, probably not. Anyway that was the start of it. At every place we stopped, Gilchrist would order wine and we both had to have a glass or two. By the end of this trip I had actually started thinking " maybe I should try wine a little more often."

I think it was on the third day that we had a discussion with the girls about the dinner we had the evening before. (They were staying at the first class hotels so they were having different dinners/desserts from those we were having.) We told them about the really good cake we had for dessert. They really let out a moan and groan. They told us that on their entire trip they had never gotten anything sweet for dessert. They were always getting fruit for dessert. Sometime during this discussion, Gilchrist and I suggested that maybe they should tell the hotel where they were staying that it was one of the girls' birthday and maybe that would cause the hotel to serve them cake for dessert. Then Gilchrist and I got the idea that maybe getting them a birthday cake for lunch that day would be a good surprise. I went up to the guide and asked if it might be possible to stop some place where we could get a cake as a surprise to the girls. She looked kind of concerned and said we were really on a tight schedule. [This was going to be a day where we had no stops. We were going to a port city on the lower (south) side of The Gulf of Corinth, then take a ferry to the north side.) She finally decided that one of the cities we would be going through would probably have a bakery where we might get a cake.

The birthday lunch!

When we got to this town, she announced that we would take a short potty break. She and I got off and hurried to the bakery. It must have been about six blocks. We got to the bakery only to find out they don't have a "big" cake like we normally have for a birthday cake, only have small cupcakes. Quickly I figured, "let's see, we have 32 total on the bus, so I'll get 16 of these and 16 of those." Then I calmly told the server I would take 8 of these and 8 of those. Back to the bus we went. When we got across the street from the bus I saw everyone waiting to get back on the bus and it hit me, WHAT THE HELL, I ONLY GOT HALF ENOUGH!! No time to go back.

When I told Gilchrist of my mistake, we covered it up by saying we only got enough for the girls and the chaperone. He and I got on last and sang happy birthday to one of the girls, who seemed embarrassed. All the other passengers sang along, not knowing we were playing a trick on the girls. That day we had lunch at the port where we took the ferry, and we had the cupcakes for dessert.

We took the ferry across The Gulf of Corinth. I don't remember where we stayed that night, but the next day we spent a lot of time at Delphi.

The navel of the earth at Delphi.

PK at Delphi. Please note that in 1964 when you were on a tour you dressed up!

Delphi is both an archaeological site and a modern town in Greece on the southwestern spur of Mount Parnassus in the valley of Phocis. Delphi was the site of the Delphic oracle, the most important oracle in the classical Greek world, and became a major site for the worship of the god Apollo after he slew Python, a dragon who lived there and protected the navel of the Earth. Python (derived from the verb pythein, "to rot") is claimed by some to be the original name of the site in recognition of Python which Apollo defeated. The Homeric Hymn to Delphic Apollo recalled that the ancient name of this site had been Krisa.

Apollo's sacred precinct in Delphi was a panhellenic sanctuary, where every four years, starting in 586 BC athletes from all over the Greek world competed in the Pythian Games, one of the four panhellenic (or stephanitic) games, precursors of the Modern Olympics. The victors at Delphi were presented with a laurel crown (stephanos) which was ceremonially cut from a tree by a boy who re-enacted the slaying of the Python. Delphi was set apart from the other games sites because it hosted the mousikos agon, musical competitions. These Pythian Games rank second among the four stephanitic games chronologically and based on importance. These games, though, were different from the games at Olympia in that they were not of such vast importance to the city of Delphi as the games at Olympia were to the area surrounding Olympia. Delphi would have been a renowned city whether or not it hosted these games; it had other attractions that led to it being labeled the "omphalos" (navel) of the earth, in other words, the center of the world.

In the inner hestia ("hearth") of the Temple of Apollo, an eternal flame burned. After the battle of Plataea, the Greek cities extinguished their fires and brought new fire from the hearth of Greece, at Delphi; in the foundation stories of several Greek colonies, the founding colonists were first dedicated at Delphi. (From Wikipedia, the free encyclopedia)

An interesting thing happened at lunch that day. For dessert we had this big great looking orange. The girl that was sitting next to me calmly took a knife and fork and was peeling and eating the orange without picking it up. I sat amazed! She asked me if I didn't like orange? I said, no, I really liked oranges, but there was no way I was going to pick up that orange and peel it with my hands when she was doing such a great job with just a knife and fork! She then quit what she was doing and picked up the orange to eat with her hands so I could eat the orange and wouldn't feel like such a fool.

After lunch that day, the girls got back on the bus to continue their week long tour. Gilchrist and I then got on the bus for the five-day tour and returned to Athens. We made arrangements to meet the girls our last night in Athens, since they would be back from their tour and would be staying in Athens. They were in a hotel that was several blocks away from the one where we were staying.

Gilchrist and I had a full day of touring Athens and got to see a lot of very interesting things. That evening we walked to the girls' hotel to meet them and go to a restaurant that they had picked out. Several of the girls were ready a bit early and Gilchrist took off walking with them while I waited to come along with the others.

As we were going out the hotel door, we heard this loud noise, like a huge crowd of people yelling. We got about a block away and came to this plaza (a park-like area about a block square). It was full of people all yelling and with banners waving. Since it was all Greek to me (Ha Ha) I wasn't sure what it was. The girls didn't know either. I had a terrible feeling it was maybe an anti-American rally. I remember so plainly that there I was, an American with a crew cut, and my head sticking up above all the crowd. There weren't very many tall people there. I told the girls I wasn't about to cross that plaza. We took a detour around and had no problems. (We found out the next day that it was a bus drivers rally for more pay!)

We had a great dinner that evening and as the time was coming to pay the bill, for some reason or another, Gilchrist and I had been asked about pictures. The girls had both our billfolds. Then the bill for dinner came and the girls with our billfolds were gone! They had tricked us so they could pay for our dinner. Of course we got the billfolds back and they had a good laugh at having tricked us. All in all it was a really GOOD R & R.

The next day it was back to Turkey for more Nuclear Alert and flying.

Athens.

I took this picture to show the openings between the columns.
Notice how the space between the columns look like a large urn.

The Parthenon is a temple on the Athenian Acropolis, Greece, dedicated to the maiden goddess Athena, whom the people of Athens considered their patron deity. Its construction began in 447 BC when the Athenian Empire was at the height of its power. It was completed in 438 BC, although decoration of the building continued until 432 BC. It is the most important surviving building of Classical Greece, generally considered the culmination of the development of the Doric order. Its decorative sculptures are considered some of the high points of Greek art. The Parthenon is regarded as an enduring symbol of Ancient Greece, Athenian democracy, western civilization and one of the world's greatest cultural monuments.

Christian church
The Parthenon was converted into a Christian church in the final decade of the sixth century AD to become the Church of the Parthenos Maria (Virgin Mary), or the Church of the Theotokos (Mother of God). The orientation of the building was changed to face towards the east; the main entrance was placed at the building's western end and the Christian altar and iconostasis were situated towards the building's eastern side adjacent to an apse built where the temple's pronaos was

formerly located. A large central portal with surrounding side-doors was made in the wall dividing the cella, which became the church's nave, from the rear chamber, the church's narthex. The spaces between the columns of the opisthodomus and the peristyle were walled up though a number of doorways still permitted access. Icons were painted on the walls and many Christian inscriptions were carved into the Parthenon's columns. These renovations inevitably led to the removal and dispersal of some of the sculptures. Those depicting gods were either possibly re-interpreted according to a Christian theme, or removed and destroyed.

The Parthenon became the fourth most important Christian pilgrimage destination in the Eastern Roman Empire after Constantinople, Ephesos and Thessalonica. In 1018, the emperor Basil II went on a pilgrimage to Athens directly after his final victory over the Bulgarians for the sole purpose of worshipping at the Parthenon. In medieval Greek accounts it is called the Temple of Theotokos Atheniotissa and often indirectly referred to, as famous without explaining exactly which temple they were referring to, thus establishing that it was indeed well known.

At the time of the Latin occupation, it became for about 250 years a Roman Catholic church of Our Lady. During this period a tower, used either as a watchtower or bell tower, containing a spiral staircase was constructed at the southwest corner of the cella and vaulted tombs were built beneath the Parthenon's floor. (From Wikipedia, the free encyclopedia)

Attachment 5

Student at the F-100 FWS

There was a joke at the FWS that they only worked half days. They told you to pick which 12 hours you wanted to work and take the other 12 off. It wasn't quite that bad, but the academics were pretty tough. The flying was also tough but the instructors were pretty darn good and that made it a lot of fun.

The first flying was aircraft handling and Basic Fighter Maneuvers. The class I was in had six F-100 students and I think six F-105 students and a number of F-4 students (both front and rear seat students). This was the very first class where all three aircraft had Fighter Weapons Instructors courses. It also allowed us to do dissimilar aircraft engagements during the air-to-air phase.

My F-100 Fighter Weapons Instructor class.

The first flight I would like to talk about is one which I wish I could forget. This was an air-to-air BFM flight with Max Templin as my IP. It also happened to be the day after we had taken our first exam and we went to the club that night to celebrate. It seemed that the IPs were right there with us all night. What we didn't realize until later in the program was the IPs would rotate. That is, it wasn't just one IP partying with us but one would be there for a while and slip away and then another would be there. Well, again, a long story short, I stayed a little too late for having an early brief and flight. I didn't do real well, and in fact when we were coming back to the pattern after the mission I came as close to getting airsick as I ever have. The debrief was very short. Max asked me if I had partied the night before and I said yes. He looked at me and said, "That's ONE!" and walked out of the room. I knew what he meant. At the FWS you got a chance to screw up ONCE. If you screwed up the second time you packed your bags and went home. Not something ANYONE would want to have happen to them.

The next flight was also a BFM flight but against the F-105 IPs and students. We were a two-ship and my IP (I can't for the life of me remember his name) was the F-100 Air-to-Air instructor. If you saw him you would think Casper Milk Toast. He had glasses he wore to read but I mean to tell you he could really fly the F-100 to its maximum. We were in a turning fight with the F-105 and he was flying fighting wing on me. I was pulling as hard as I thought possible, and he was right there and he was saying, "PK, if you are going to get inside these guys, you are going to have to pull it a bit tighter." I couldn't believe he was pulling as hard as I was and taking in the entire fight and telling me what to do. I learned a lot that day.

We had a chance to fly air-to-air against the dart firing all four guns. It was called Combat Dart. You and the dart tow aircraft would separate for about maybe two miles and then come back head on to each other. When you passed line abreast the fight was on and the dart tow aircraft would start a turn into you. Your mission was to get into position and fire at the dart as quick as possible. Object of course was to get a hit on the dart. I think we had three missions like this and I don't believe I ever got a hit although I did fire out all the ammo on each of the missions. On one of the missions the IPs had told us one approach to getting into position quickly was to roll inverted just as you passed abreast and pull as many g's as you could; completing the maneuver coming back up, you should see the dart and have plenty of closure airspeed to get in position quickly. I did this, and pulling g's going down and coming back up, I got tunnel vision for the first time. I almost blacked myself out. I did get to the dart pretty fast but again I wasn't worth a crap shooting at the dart.

The Combat Mission Profile missions were some of the most difficult missions of all. You were given a target out on the Tactical Range, and they were not real big or easy to see targets. You had to plan a low level, do the maps, brief the mission, and lead the IP as you flew the route to the target. Finding the target and time on target were the real important scoring parts of the mission. I think we had three of these missions. A real learning experience but very hard missions.

The missions on the conventional range, dive bomb, skip, rocket and strafe were all about learning new techniques and learning how to teach the basics. One such mission had a somewhat unusual ending for me. It was the day that the last event would be doing 500 kt strafe. You set up in a larger than normal strafe pattern and on the base leg, light the afterburner and attempt to get to 500 kts as you arrived into firing position. You only had enough fuel for about three passes after doing all the other events. I will put in here the actual report that was filed.

REPORT OF MAJOR AIRCRAFT ACCIDENT INVOLVING F-100D, S/N 56-2957, 4 NOVEMBER 1965, PILOT - CAPT KIMMINAU HISTORY OF FLIGHT: *On 4 November 1965, Captain Paul F. Kimminau, a student pilot attending the Fighter Weapons School Instructor Course, was scheduled to fly #3 in Oak-leaf Reno, a flight of four F-100D's as follows: Capt McEntee, Capt Burden, Capt Kimminau, and Capt Templin. Scheduled takeoff time was 10:55 for Range #4 to practice rocketry, bombing, and strafing. After the flight briefing, Captain Kimminau proceeded to the aircraft, performed a standard pre-flight, started the aircraft and taxied to the active runway, passing through the arming area for gun arming and final safety check. After takeoff at 10:55, the flight joined up and proceeded to Range #4. Range work consisted of 20 degree rockets, 10 degree glide bomb, 20 degree dive bomb, 1,000 foot level bomb and 500 knots low angle strafe. Range work was normal and as briefed with no pattern irregularities in regard to fouls, low passed or pressing minimum altitudes. Upon completion of the range work, Captain Kimminau engaged the afterburner to expedite join-up. After a few seconds in afterburner, the engine oil overheat light illuminated. The throttle was brought inboard and power was reduced. The warning light went out and all cockpit instruments appeared normal with the exception that a slight trace of fumes was noticed and the oxygen lever was placed at 100 percent. The throttle was re-advanced to military power to effect a join-up at 15,000 feet. At this time, the wingman joined up in formation on the right wing and observed nothing out of the ordinary as they closed on the lead element. As join-up was being accomplished at 15,000 feet, the engine oil overheat light illuminated for the second time. As the* *throttle was retarded, it was noticed that the oil pressure was decreasing from 40 psi to 20 psi. The fire warning light then illuminated. This information was transmitted to #4 who immediately advised #3 to go to Guard frequency and set up a precautionary landing at Indian Springs, which was approximately five miles to the left. Shortly after starting a gentle left turn toward Indian Springs airfield, both rudder pedals went full forward. Utility pressure was checked and found to be reading 3,000 psi. Airspeed was reduced to 220 kias. Oil pressure was now indicating zero. The gear handle was placed in the down position. Shortly thereafter, the Instructor Pilot (Reno #4) advised that smoke was coming from the left side of the fuselage. At this time the oil pressure pegged on the high side and Captain Kimminau called that he was ejecting. Successful ejection was accomplished at 15,000 feet and 200 kias. Rescue was effected by helicopter. Captain Kimminau was uninjured and the aircraft was destroyed.*

That is the official report. Just a couple additions. When the oil overheat light first came on and I pulled the throttle out of AB and back a bit and it went out, I called all this to #4. I said everything looked OK and I was going to continue. One thing the students tried to do on these missions was to all three be back in close formation BEFORE the IP as number four was joined up. Since I went back to full power I thought I would get joined up before #4 joined up on me. I was still a good way from being joined up when I saw #4 on my wing. Well, as the report said, just as we were joining up in close formation on the lead element, all the stuff starts to happen. You cannot imagine just how BIG that fire warning light looks when it comes on in flight!!

When the report says #4 calls to go to Guard, I reached down and flipped the three position switch to the outboard position. This was just habit kicking in. The three positions on this switch were outboard you were selecting the manual frequency you had set. If in upright position, which is the position it was in, you were operating on the preset frequency of the channel selected. The inboard position was Guard. What happened was as I went outboard, going to manual, I heard it cycle and lock on. At the very same time #4 checked to see if I was on Guard. I heard him because I had the on/ off switch set to TR&G (Transmit, Receive, & Guard). This was a position that allowed you to monitor Guard channel all the time, regardless of which frequency/position the other switches were in. So I heard #4 ask for the check in and immediately answered back that I was on frequency. Of course he didn't hear me because I was transmitting on the manual frequency (which was the Range 4 frequency). I remember looking out at him and asking which direction the traffic at Indian Springs was and he wouldn't answer. He kept asking if I was up on Guard. I, thinking I was, kept yelling at him that YES I was up and hearing him.

He had to make the Mayday call to Indian Springs several times before they answered. This was a bit unusual as they normally answer real fast to a Mayday call. I was transmitting all the information about oil pressure, gear coming down, etc., when I heard #4 tell me about the smoke. I rolled wings level and ejected. There were a lot of stories about guys not being able to raise the handles because they forgot about the device that kept the handles locked down. I had no problem with that. There were also stories about guys then getting confused thinking that that device was the trigger. Again I did not have a problem. I just extended my fingers, found the trigger, squeezed, and shot out of the airplane.

The report has another section telling about the ejection but I'll keep it short by saying I deployed the survival kit, had the lanyard that the dingy was attached wrap around my legs a couple times until I just jettisoned the survival kit. I had plenty of time floating down from altitude, watching all the vehicles running around the desert. When I got down to what I thought was about 300 feet, I saw a Joshua Tree and thought, way out here in the desert and I am going to land in a cactus? Well, a slight breeze out of the west had me floating gently to the east. I landed on the west side of a very shallow drainage ditch, with soft dirt in the bottom, and did a perfect PLF. Laid there for a few seconds, realized nothing hurt, so I got up, took my helmet and G-suit off, and waited for a truck I saw coming my way. It turned out it was an ambulance from Indian Springs and the guy couldn't drive right up to me because of a large ditch. He ran over and asked if I was OK. I said, yeah, I am just fine. He said I could either ride in with them or wait a minute or two because a helicopter was on the way. I said I would just wait.

Sure enough in a couple minutes one of the base rescue helicopters arrived and I jumped on board. It turned out this helicopter was actually taking some VIPs on a tour of the nuclear test site, and when they heard I had ejected, the guy landed out in the desert and let the VIPs out, then came to get me. He took me as far as Indian Springs and dropped me off, then went back to his VIPs.

In about 30 minutes the base rescue helicopter from Nellis arrived and took me to the hospital at Nellis. I got a physical and they said everything was OK, what did I want to do now? I got the ambulance to take me down to the squadron

I came walking in with my helmet and G-suit and the IPs all wanted to know what happened. I told them and asked what I should do then? They said why not go to the academic class that was going on. (It happened to be a class on bombs and fuzes which was the same for all three aircraft, so all the F-100, F-105, and

F-4 students that weren't flying were in class.) So that is what I did. Of course as I came into the class they took a break and wanted to know what happened. I told them and we went back to learning about bombs and fuzes.

It was only about about 20 minutes later when the secretary stuck her head in through the door asking if there was a Captain Kimminau in class. I answered and she said, "They want you up at the Wing Commander's office RIGHT NOW." I just knew there must be someone who wanted to talk about this. The Wing Commander was off base at TAC Headquarters so the Vice Commander, Ops Officer, Flying Safety Officer, and my IP —Max Templin—were all in the office with the Wing Commander on the phone. Max had already explained to him what happened and he asked me if I were alright. I said yes, no problems. They talked a few minutes deciding that it was just an accident and no pilot error involved, so start the investigation. I went to the club and had a few beers.

I didn't have many beers and did not stay very late at the club because I had a very early brief the next morning for a 500 knot low level mission. Nowadays no one believes me when I tell them I ejected about 11:45 one day and the next day at 05:30 I was briefing for another flight. This was also an F-100D, single seat airplane. No flight check required, just go fly. I never really thought about having to eject and maybe it still being on my mind the next time I went to fly. Well, sure enough the crew chief that morning, after he put my helmet in the cockpit, came back down and asked me if I was the one who had ejected the day before. I said sure and then told him I wish he hadn't asked me that!!

One other side note about this incident. Years later I was telling this story at a family get-together and my daughter-in-law's father (Richard Lambert) heard me telling it and stopped me. He asked me a couple questions and then said, "Hell, I was in the control tower at Indian Springs that day." He said that the Thunderbirds were over Indian Springs airfield practicing their maneuvers when the call came on Guard channel that I was in trouble and maybe going to land at Indian Springs. They had a little trouble getting the Thunderbirds out of there and that was the reason for not answering the Mayday call right away. Man, the world is really small.

I left Nellis before the final graduation ceremony because Lois was pregnant with our youngest son and with no hospital at Woodbridge or Bentwaters, she would have to go to Lakenheath where the Air Force had a hospital. It turns out she did not have the C-Section until January but in mid December the doctors were unsure just when they would have to do it. The F-100 students had a graduation dinner with all the students and F-100 IPs. For the guest speaker we invited Vincent

Roy, one of the F-105 students, to give the speech. I am going to include it in here even though it doesn't directly concern flying.

Col. Coury, prospective graduates and guests. Since my arrival here in September, I have managed to maintain some semblance of a physical conditioning program by regular workouts at the base gym. After being invited to this affair as guest speaker and reading my speech, I decided to up the tempo of my workouts and also keep my automobile running outside.

I have to say that it is a rather dubious distinction to be the speaker at a function such as this with a mixed audience of F-100 pilots and untouchables. However, I do want to congratulate the party chairman on his excellent taste in selecting me as guest speaker.

In the process of preparing this subject for tonight, I became so enthralled in my literary genius that I could hardly wait to hear the speech myself, as I'm sure you can't.

In looking out at this collection of fighter pilots, I can only say that in two trips around the world, 3 pig stickings, and 4 county fairs, I have never seen a greater gathering of experts.

With regard to the prospective graduates, I can only say, SHAZAM! For you see, a school I judged and a reputation established through the caliber of the students it produces. In looking at these fellows I can say without reservation that they should set the FWS back a good ten years.

It hasn't been easy for the Operations Staff to keep the books on this class because of their erratic performance. Such events as strafing the FAC van, scaring Petey Potts on formation join-ups, and getting lost on low-level CPM's, can only be considered an anti-climax when you have a sports parachutist like Paul Kimminau in the group. That sky dive caused old J. C. Nabors all sorts of problems for it gave the F-100 section one more takeoff than landing. Had it not been for Edelblut's multiple landings on a single flight you would still be behind one landing. As it is, I think you are now one landing ahead—Good Show, Blute.

You may be thinking that I have an awful lot of audacity and lack of discretion to speak to you tonight but I believe that this can be attributed to my recent assignment to S.E.A. You see once you get orders to go PCS to S.E.A. you develop a certain degree of infallibility and a "I don't give a damn" attitude.

Lastly before beginning, I do want to say that I agree with the F-100 students on what they consider to be the highlight of the F-100 program which as you probably all realize occurred when the F-105 students consented to join in Lou Busch's philosophical presentation of fire crackers and caps. I think the F-100 students benefited remarkably from our presence.

This brings me to my subject for tonight. I gave this much thought and decided that the best method of presentation would be the only one you IP's obviously understand, so on with the speech.

As you will note, I used The Spradling Special format for a speech.

SPEAKER'S NAME: ME
SUBJECT: Hostilities in Little Known Areas or the Air War In S.E.A.
TRAINING AIDS :   Liquor
MOTIVATION: None
OVERVIEW: An insight into the conduct of a civil war.

As all of you six gentlemen know, and as some of you may have heard from the Blute, there is an armed conflict being waged in S.E.A. Trivial by some standards and not accepted by some groups but nevertheless a war.

What is a War?

The basic reasoning and planning behind a war is very fundamental and so simple that even a Petey Potts can understand it. Wars are usually categorized by the amount of Geography they cover which is why WW II made the front page. With this thought in mind, you can see why Vietnam ranks with Selma, Alabama, and the Watts area in Los Angeles.

This reflects fairly accurately the interest of the American citizen and also shows the contrasting metamorphical complexion of war.

To start with, in the Civil War, as some of you like Col. Coury and J.C. may remember, the good guys were on the North team and the bad guys on the South.

However, every war since then has found a complete reversal of this primarily basic Wellington composition. For example Korea: The teams switched and we found the good guys on the South and for the first time the bad guys in the North.

And now in Vietnam we find the Ho Chi Minh panthers from the North engaging the General Key tigers in the South.

Recognizing all these factors as being synonymous with our own historical, rebellious, early years, we can see the pattern for sympathy expressed for South Vietnam by our own Southern-born president. As the President well knows, the South has never won a war anywhere and he figures this is as good an opportunity to break the ice as any. However, his personal war manager, Mr. Edsel, is a Northern-born boy and although the boss wants to help the South, Edsel secretly, perhaps, subconsciously is pulling for the North. When you recognize this fact you find it easier to understand our program in Vietnam. Mr. Edsel has planned the war to show Mr. President that we are flying a maximum number of sorties daily but he never relates to him the ordnance load or the type target.

So now understanding as we do the basic reasonings behind Mr. Edsel's subconscious, emotional, Northern ties, we cannot readily accept the reason for conducting the war as we are.

To strengthen our world image, we have taken our WW II deterrent force and stationed them at Guam and assigned them the task of leveling the forests of South Vietnam. In so doing, this Guam bunch has in fact killed numerous monkeys, tigers, and snakes which were previously a hinderance to the Viet Cong.

In addition to the deterrent force at Guam Edsel has located within the war zone itself some of our best peacetime cross-country aircraft and trainers. We are using the F-100, A-1, and F-5 extensively to destroy villages, rice paddies, and suspected enemy strongholds: in some cases as far away as 100 nm from their home station, and with as much as two bombs and 800 bullets per aircraft.

As you can see thus far in our examination of this "War," we have really torn up the good guys real estate and haven't touched the bad guys Fatherland, so now let's examine that aspect of the war next.

Mr. Edsel has consented to let a choice few go up North to irritate Uncle Ho Chi Minh. However, in so doing he has placed many restrictions on the effort which have proved to be tighter than a frog's ass—and that's waterproof!

These choice few who are sometimes jokingly, lovingly, and enviously called the "squash bombers" are as we all agree carrying the load in this war.

While everyone else is tinkering in the South, the "big boys" are going up North every day and destroying all kinds of good non-military targets. In fact what has happened is, Uncle Ho has requested additional free time to defend his military targets but we found it impractical to afford him the time he wanted so we became calloused and adamant and insisted he be ready by June 1967. I don't mean to infer that the boys going North are not directed on to sound, strategic targets, it's just that when they are they are not allowed to carry bombs.

And so the war goes on...and now with SAC assuming a bigger and bigger role in the war we find that our stockpile of bombs and medals has dwindled to a mere pittance.

And so the war goes on...and we have found a simple method of attritioning the fleet, and as Ho Chi Minh develops his own F-105 wings, I'm sure that he will encounter the same logistics problems that we have. Soon, I'm sure, he'll be ready to sell them back to us.

And so the war goes on… and as the F-100 continues to fly in Vietnam it proves more each day the soundness and wisdom behind the Pentagon's earlier decision to convert it into a crop duster.

And so the war goes on… as you know in the near future I will leave this hostile nation to take up residence in Hootch #9 Takhli Air Base and I say to you who might venture that way—-drop by and we'll share a cobra. I want to thank you for letting me express my views on the war and remind you that this opportunity to speak to you, like my #*%^@, is no big thing.

As you read that you may not think it funny. Myself, reading it I remember very well when Vincent gave the speech and just how funny it was. Maybe it was the training aids he used. Col. Coury was the School Commandant and J.C. Nabors was just taking over the F-100 Section. Spradling was an instructor who didn't teach anything about flying; he taught us how to prepare and present our briefing/presentations. Petey Potts was one of the instructors who wasn't assigned to the section but assigned to the wing and flew with the F-100 section.

Attachment 6

NORTH STATION aka LIMA SITE 85

From Wikipedia, the free encyclopedia:

Laos Site 85 (LS-85 alphanumeric code) was a clandestine Laos military installation of the Hmong "Secret Army", the Central Intelligence Agency, and the United States Air Force used for Vietnam War covert operations against communist targets in ostensibly neutral Laos. Initially created for a CIA command post to support a local stronghold, the site was expanded with a 1966 TACAN area excavated on the mountaintop where a 1967 command guidance radar was added for Commando Club bombing of northern areas of North Vietnam. The site ended operations with the Battle of Lima Site 85 when most of the U.S. technicians on the mountaintop were killed, including SMSgt Richard Etchberger who was awarded the Medal of Honor.

The LS-85 military installation began as a supply site and command post for "Hmong officers and CIA paramilitary advisers [to control] harassing operations against the PL [Pathet Lao] and North Vietnamese". LS-85 was supplied via an "Air America STOL airstrip… two-thirds of the way down the mountain" and the command bunker was down the hill from the summit (identified by the North Vietnamese as the "communications center".) The airstrip was also used for refueling USAF rescue helicopter.

The LS-85 TACAN area with the AN/TRN-17, generator, diesel supply, and "Comm and Relay Center" was operating on September 24, 1966; and the portion of LS-85 serviced by the landing zone was supported (supplies, etc.) by Continental Air Services, using PONY EXPRESS Sikorsky CH-3 helicopters. Fuel drums for the MB5 were landed directly at the mountaintop.

From Wikipedia, the free encyclopedia
LS 85 Phou Pha Thi

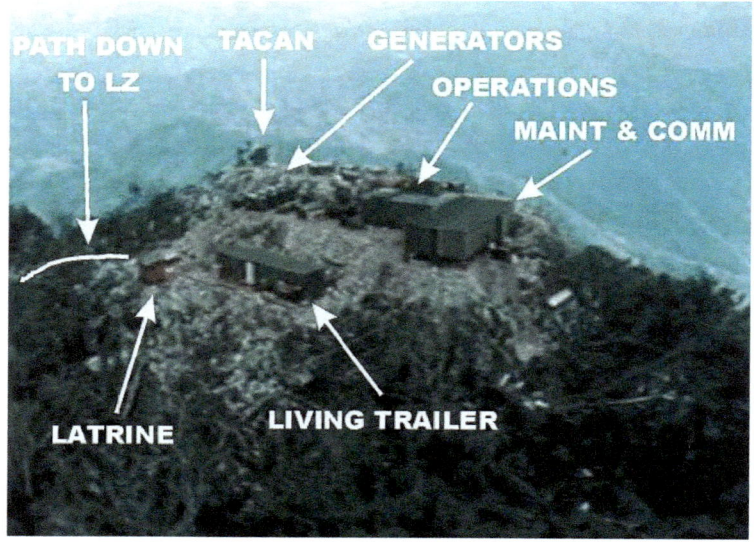

Heavy Green was the military operation to emplace a Reeves AN/TSQ-81 Bomb Directing Central on the LS-85 summit adjacent to the TACAN area particularly for monsoon season bombing of northern North Vietnam. The site's Initial inspection regarding suitability for ground-directed bombing was by its eventual 7th AF coordinator, and geodetic surveying was by a 1st Combat Evaluation Group team manned from existing Combat Skyspot operating locations. The site was developed under USAF Major Richard Secord (assisted by Tom Clines) by first "clearing additional space on the white karst limestone mountaintop" with blasting by a "Navy Seabee demolitions expert". Construction included leveling steel girders on vertical posts to allow a Corps of Engineers CH-47s to airlift the "new equipment, vans [rigid shelters], and prefab crew quarters". Defenses included a defensive bunker and an inner perimeter with outpost, and a frequency converter shelter provided the 3 phase 400 Hz power needed for precision pointing by the radar's antenna motors. The camouflaged Cassegrain antenna was on the roof of the operations shelter, while the connected shelter had a rotating identification friend or foe antenna and mast antennas for UHF and VHF communications. A calibration in September 1967 included an estimation of the AN/TSQ-81 antenna coordinates by "fly-in" using aircraft tracked by LS-85 while overflying previously-surveyed nearby peaks (surveyors at the peaks observed the fly-over precision). [NOTE: On a couple of my Fire Fly missions I actually was used as an observer for drops from the site on a bend in a river to the Southwest of LS-85.]

The initial assessment by the site's 7th AF coordinator was that after radar operations began LS-85 would be attacked within 6 months, which a February 25 CIA report accurately predicted would be after March 10. Summit structures at LS-85 had originally been outfitted with demolition charges (later removed by the technicians), and the personnel eventually had small arms (e.g., M16 rifles) for defense. TACAN and AN/TSQ-81 personnel were included in the February plan to evacuate when the site's risk became too high, and defense training had been provided. An enemy patrol was dispersed from the base of the mountain on January 10, a January 12 air strike bombed LS-85, and a mortar attack was on January 30. On February 18 near the head of the road an NVA survey party was defeated (the NVA map with planned artillery positions was captured.) On March 10 (1800–1945 hours), an "artillery barrage" preceded an attack toward the southeast slope by 3 battalions ("a kilometer or two from the hill"), and commandos including Hmong defectors— instead of assaulting in a direct infantry attack upslope toward the radar station— scaled the north mountain cliff and after midnight killed the majority of the onsite technicians. All areas of LS-85 were captured, and the remaining mountaintop structures were destroyed by US air strikes through the next week.

Battle of Lima Site 85: The Battle of Lima Site 85, also called Battle of Phou Pha Thi, was fought as part of a military campaign waged during the Vietnam War and Laotian Civil War, in which the Vietnam People's Army (then known as NVA) and the Pathet Lao fought against airmen of the United States Air Force 1st Combat Evaluation Group, elements of the Royal Laos Army and Royal Thai Border Patrol Police, and the Central Intelligence Agency-led Hmong Clandestine Army. The battle was fought on Phou Pha Thi mountain in Houaphanh Province, Laos, on 10 March 1968, and derives its name from the mountain top where it was fought, or from the designation of a landing strip 700 feet (210 m) in length in the valley below, and was the largest single ground combat loss of United States Air Force members during the Vietnam War.

Towards the end of 1967, North Vietnamese units increased the tempo of their operations around Phou Pha Thi, and by 1968 several attacks were launched against Lima Site 85. In the final assault on 10 March 1968, elements of the VPA 41st Special Forces Battalion attacked the facility, with support from the VPA 766th Regiment and one Pathet Lao battalion. The Hmong and Thai forces that were defending the facility were overwhelmed by the combined North Vietnamese and Pathet Lao forces.

Successes of the system also brought about concerns for the personnel on the ground. Major Richard Secord, who was responsible for the security of Lima Site 85, was concerned about the safety of the unarmed USAF technicians who were working under disguise as civilians. Secord's concerns were justified by the events of 1967, as USAF reconnaissance aircraft that were regularly flying over northeastern Laos showed that roads constructed by the North Vietnamese were approaching Phou Pha Thi. Activities associated with road construction were observed along Routes 6 and 19, which connected Dien Bien Phu in North Vietnam with Phou Pha Thi and Nam Bac in Laos respectively.

Although Ambassador Sullivan repeatedly stated that USAF personnel at Lima Site 85 should not be armed, Secord decided to equip the technicians at the facility with weapons, so M-16 assault rifles, fragmentation grenades, concussion grenades and other small arms were brought in for use by the technicians. Sensing that the North Vietnamese would attempt to destroy the facility, Secord advised the U.S Embassy in Vientiane to evacuate all U.S. personnel from the installation. However, high-ranking U.S. officials insisted that Lima Site 85 should operate for as long as possible, as it was saving the lives of U.S. pilots each day it remained in operation. In December 1967, the Communist military offensive in the region was signalled by a series of skirmishes. On 15 December, CIA-led Hmong reconnaissance patrols detected several North Vietnamese and Pathet Lao battalions moving against Nam Bac, then the stronghold of the Royal Laos Army.

On 16 December, two Pathet Lao companies overran Phou Den Din, which was only 12 kilometers (7.5 mi) east of Lima Site 85. Shortly afterwards, Hmong units recaptured the site. Towards the end of 1967, U.S. controllers at Lima Site 85 directed F-4, F-105 and A-1 fighter-bombers based in Thailand and South Vietnam, to conduct air-strikes against North Vietnamese and Pathet Lao formations that appeared to be massing around the U.S. facility at Phou Pha Thi. A-26 Invaders were even called in to undertake night missions, targeting movements of the opposing forces on Route 6 and Route 19. On 14 January 1968, the situation in north-eastern Laos continued to worsen when an estimated four North Vietnamese battalions captured the Laotian Government stronghold at Nam Bac. Despite the growing threat from North Vietnamese forces, the U.S. military was not permitted to reinforce their facility on top of Phou Pha Thi Mountain due to political sensitivities.

Instead, the defense of Lima Site 85 was entrusted to two CIA paramilitary officers who led about 1,000 Hmong soldiers, with 200 guarding the ridge-line and the remaining 800 soldiers were positioned in the valley below. They were reinforced by a Thai Border Patrol Police battalion of 300 soldiers. In the first week of 1968, the combined North Vietnamese and Pathet Lao forces probed Royal Laos Army positions in the region, by launching several artillery attacks. On 10 January, a Pathet Lao patrol was driven away from the area by the Hmongs. Fearing that the explosives attached to their equipment could be detonated by artillery strikes, the U.S. technicians dismantled all the charges and threw them over the cliff.

On 12 January, CIA spotters reported a four-aircraft formation flying in the direction of Lima Site 85. The aircraft spotted were Soviet-made Antonov An-2 biplanes; two aircraft flew towards Lima Site 85, while the other two split off. The Vietnam People's Air Force, in one of their few air attacks during the entire conflict, was attempting to destroy the radar at Lima Site 85. As the two AN-2s flew over Phou Pha Thi, their crews dropped 120 mm mortar shells through the aircraft's floor and also strafed their targets by firing 57 mm rockets from the wing pods. However, as the two aircraft flew back and forth to attack the facility, CIA officers and U.S. controllers at Lima Site 85 managed to call in a Bell UH-1D helicopter operated by Air America, which proved to be faster than the Soviet-made biplanes. Once the pilot of the helicopter, Theodore Moore, sighted the An-2s, he *quickly chased the aircraft and pulled alongside one. Crew member Glenn Woods, who was armed with an AK-47 assault rifle, fired on the biplane and caused it to crash. Moore then chased down a second An-2 and Woods shot it down too.*

The two remaining An-2s that had observed the attack from a distance escaped from the scene without any damage. On the ground four Hmongs were killed by the attack, which included two men and two women, but the TSQ-81 radar and all associated equipment were not damaged. Shortly afterwards, the wreckage of one of the An-2 biplanes was put on display in front of the That Luang Monument, Vientiane's most important Buddhist shrine, as evidence of North Vietnamese activities in the country. [NOTE: I don't remember where I got the information but supposedly the AN-2 wreckage was picked up by a US Army crane helicopter. I got to see the wreckage of this aircraft one day when I made an unscheduled stop at Lima Site 36.]

Image from Wikipedia, the free encyclopedia.

Despite the severity of the attacks, the U.S. Embassy in Vientiane and the USAF did not change their strategy for the defense of Lima Site 85. Lieutenant-Colonel Clarence F. Blanton, the commander of USAF personnel at the facility, was not given the authority to supervise his own defenses or to order a retreat if the facility came under attack. Throughout January and February, intelligence collected by the Hmongs confirmed that a major assault on Lima Site 85 was in the making, but nothing was done by Sullivan or the U.S. military to strengthen the facility.

North Vietnamese plan and preparations: *On 18 February 1968, a North Vietnamese artillery survey team was ambushed near Lima Site 85 by Hmong reconnaissance teams, killing a North Vietnamese officer in the process. The dead officer, who was a major, carried a notebook which revealed a plan to attack Phou Pha Thi by using three North Vietnamese battalions and one Pathet Lao battalion. Consequently, U.S. personnel at Lima Site 85 directed 342 air strikes within 30 meters (98 ft) of their own facility to disrupt their opponent's build-up during the periods between 20–29 February. Unknown to the USAF, however, the Vietnam People's Army had also drawn up a plan to capture Lima Site 85 by deploying its Special Forces. The task of capturing the U.S. facility was entrusted to a platoon from the VPA 41st Special Forces Battalion, led by First Lieutenant Truong Muc. The platoon numbered 33 soldiers, and they were reinforced by a nine-man sapper squad and a communications and cryptography squad.*

Prior to their mission, Muc's soldiers had undergone nine months of special training which mainly focused on methods of fighting on mountain tops, scaling on cliff rocks and jungle operations. They also conducted physical conditioning, to improve their physical fitness and stamina to undertake operations in the most extreme conditions on Laotian territory. On 18 December 1967, following their intensive training, soldiers of the VPA 41st Special Forces Battalion launched the first phase of their operation by conducting terrain reconnaissance and watching activities on Lima Site 85 to learn their opponent's routines. As part of the second phase, commenced on 22 January 1968, six North Vietnamese sappers were sent out to climb Phou Pha Thi Mountain, in order to pinpoint their opponent's positions in and around Lima Site 85, as well as their routes of withdrawal. On 28 February 1968, the North Vietnamese Special Forces completed their preparations, and they began marching towards their assembly point on 1 March.

To maintain the element of secrecy, Muc was ordered to avoid contact with local civilians and opposing military forces. In the event they were engaged by opposing forces, the North Vietnamese would have to deploy a small force to deal with the situation, while the main formation would continue marching towards their objective on Phou Pha Thi. Once the North Vietnamese formation had arrived at their assembly area, they were to be divided into two assault groups. The first assault group, under Muc's direct command, was divided into five 'cells' to attack key targets at Lima Site 85. Accordingly, Cells 1 and 2 were given the mission of capturing the communications center, with the latter given the secondary role of supporting Cell 3, which was given the main mission of seizing the TACAN site and eliminating all U.S. personnel. Cell 4 was ordered to capture the airstrip, and

Cell 5 was placed in reserve to support other units. Meanwhile, Second Lieutenant Nguyen Viet Hung was given responsibility to lead the second assault group, and their mission was to destroy Thai positions. The attack would commence during the early hours of 9 or 10 March.

To capture Lima Site 85, the North Vietnamese Special Forces were equipped with three Chinese-made K-54 pistols, 23 AK-47 assault rifles, four 7.62mm carbines and three RPG-7 rocket propelled grenade launchers. Furthermore, there were 200 rounds of ammunition for each AK-47 rifle, six rounds for each RPG, 400 grams (14 oz) of explosives and six hand grenades. The weapons load, in addition to 15 days of rations and other personal items, required each North Vietnamese Special Force soldier to carry between 42 kilograms (93 lb) to 45 kilograms (99 lb) worth of supplies. Shortly after the North Vietnamese Special Forces had arrived at the assembly point, they moved off to an undisclosed location for two days to test-fire all their weapons, and to ensure their explosives were in good working order. Then, in an attempt to fool Hmong and U.S. intelligence, the North Vietnamese made diversionary movements against Muong Son to cover their main assault. On 9 March, elements of the VPA 41st Special Forces Battalion arrived in the vicinity of Phou Pha Thi, where they made final preparations for their assault.

By 9 March 1968, the U.S. facility on top of Phou Pha Thi was surrounded by North Vietnamese and Pathet Lao units, with the VPA 766th Regiment and one Pathet Lao battalion totaling more than 3,000 men, were reported to be in position to attack Lima Site 85. Despite the seriousness of the situation around the facility, Sullivan did not issue an order for the evacuation of U.S. personnel from Phou Pha Thi. At around 6:00pm on 10 March, Lima Site 85 was subjected to a series of artillery barrages. Under the cover of the artillery bombardment, the North Vietnamese Special Forces sent a small team up the mountain to defuse the mines and quick-fuse grenades, to establish their routes of infiltration. Inside the facility, U.S. technicians immediately grabbed their weapons and ran into trenches and bunkers, thereby abandoning the very equipment which could enable them to call for air support. At 7:45pm the barrage stopped, and the U.S. technicians returned to their positions.

The TSQ-81 antenna only received minor damages during the attack, and the U.S. suffered no casualties. However, the only 105 mm howitzer operated by the Hmongs received a direct hit, and was rendered ineffective. At around 8:20pm, Sullivan gave the U.S. commander at Lima Site 85 the authority to direct air strikes against targets at the lower slopes of the mountain, on the basis that the situation had become critical. About 20 minutes later, the 33-man North Vietnamese platoon began climbing up towards the U.S. facility at Lima Site 85. At 9:15pm Sullivan was considering evacuating all U.S. personnel from the facility at first light. However, officers of the Seventh Air Force contacted the U.S. Embassy in Laos and indicated that evacuation should only occur as the last resort, when the situation on top of Phou Pha Thu was no longer within their control.

At 9:21pm the North Vietnamese resumed their artillery attack on Phou Pha Thi, followed by several infantry assaults by the VPA 766th Regiment, which prompted Sullivan to order the evacuation of six technicians by 8:15am on the next morning, from a contingent of 19 U.S. personnel. Starting at 1:00 am on 11 March, the North Vietnamese Special Forces moved into their assigned positions in order to launch their attack. About 2:00am, a U.S. adviser at the airstrip reported to Secord and CIA officers at Udorn that he heard gun-fire on top of Phou Pha Thi, and communication with the U.S. technicians at Lima Site 85 was completely cut off. Afterwards, Secord briefed U.S. A-1 Skyraider pilots in Thailand on the situation at Lima Site 85, to familiarize them with friendly positions around the facility, so they could cover the evacuation of U.S. personnel and support Hmong's counter-attack.

About 3:00am Cell 1 moved to within 150 meters (490 ft) of their objective, with Cell 5 positioned behind them. At the same time, the commander of Cell 4 decided to maneuver his unit to the west side of the airstrip instead of the east side as originally planned, because the terrain on the east side was higher and was covered by buildings. Precisely at 3:45am, Cell 1 moved to within 30 meters (98 ft) of the communications center, when they bumped into a Hmong outpost. Both sides exchanged fire, and the outpost was destroyed by a grenade while the Hmong soldier guarding the post ran away. Shortly afterwards, a soldier from Cell 1 fired an RPG-7 grenade which immediately destroyed the TACAN antenna. Within 15 minutes, Cells 1 and 2 had secured the communications site. Signaled by the explosion of Cell 1's RPG-7 round, Cell 3 immediately attacked the TACAN installation by firing one of their own RPG-7s, which destroyed the electrical generators.

Upon hearing the noise of explosions, the U.S. technicians who were on duty rushed out the front door of their operations building where they were met by North Vietnamese gunfire. Blanton, the U.S. commander at Lima Site 85, was killed along-side two other U.S. technicians. Those who were not killed retreated to the west side of the mountain, where they hid on the edge of the cliff. From their hideout, the U.S. technicians fired on the North Vietnamese with their M-16 rifles and hand grenades. At 4:15am, in response to the gunfire from the U.S. technicians, Muc ordered Cell 5 to reinforce Cell 3, and they captured the TACAN installation at 4:30am after 45 minutes of fighting. Meanwhile, Cell 4 had much greater difficulties in their attempt to seize the airstrip, where they were blocked by a Hmong mortar position. Le Ba Chom—the commander of Cell 4—was isolated from the other three soldiers of his cell. To avoid being captured alive by the numerically superior Hmong forces, Chom and his soldiers held onto their position and fought till daybreak.

At 5:15am Sullivan, from the U.S. Embassy in Vientiane, decided to evacuate Lima Site 85 and he gave a signal to U.S. pilots at Udorn to begin the operation, which was due to start at 7:15am. However, Sullivan did not realize that U.S. technicians were no longer in control of their TSQ-81 equipment. Starting at around 6:00am, Pao's Hmong soldiers launched a counter-attack against North Vietnamese positions at the communication center, which was guarded by Cells 1 and 2, but their attacks were repelled and the North Vietnamese held their positions. When the final Hmong counter-attack on the communication site was defeated at 6:25am, Cell 2 was ordered to support Cells 3 and 5 in their fight at the main TACAN installation. By 6:35am, the North Vietnamese established full control of the TACAN site. At the airstrip, Cell 4 was encircled by an estimated two Hmong platoons, but Chom and his unit were able to fight their way out by taking full advantage of the rough terrain which covered their positions. Later, Cell 4 linked up with other units at the TACAN site.

At sunlight Air America helicopters hovered over Lima Site 85 to start the evacuation, which was covered by USAF A-1 Skyraiders. Immediately, Hmong soldiers and their CIA commanders rushed the TACAN site and shouted to the U.S. technicians that help was coming. In response, the North Vietnamese Special Forces organized a defense around the TACAN site, and hid their dead and wounded comrades under the large rocks which dotted Phou Pha Thi. While U.S. fighter-bombers strafe the TACAN site, the Air America helicopter landed on the airstrip and they picked up two CIA officers, one forward air-controller and five technicians who were hiding during the fire-fight. Later during the day, Air America was able to recover or account for eight of the dead U.S. personnel on Lima Site 85, along with a number of wounded Hmong soldiers. By midday, Lima Site 85 was fully controlled by the VPA 41st Special Forces Battalion, and they held the facility until 14 March when they withdrew from the area.

Aftermath: *Just before midday on 11 March, the USAF turned their attention from looking for their missing personnel to that of destroying the TSQ-81 'Commando Club' radar, along with all the documentation and operation information left behind at Lima Site 85. Between 12–18 March, the USAF conducted a total of 95 strike sorties against the radar site, and on 19 March an A-1 fighter-bomber* destroyed every building at the old facility. In addition to the destruction of their own radar equipment, the USAF bombing of Lima Site 85 may also had the effect of obliterating the bodies of deceased U.S. personnel who were left behind at the site. In the days following the loss of Phou Pha Thi, Sullivan reflected on the disaster at Lima Site 85 and commented the U.S. technicians operating there should have been evacuated on 10 March, when it became amply clear the North Vietnamese were preparing to launch their assault.

For the USAF, the loss at Phou Pha Thi was not a result of intelligence failure, because they had been provided with accurate information from the very start. Instead, it was clearly a failure of command and control, as the U.S. personnel and their Hmong allies were not permitted to carry out their own defense in order to hold the radar facility. The Battle of Lima Site 85 resulted in the largest ground combat loss of USAF personnel during the Vietnam War. A total of 12 U.S. personnel were missing or killed as a result of the fighting on Phou Pha Thi; 11 were killed or missing on the ground and one was shot down during the evacuation process. The single fatality occurring during the evacuation was Air Force Chief Master Sergeant Richard Etchberger who was awarded the Medal of Honor posthumously in September 2010 for his role in helping four injured airmen into the evacuation helicopter lift sling. In addition Captain Donald Westbrook was shot down and killed while searching for survivors.

The total casualty figure for all North Vietnamese, Pathet Lao, Hmong and Thai units are unknown. According to official Vietnamese history, the VPA 41st Special Forces Battalion lost one soldier killed and two wounded in their fight for Lima Site 85. Against those losses, the Vietnamese claimed a total of 42 Hmong and Thai soldiers were killed, and a number of others were wounded. Furthermore, a large cache of weapons were captured which included one 105 mm howitzer, one 85 mm artillery piece, four recoilless rifles, four heavy mortars, nine heavy machine guns and vast amounts of ammunition. The North Vietnamese victory proved to be a significant one, as they had succeeded in knocking out a major asset of the USAF, which had inflicted heavy damages to North Vietnam's limited industrial infrastructures.

The fight at Phou Pha Thi, which was part of a larger military campaign waged by the North Vietnamese and their Pathet Lao allies, marked the beginning of the Communist dry-season offensive against Laotian Government forces in north-eastern Laos. By September 1968, the strength of North Vietnamese and Pathet Lao forces in the Sam Neua area were estimated to have numbered more than 20 battalions. Against such heavy odds, General Vang Pao insisted on recapturing

Phou Pha Thi, which the U.S. Embassy believed was unnecessary. On 20 October 1968, Pao returned to Laos following a month-long vacation in the United States, and he immediately planned his next move. However, by that stage the Hmong Clandestine Army had lost about half their strength due to heavy casualties. On 1 November 1968, Pao launched Operation Pig Fat in attempt to retake Phou Pha Thi, but the operation quickly turned into a rout for the Royal Laos Army and the Hmong guerrillas and Phou Pha Thi was never retaken.

Although airpower was to be a major factor in the defense of Lima Site 85, it could not be applied without limitations and restrictions. The defense of Lima Site 85 was not the sole task of limited air resources in the Southeast Asian conflict. For example, during this same period, the 1968 Tet Offensive was underway in South Vietnam, the Marine Khe Sanh Combat Base was under siege, and there existed an unprecedented flow of enemy logistic traffic which had to be interdicted. The Lima Site 85 had provided direction to about a quarter of the USAF missions over North Vietnam and Barrel Roll from November 1967 to 11 March 1968. No other facility existed to provide a similar coverage over these areas. While this loss was a serious blow to the USAF air effort, it was not crippling.

Eleven of the twelve USAF personnel lost on the day of the battle were listed first as missing in action (MIA), then later as KIA/body not recovered. Between 1994 and 2004, 11 investigations were conducted by both Joint POW/MIA Accounting Command (JPAC) and unilaterally by Lao and Vietnamese investigators on both sides of the border. In 2002 two of the former VPA soldiers who had taken part in the attack told investigators that they threw the bodies of the Americans off the mountain after the attack as they were unable to bury them on the rocky surface.

In March 2003, JPAC investigators threw dummies over the edge at those points indicated by the VPA soldiers while a photographer in a helicopter videotaped their fall. That pointed the investigators to a ledge, 540 feet (160 m) below. Several mountaineer-qualified JPAC specialists scaled down the cliffs to the ledge where they recovered leather boots in four different sizes, five survival vests, and other fragments of material that indicated the presence of at least four Americans. On 7 December 2005 the Defense Prisoner of War/Missing Personnel Office announced that the remains of Technical Sergeant Patrick L. Shannon had been identified and were being returned to his family. On 14 February 2007 the remains of Captain Donald Westbrook, who had been shot down in 1968 while searching for possible survivors of the battle, were positively identified from remains which had been returned in September 1998. The remains of Lt Col Blanton were identified on July 26, 2012.

I have read a book about the loss of North Station. It is called *ONE DAY TOO LONG*. As I noted earlier, with the few Thai and Hmong special forces guys they had, they could hold off an attack for at least long enough so they could extract the Americans and destroy the equipment. However, the North Vietnam Army had a special group formed that climbed the steep sides at night and were shooting our guys before they even knew the bad guys were there. They did get five guys out but they lost eleven. One of the guys that the Air America Huey picked up took a round that was fired up through the floor as they were leaving and died later as they were going to Lima Site 36. (He was awarded the Medal of Honor for his efforts to get him and the others out of there.) Three of the eleven that were lost are still unaccounted for. (As I write this, October 2012, the remains of one of these three were returned within the last month or so.) Twenty-twenty hindsight tells us that there was plenty of warning that they were building up forces to take the place. It was just another example of someone not making a decision when it should have been made.

Attachment 7

AWARDS & DECORATIONS

(Left to right, top to bottom)
Silver Star, Distinguished Flying Cross [3 Oak Leaf Clusters], Bronze Star, Purple Heart, Air Medal [8 Oak Leaf Clusters], Air Force Commendation Medal, Air Force Outstanding Unit Award [2 Oak Leaf Clusters], Combat Readiness Medal, National Defense Service Medal, Armed Forces Expeditionary Medal, Vietnam Service Medal [4 Bronze Service Stars], Republic of Vietnam Gallantry Cross with Palm [1 Bronze Service Star], Republic of Vietnam Campaign Medal